The Mind Games *of* Art *and* Entertainment

Also by James Sloan Allen

The Romance of Commerce and Culture: Capitalism, Modernism, and the Chicago-Aspen Crusade for Cultural Reform

Worldly Wisdom: Great Books and the Meanings of Life

William James on Habit, Will, Truth, and the Meaning of Life (editor)

Aloha: The Surprising History of an Idea and a Culture

Life Line: A Novel of Romance and Rebirth

Dreamers, Runaways, and Mysteries: A Traveler's Tales and Essays

Cabbages and Kings: To Talk of Many Things, of Style and Humanism, Politics and Culture, Literature, Laughter, and the Meaning of Life

Photographs: Travel, History, Memories

The Mind Games *of* Art *and* Entertainment

And How They Gave Us *the* Culture *of* Entertainment
— *with the* Perils *of* Unseriousness

James Sloan Allen

ISBN: 978-1-7349787-4-2

E-ISBN: 978-1-7349787-5-9

Cover art: Giorgio de Chirico, *The Mystery and Melancholy of a Street*, 1914.

Fig. 16 and Fig. 54 from Adobe Stock.

Book design by Rachel Davis Mariano.

To Stan Burnett,

Modest polymath, music aficionado, influential author,
seasoned diplomat, gracious gentleman, valued friend,
and all-around exceptional human being.

Contents

Acknowledgments

I do not have a large number of people to acknowledge here, but those I must recognize have been more than helpful. They have been indispensable as enduring friends, knowledgeable readers, thoughtful critics, and encouraging allies.

Stan Burnett, to whom the book is dedicated, is a friend with whom I have discussed many things over the past two decades—often by email, which has yielded reams of correspondence—and whose intellectual penetration, wide-ranging knowledge, and light touch have brought me much enlightenment and pleasure, through disagreement no less than agreement. His natural modesty belies his capacious mind and many worldly accomplishments. I am grateful for his sagacious observations on this and other books and for his generous support.

My sisters Barbara Allen and Mary Allen Redd have been my loving intellectual and artistic companions for more years than I can count, and have been willing and incisive readers of my writerly ramblings for many of those years as well. I would not want to write anything of substance without drawing on their astute criticism, friendly interest, and familiarity with things largely unknown to me. They always improve whatever I write. How fortunate I am to have sisters who are also such good friends. Words can only graze the surface of what I owe them.

The last person I wish to acknowledge here is my friend of over fifty years Tom Thompson. Not only does his good nature and embracing spirit make him an exemplary friend, his sharp mind and wide-ranging curiosity about life make his friendship priceless—and fun. He has awakened me to many things, like the delights of jazz and the pleasures of New York nightlife—albeit back in the day when that nightlife had more variety and life than it does now—and even the character of popular culture overall. Without Tom's influence, I would either have not written this book, or it would surely have been very different. And my life would have been much the poorer in many ways.

But I cannot close these Acknowledgements without a note of gratitude to the person who designed and gave this book physical life, Rachel Davis Mariano. Her deft expertise and remarkable ingenuity in all kinds of technical and artistic things truly made the book possible. And her enduring good nature has made working with her on this and other books a pleasure. She is indeed a treasure. I am lucky to have "found" her.

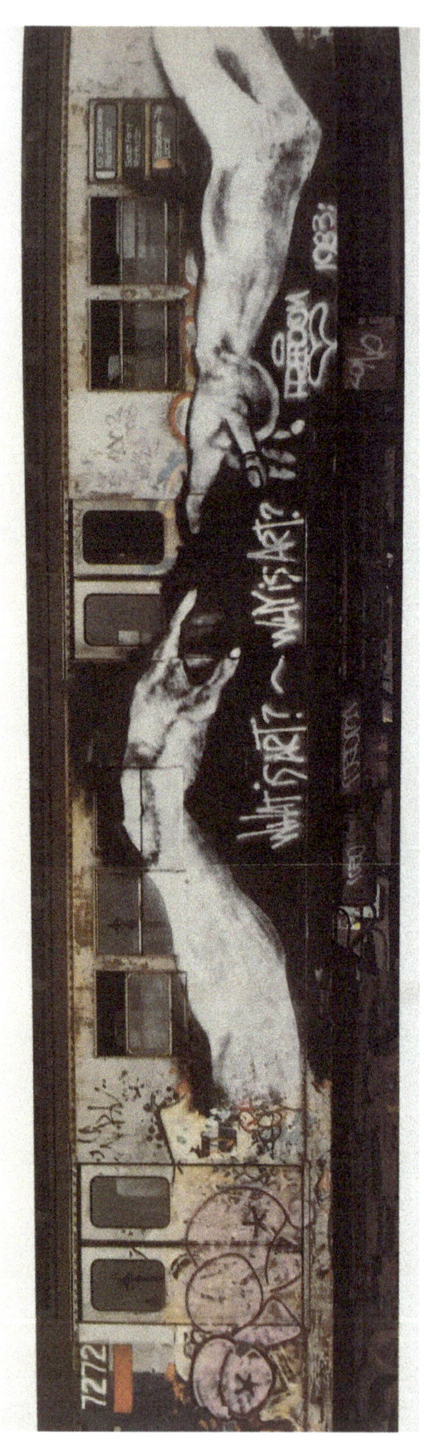

Fig. 1 — What is Art? Why is Art? *by FREEDOM (a.k.a., Chris Pape) New York City subway graffiti, 1983. Composite photograph, Henry Chalfant.*

Prologue: Why Art Matters

"Art is a great matter."
—Tolstoy

In one way or another, art, high and low, pervades our lives. It adorns all kinds of public places—sidewalks, squares, entrance lobbies, building walls, and so on. Schools encourage children to express themselves through it, and they model teaching practices on entertainment. Radio, television, movies, computers, and smart phones make art, mainly as entertainment, omnipresent in sight and sound. Publications disseminate news of the arts from museum exhibitions, concert hall programs, and current artistic creations to the latest movies, television fare, and fads in pop music. They also report prices paid for artworks at auction and ticket sales of current movies, as though that is big news. Museums stage "blockbuster" shows marketed to attract hordes, and they reproduce thousands of art-objects for sale. As "design," art is a saleable commodity grafted onto every commercial product and its packaging. No large community goes without organizations and performance centers devoted to the arts. Families vacation in theme parks modeled on cartoon fantasies. The popular arts earn their creators, performers, and producers astonishing riches. Entertainment and athletic "stars" have become idols of the culture, shaping the lives of the young. The mass media have made celebrity the measure of human worth, while the personal possessions of celebrities have become cherished collectors' items and their homes have become shrines. People live for their favorite television shows and live through their favorite celebrities, often imitating them in appearance and manner. And many people would do anything to appear on television, becoming momentary celebrities themselves. The list could go on and on. Clearly, this is not an environment where art is neglected. It is one where art, in countless manifestations—especially entertainment—is part of the lives we live.

But for all of the "art"* we live amidst, do we sufficiently understand its powers and how they work on us for good and ill? I think not. Does it matter? I think it does. And it is the purpose of this little book to shed some light on the wiles and the influence of art, high and low—especially the low—in our lives. Although there has been no scarcity or variety of efforts to do that before—many of which are, indeed, illuminating, and several of them show up in these pages—none has gone about it quite as this book does.

As a prologue, we start about 125 years ago in the waning twilight of the nineteenth century, when one of that era's greatest artists, Leo Tolstoy, published the most provocative, impassioned, and eccentrically brilliant book ever written on the nature and effects of art. Plainly entitled *What Is Art?*, the book blasted virtually every European artist and artwork of modern times—including Tolstoy's own literary works written before his conversion to a higher morality—for betraying what he deemed "true art" and perpetrating a variety of evils through "false art" that were driving the entire culture into the ground. Few thinkers, if any, have granted art as much power to do harm, and good, as Tolstoy did. He judged art to be not only a primary cause of the degradation of Western culture but the chief hope of redeeming that culture and humanity itself. "Art is not a pleasure, a solace, or an amusement," he cried, "art is a great matter." And he blamed the entire art establishment—artists, museums, critics, schools, arts organizations, etc.—for ignoring and violating that truth, sending art down a wayward path, blind to the evil that art can do and oblivious to the good.

Tolstoy complained that so many people are caught up in the arts—some as artists who give their lives over to it, others as art-lovers whose

* I have sometimes put quotation marks around "art" to emphasize the encompassing idea and singular status of art in modern Western culture, for reasons that will become clear.

emotions and sensibilities are molded by it, and others still whose livelihoods depend on what has come to be known as the "artworld"—that the powers of art shouldn't be taken lightly. For society pays a heavy price by misunderstanding what "true art" is and can do for us, and how "false art" does great damage. At heart, Tolstoy's distinction between the two is simple, if questionable. "True art" affects, or in his term "infects," people with deep and universal emotions that unite humankind in a benign, spiritual brotherhood. "False art," by contrast, merely stimulates the senses, or teases the intellect, breeds elitist tastes, divides people, perverts morals, and debases humanity. Few readers can nod assent to Tolstoy's impassioned moralism, and some probably hurl the book against a wall with laughing contempt. But we do not need to accept Tolstoy's moralistic view of art in order to take his questions about the effects of art, good and bad, seriously.

In fact, ever since antiquity in the West thinkers have tried to explain—and sometimes to manage—the powers of art. Conservative thinkers going back to Plato have stressed the dangers of art and urged curtailing it to head those dangers off, whereas the more liberal-minded, beginning with Aristotle, have stressed the good art can do and encouraged freedom for art to promote that good. Even today, politicians, teachers, and parents get embroiled in controversies over what kind of art is benign and what kind is dangerous—as I write this, a school in Florida has recently fired its principal for allowing an art history class to see Michaelangelo's nude sculpture of David. In the light of this tradition, and the culture of art and entertainment that enfolds us as never before, it is arguably more pressing than ever to ask: What is art? What is entertainment? What do they do to us, and how do they do it? And how can we use them for the better and not the worse?

But before delving into those prickly questions we must first acknowledge an important historical fact about art. It is this: The idea of "art" did not exist for most of human history in the West or anywhere else. No one had a word for "art" as we know it. That does not mean, of course, that there was no *art*. Just that no one thought of it as "art." The English word "art" itself comes from the Latin *ars*, for technical skill in making things—preceded by the kindred Greek terms *ararisko*, for fitting something together; *techne*, for the skill and rules in making something; and *poieîn*, for making or bringing something to pass (hence our words *technique* and *poetry*). Traditional cultures have therefore tended to view what we now label "art" as what we would call "crafts," and the makers were not creative "artists" but skilled "craftsmen" or "artisans." The Greeks called them *demiourgoi*, makers of things. The objects produced or performed with *technical* skills, would not even fall into a generic category like "art," but would instead have their own individual names, or clusters of names, like poetry, dance, music, and painting—all of which became linked in ancient Greece under the *muses* and collectively taught as *mousikē*. These arts were also entwined so thoroughly with the rest of life, from religion to the social order, that no one could think of them as separate and unique, providing people a distinctive experience. Just look, for instance, at the culture of Bali today, where the lack of a word for "art" still goes unnoticed amidst an unsurpassed abundance of artistic activities in the name of Hindu worship, and where almost everyone is an artist of some kind.

All of that changed in the West when the objects made through these activities became "art," and the makers became "artists." But that did not happen until very modern times. Not that artists had gone altogether unappreciated. The ancient Romans had crowned poets and war heroes alike with laurel wreaths for their notable accomplishments. That practice had been abandoned with Rome's decline but was revived in that city centuries later with the poet Petrarch's ceremonious crowning with laurel in 1341 (the slightly earlier Italian poet Dante Alighieri is often depicted wearing a laurel wreath but that is a later symbolic addition). Still, these honors did not go to "artists" by that name. Over the next couple of hundred years, the Renaissance elevated figures like Michelangelo and Leonardo da Vinci into cultural heroes exemplifying the *homo universal* gifted in many pursuits, especially the arts. But even they were not celebrated as "artists." After the idea of the "fine arts" emerged in the seventeenth and eighteenth centuries, bringing the notions of "taste" and the "connoisseur," the "artist" ascended from the "artisan" with the rise of Romanticism that ushered in ideas of genius, the creative imagination, artistic "originality," and a cult of "art." The late-nineteenth-century creed of "art for art's sake" completed this new tradition, rendering "art" a thing unto itself, unrelated to other pursuits and practices of society, and for the most part superior to them. That is where Tolstoy entered the scene to decry the divorce of art from ordinary life and to deplore the consequences for society and humankind. That is also where the flights of "modern art" took off and sailed on through the twentieth century toward the peculiar condition of "art" today, when pretty much anything can be art, as well as to the Culture of Entertainment that gathered steam in the later years of Modernism and has gone on to achieve preeminence over practically everything.

This tiny historical outline brings us to the particular character and powers of art. Being the very large subject that is, this little book can barely touch it. But I will sketch some ways of looking at the character and powers of art and their effects on us that I think are useful. I will do that first by identifying what I call the three faces of art: artistic creation, the created artwork, and the effects of art. From there, I will concentrate on the third of these faces through what I call the "art experience," for here lie the best clues to understanding the distinctive character and effects of art, both high and low. Next, I look into what happens to us within the art experience overall. That is where *mind games* come in. Then I look more closely at the similarities and differences within the art experience of what high art and low, or art and entertainment, can do to us, and how, in effect, they play mind games with us. That will lead me to the Culture of Entertainment, where I will outline how it gained ascendancy and illustrate some of this culture's most consequential influences in human life, including its effects on politics and the events of January 6, 2021. Finally, I will conclude with a few thoughts on future prospects for the Culture of Entertainment, and for humanity.

In short, this little excursion into the large realm of art and entertainment has limited and specific aims. But it also echoes Tolstoy's judgment that "Art is a great matter."

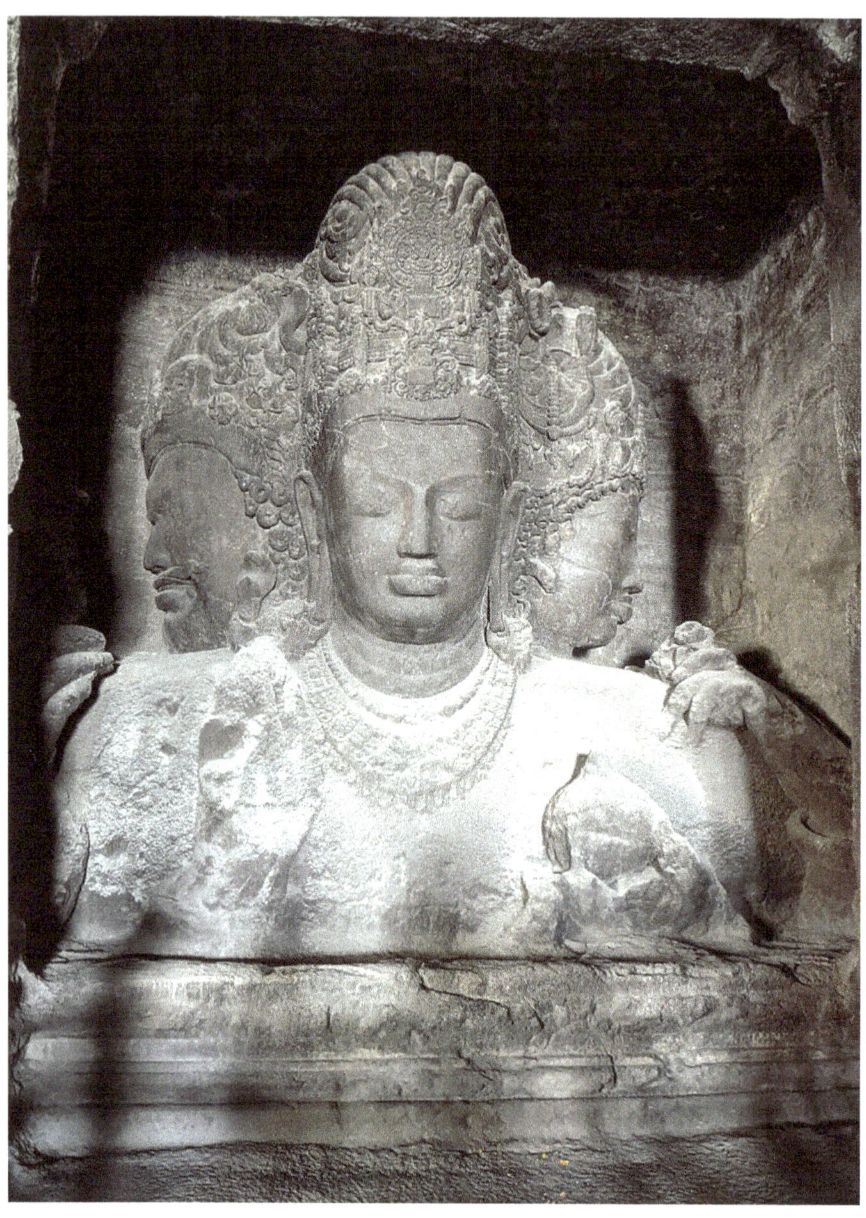

Fig. 2 — Three Faces of Shiva*: his destructive side (left), his creative or restorative side (right), and his calmly preservative side (front). Elephanta Caves, Mumbai, India. Mid-fifth to -sixth centuries.*

I
The Three Faces of Art

"Anything can be a work of art."
—Arthur Danto

Like the divine Hindu triumvirate of Brahma, Vishnu, and Shiva, whose faces sometimes appear on three sides of a single sculpture representing the three distinctive dimensions of existence in Hindu theology (creation, preservation, destruction/renewal),* art could be said metaphorically to have three faces representing the three principal aspects of art. One is the act of artistic creation. Another is the created artwork. And the third is the effect of the artwork on observers or audiences—through the mind games of what I call the art experience. These three faces show us how to define art, and how not to.

The Creation of Art

Artistic creation comes first because without it there would be no art of any kind. And yet it proves to be both the most elusive and the least helpful in understanding what "art" is by contrast to things that are not "art." After all, artistic creation remains one of the unsolved mysteries of human nature, even though thinkers have studied and pondered it for millennia.

In the early years of Western philosophy, Plato viewed artists with a wary eye (he did not call them "artists," of course, but rather, in general,

* Shiva is also often depicted alone with three faces representing those same characteristics, as in the sculpture pictured here (Fig. 2).

demiourgoi, craftsmen or makers of things).* And he considered the act of creating, or rather *making*, artworks to be quite simple. It was an act of imitation, *mimesis*: an imitation of physical things perceived by the senses or of mental images perceived by the mind's eye. He thought artists made these imitations in one of two ways. First, as he wrote in the *Republic*, they could have the technical skill to imitate anything well enough to appear like the original. Second, artists might fashion imitations through a kind of "divine madness," as he called it in *Ion*, that inspires them independent of technical skill or deliberate effort. Either way, artists misrepresent whatever they imitate: they tell stories of the gods but are blind to the gods' true nature and ways; they mimic war and its heroes but never fight in it; they treat moral subjects but don't really care about morality; they depict people and gods and objects in sculpture and painting but know little of people, nothing of the divine, and they could not even make the physical objects they imitate. In all, they deal in deceptive appearances of things while being ignorant of things in themselves. No wonder Plato distrusted artists and proposed in the *Republic* to banish or at least to control them—notwithstanding his own gifts as a literary artist, which gave his dialogues an artistry admired through the ages, of which more later.

Plato's grumpy judgments of artists aside, the idea of "making" as an act of imitation, *mimesis*, whether arising from technical skill or divine madness, held sway in the West until the eighteenth century. And it was not confined to the imitation of physical things or ideas. The act of imitation could include borrowing from the works of other artists, too. As a result, artistic originality was not prized, and plagiarism was unknown as an offense until the seventeenth century. So it was that the act of artistic creation continued to be understood as primarily one of making imitations for over two thousand years.

Then came a new discovery: the creative imagination. The imagination had long been thought of primarily as a faculty of mind that can imi-

* The act of making things was *poieîn,* and the things made were *empoieîn*—hence the English words *poets* and *poetry*—terms Plato uses in his condemnation of poets in particular.

tate existing things, although it was also sometimes scorned as a perverse power of fantasy that can cloud reality and do harm. Sir Joshua Reynolds, the doyen of eighteenth-century British artists and authorities on art, echoed the first of these traditional ideas when he wrote in his *Discourses on Art*, "The imagination is incapable of producing anything originally of itself, and can only vary and combine those ideas with which it is furnished by means of the senses."[1] For good measure, he added that "genius is not [to be] taken for inspiration, but as the effect of close observation and experience."[2] Reynolds was a thoroughgoing empiricist to be sure, in the manner of British intellectuals of his day. Empiricists declared sensation, mind, and imagination to be essentially passive faculties that receive information from the outside and fit it together in thoughts and possibly artworks (Reynolds' contemporary, Laurence Sterne, poked ribald fun at this theory throughout his great comic novel *Tristram Shandy*). Reynolds did not even grant the imagination the powers of inventive fantasy. But those who did, going back to Montaigne and including Reynolds' contemporaries Jean-Jacques Rousseau and Samuel Johnson, scorned the imagination as, in Johnson's words, "a licentious and vagrant faculty, unsusceptible of limitations, and impatient of restraint."[3] In all, the idea of imaginative "creation" beyond imitation or wild-eyed fantasy had long been, well, we might say, unimaginable.

But it wasn't unimaginable to the Romanticists. They embraced the imagination as a power of creation, with all of the fantasies it could conjure up. The mental passivity of empiricism was anathema to them. The Romantic poet William Blake attacked Reynolds on just those grounds. "Damned fool," Blake scrawled beside Reynolds' words on genius quoted above (among the scores of contemptuous marginalia he wrote in his copy of Reynolds' *Discourses*), adding, "Genius cannot be bound."[4] And, setting forth his own anti-empiricist conception of the mind and senses in his illustrated book of philosophical aphorisms, *There is No Natural Religion*, he proclaimed (on Plate 10), "Man's perceptions are not bounded by organs of perception; he perceives more than sense (tho ever so acute) can discover." Stressing the idea, he declared: "Inspiration & Vision . . . will always Remain my Element my Eternal Dwelling place."[5] Convinced that the imagination yields powers of sheer creation,

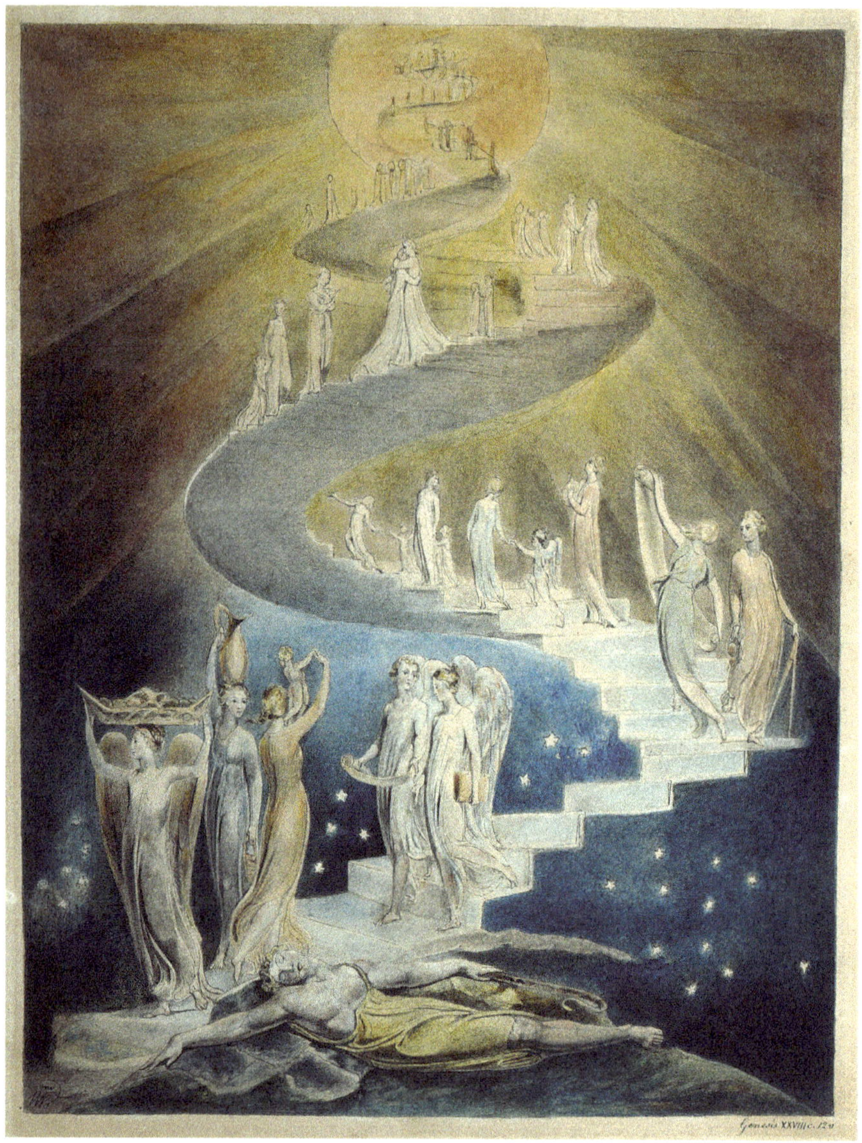

Fig. 3 — William Blake, Jacob's Dream, *c. 1805.*

Blake imagines the stairway to heaven in Jacob's Biblical dream as an irenic, curvilinear passage rising beyond the stars with angelic ladies and children drifting along its gentle and magically suspended incline. He would insist that he did not just assemble sensations here; his imagination created something new.

he created artworks—visual and literary—that no one could deny were truly *imaginative* (see Fig. 3). Later, the poet Samuel Taylor Coleridge rhapsodized in *Biographia Literaria* (1817) about the "Imagination" as "the living Power and prime Agent of all human Perception," which stirs thought and resembles "the eternal act of creation in the infinite I AM."[6] Coleridge's imagination might have got the better of his words here, but, like Blake, he demonstrated his ideas in imaginative and often mysterious poems like "The Rime of the Ancient Mariner" and "Kubla Khan"—he also smoked a lot of opium.

The literary historian M. H. Abrams notably described the passage of the imagination from imitating existing things to creating something brand new as that *From the Mirror to the Lamp*, the title of his enduring book. This passage so exalted the creative imagination that the "creative artist" became a figure of nearly divine powers. And with those powers went the assumption that the artistic imagination arises from "genius" and yields truly "original" art far from mere imitation. Even the sober-minded philosopher Immanuel Kant, an older contemporary and intellectual mentor of Coleridge, lent support to these claims in his pioneering book on art and aesthetics, *Critique of Judgment* (1790), where he declared (contradicting Reynolds) that "genius is a talent for producing that for which no rule can be given . . . consequently, originality must be its primary property."[7] The near obsession with the creative imagination, genius, and originality brought the condemnation of plagiarism—a term derived in the seventeenth century from the Latin word for kidnapping—as a kind of artistic crime. That obsession also wrapped the act of artistic creation in more mystery than ever.

In the twentieth century, artistic creativity became a recurrent topic among philosophers who theorized about it and psychologists who studied it. Arthur Koestler's expansive *The Act of Creation* (1964), for instance, found the act of creation to be similar in all branches of human activity from humor to art and science. But because he equated this creativity with an intellectual act of linking normally incompatible ways of thinking, he still did not capture the illusive character of "artistic creation." The psychologist Howard Gardner also aspired to a generic understanding of "creativity" in *Creating Minds: An Anatomy of*

Creativity Seen Through the Lives of Freud, Einstein, Picasso, Stravinsky, Eliot, Graham, and Gandhi (1993). His notion that creativity occurs in every area of life where people manage to come up with something at least relatively original—whether an artwork or an advertising slogan or the solution to a problem—did spark a widened perspective on what "intelligence" and "creativity" are. Surely the act of creation, whatever it is—and Gardner says nothing much about how it actually works—has kinships wherever we find it. And many a student of the subject has found "stages of creativity" or the equivalent in practically every pursuit. For instance, the enterprising record producer and author Rick Rubin proclaims right off in his book *The Creative Act: A Way of Being* (2023) that "Everyone is a Creator," then proceeds to demonstrate this through every endeavor imaginable. But none of this sheds much light on the uniqueness of "artistic creation" among creative activities, much less on the uniqueness of "art" itself. Perhaps they are not unique.

A sampling of twenty-first-century philosophical books might bring us closer to understanding artistic creation. And we do find efforts—surprisingly scarce compared to the plethora of books on this subject in psychology and the mass market—to penetrate the mystery, e.g., *The Creation of Art: New Essays in Philosophical Aesthetics,* eds., Berys Gaut and Paisley Livingstone (2003) and *Artistic Creation: A Phenomenological Account,* Jeff Mitscherling and Paul Fairfield (2019). But those, often abstruse, philosophical forays don't come close enough. For in the end they leave us with generalizations on artistic creation that might apply to other pursuits. This suggests that whatever might be truly unique in artistic creation still remains too wrapped in mystery to fully discover. So, maybe we should just call it "divine madness," and let it go at that.

But, if we leave artistic creation uniquely wrapped in mystery, it can tell us nothing much about the created artwork. And if we think of it as essentially the same as other types of "creative" activities, we make art, as the fruit of that activity, pretty much the same as the fruits of the other activities. Maybe "art" is, indeed, no more than that. But I think human experience tells us otherwise. And this leads me to the conclusion that, whether artistic creation is mysteriously unique or a generic act like all other creative acts, it simply cannot tell us enough about what art itself is and what makes art so important in human life. Perhaps the created artwork can do better.

The Artwork

Compared to the act of artistic creation, the created artwork more readily discloses its secrets or, at any rate, lends itself to scrutiny. For unlike the illusive act of artistic creation, the work of art is something we can, in a manner of speaking, hold up to the light and examine closely. This accessibility of the artwork has yielded shelves of books on how artworks can help us answer the venerable question: What is Art? That accessibility has also tended to focus the attention of critics and connoisseurs on the aesthetics of artworks as the best way to answer that question, at least by contrast to things that aren't "art." But taking aesthetic form as the measure of art raises some perplexing questions.

One of those questions is this: If aesthetics is the measure of art, wouldn't an exact duplicate of an artwork have as much claim to being art as the original? Or, in the words of the influential philosopher of art Arthur Danto, "What makes the difference between a work of art and something not a work of art when there is no interesting perceptual difference between them?"[8] This question would have had no meaning before the rise of "creative originality" as a standard of artistic value—and the invention of technologies that can mechanically reproduce art. But it means a lot nowadays. And yet, as esteemed as originality has become, if there is no perceptible aesthetic difference between the original and a copy, what makes the original true "art" and the copy, or forgery, however exact, a mere imitation?

We might dismiss this question as a hypothetical philosophical exercise since no two artworks could ever be exactly alike. But the question amounts to more than that. And the artworld takes it very seriously indeed. For much can be at stake in distinguishing an original artwork from a virtually identical copy. Some critics—led by Walter Benjamin, who was probably the first to explore, as he put it in the title of his seminal essay, "The Work of Art in the Age of Mechanical Reproduction" (1935)—make that distinction by discerning an "aura" that emanates from the original artwork as created by the artist and embedded in its historical context, which a copy lacks. But I dare say one would have to know which is the original before one could sense that aura. And museums go to great pains to ensure that the artworks they display are originals and not copies, since "aura" tends to follow the authority of the museum. When, for instance, a painting long attributed to a master like Rembrandt is discovered to have come from a lesser contemporary, or worse, to be an outright forgery, the painting comes off the wall or is relegated to the shadows as a curiosity. "Aura" be damned. And when the Metropolitan Museum of Art in New York had to revise—more than once—its historical attribution and aesthetic evaluation of a famed ancient Greek bronze horse (see Fig. 4), and did so based on highly technical scrutiny surpassing any perceptions by the ordinary naked eye, we have to conclude that the observable aesthetics of the original artwork is not the measure of what "art" is, or even the value of an artwork. It must be something else.

We can find a clue to what that is by looking at the "original artwork" from two perspectives. From one, we see the artwork as an original creation by an artist who endowed it with aesthetic properties that are distinctive to that artist's imagination, talent, and style. The value of the original artwork in this sense is primarily aesthetic. From the other perspective, we see the original artwork as simply a unique object created by an individual artist at a particular time. The value of the original artwork in this sense is primarily historical and economic. Art appreciation teachers and museums guide us more toward the first perspective, since they want us to value artworks for their aesthetic qualities as fashioned by an artist's hand. But many experts in the artworld nowadays view artworks primarily from the second perspective, because these professionals deal so often with the economics of art, namely, the market value of individual art objects themselves.

And in recent times the economics of art have gone kind of crazy. For the financial value of original works in the visual arts, especially by well-known artists, has quite overshadowed their aesthetic value. When the Metropolitan Museum of Art in New York purchased Rembrandt's great painting *Aristotle with a Bust of Homer* for $2.3 million in 1961, it was the highest price ever paid for a painting anywhere (see Fig 5).

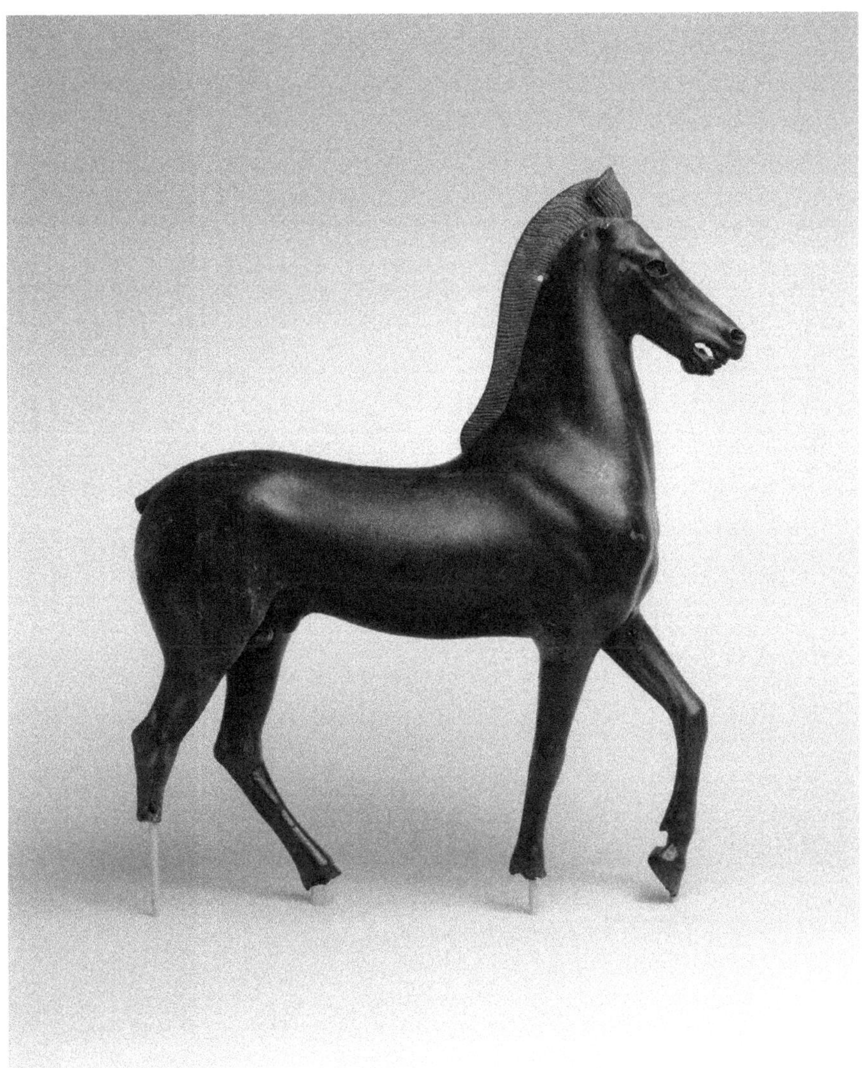

Fig. 4 — Ancient Greek bronze horse.

Acquired by the Metropolitan Museum in 1923, the sleek bronze horse was proudly and popularly displayed as a supreme example of Greek artistry from the classic age of fifth century BCE. Then in the 1960s, a curator declared, after close scientific scrutiny, that it was actually a twentieth-century forgery and it was pulled from public view. A brouhaha erupted in the museum world over the age and artistic integrity of the horse. Finally, following further scientific analysis of the sculpture, a loose consensus formed in that artworld around the conclusion that, although the horse was not of the fifth century BCE, it was most likely sculpted in late Hellenistic times, the later second or early first century BCE, and possibly for the Roman art market. Back on display, the horse still looks to the naked eye as splendid as it always did, but can museum goers really see it as they once could?

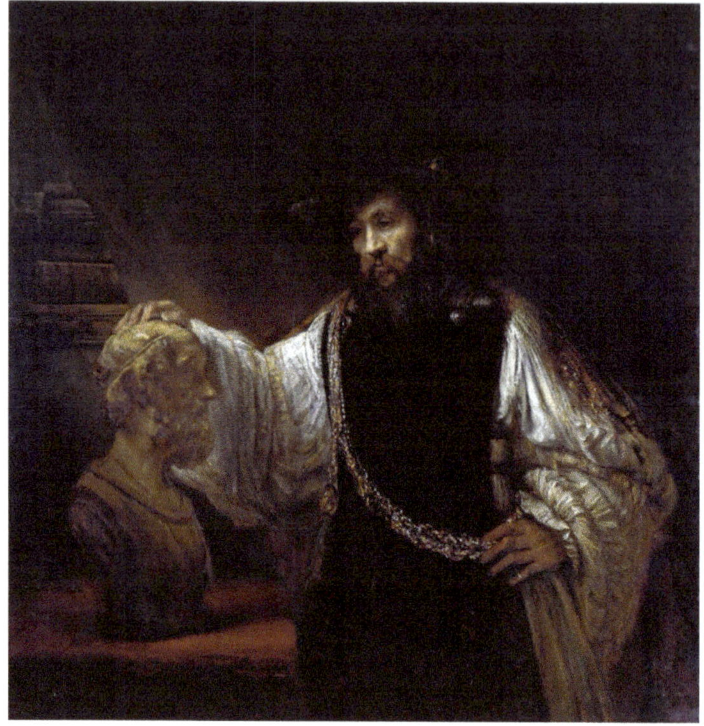

Fig. 5 (above) — Rembrandt van Rijn, Aristotle with a Bust of Homer, *1653.*

Fig. 6 (right) — Leonardo da Vinci, Salvator Mundi *(Savior of the World), c. 1499–1510.*

This painting has had a peculiarly checkered history since it left the hand of its creator, starting with its neglect and virtual disappearance, then followed by questions about who that creator actually was. It was generally thought (by anyone who knew of its existence) to be by many hands. And it had been touched up so many times over the years that the very idea that Leonardo could have painted it all became absurd. As a measure of its status, when it surfaced at auction in the 1950s it sold for about $120. Later, some art connoisseurs and restorers hit upon it, cleaned it up, and found, beneath centuries of neglect and misguided "improvements," what they judged to be an authentic Leonardo. Although the attribution was still questionable—and several art experts denied it altogether—that was good enough for the money-hungry art market. In 2017, it fetched $450 million, the highest price ever paid for a painting as of now. But the saga of Salvator Mundi *was not over. Purchased by the Saudi Prince Mohammed bin Salman, for whom $450 million was pocket change, it has not been publicly exhibited, despite bin Salman's promises to do so by loaning it to museums, including the Louvre. The reasons are shrouded in mystery. The ongoing saga of* Salvator Mundi *has by now become the stuff of fable—and of documentary films, such as Antoine Vitkine's* The Savior for Sale *and Andreas Koefoed's* The Lost Leonardo *(2021). A symptom of an art-crazed culture.*

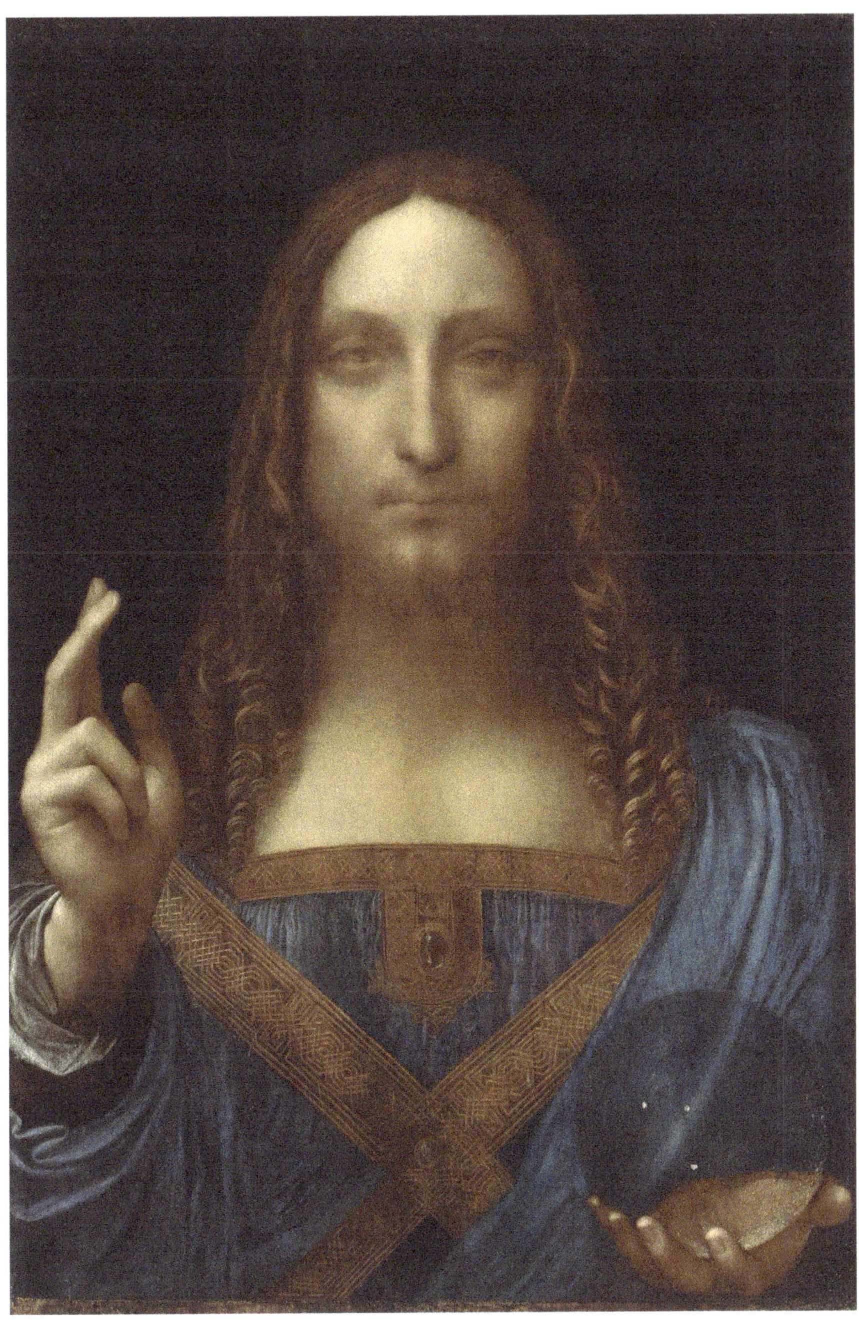

So impressed was the museum with that mighty price tag, and aware of the public's interest in it, that the figure was posted on the wall along with the painting's identity—until $2.3 million became a pittance in the art market and the notice was removed. The current holder of the top price paid—and we can be certain this will not last long—is a painting by Leonardo da Vinci entitled *Salvator Mundi*, for which an Arab billionaire dropped $450 million in 2017 (see Fig. 6). However splendid an artist Leonardo might be, it is surely not the aesthetic quality of *Salvator Mundi* that makes it "worth" that price—much less is it aesthetics that got $110 million that same year for a creation by the dubious, novelty artist Jean-Michel Basquiat, or $195 million in 2022 for a silkscreen of Marilyn Monroe by Andy Warhol, or even $10 million in 2021 for a painting of Marrakesh by the amateur artist Winston Churchill. That these objects are artworks is almost incidental to their economic value. They are primarily rare objects to hang on the wall in an artworld awash in money and possessed by the value of artistic celebrity.

In Voltaire's *Candide*, the innocent hero finds himself in Eldorado, where the inhabitants treat gems as indifferently as they do pebbles on the ground. That is because gems lie on the ground as plentifully as the pebbles among them. This stuns the naïve Candide and sets him to dreaming of riches if he gathers a bunch of the gems and takes them back to Europe with him. Even if their colors and glitter gave them aesthetic value to the Eldoradans, the gems had no economic value. Copies or prints of paintings work largely the same way. Despite their aesthetic value they have little economic value because they are plentiful.

Here we must draw another, and quite obvious, distinction pertaining to "original artworks." It separates the visual arts, in which paintings and sculptures are created as aesthetic objects in themselves, from the arts in which artworks are created to be reproduced or performed, like manuscripts in literature, scores in music, and the prints of films. An "original" painting has a status and value as "art" that simply does not apply to the "original" manuscript of a book or a score of music or a print of film. However aesthetically *original* Dante's *Divine Comedy* or Shakespeare's *Hamlet* or Beethoven's *Ninth Symphony* or even films like Orson Wells' *Citizen Kane* may be, the physical originals have no particular aesthetic value. It is Dante's poetry as read that has aesthetic value, not Dante's original pen marks on the page; it is Shakespeare's plays as put on a stage, or even read, that have aesthetic value, not the pages containing his written words; it is Beethoven's symphony as performed by musicians that has aesthetic value, not the notes Beethoven inscribed on the staffs; and it is Wells' film as shown in theaters that has aesthetic value, not the original physical print of it. Of course, such original manuscripts, musical scores, and film prints do have great value, but it is historical and above all economic, for they are prized as rare objects created by notable individuals. Historians might pore over those objects, and collectors might pay dearly to own and proudly display them. But art and aesthetics have nothing much to do with it.

Every day museums, auctions, and collectors prove that original artworks have primarily economic rather than aesthetic value. Exact reproductions will not do for them, even if the reproductions have the same aesthetic value as the original. So, apart from economics, if a copy can have the same aesthetic value as the original, why should anyone fuss about reproductions?

Auguste Rodin didn't. And his attitude toward reproductions marked a kind of watershed in the very idea of the "original artwork." For he gained renown with highly evocative, often moody, rough-hewn sculptures that were not fashioned to stand as unique original artworks. He rather molded plaster casts that he used to produce multiple reproductions, sometimes recasting them again and again in alternative versions or combinations of images. It is true that sculptors since antiquity had been creating models of sculptures to be cast in bronze or other materials, sometimes reproduced for buyers. But Rodin took this practice much farther. He made reproduction central to his artistic creativity (see Fig. 7). As one art historian observes, "Rodin's deployment of the replicable plaster cast was largely unprecedented" because "he made sculpture from his own sculptures" and "reminded viewers that the individual figures were replicable objects." Far from being an artist preoccupied with creating original artworks, he wanted to produce many copies to share. And it was as an expression of his "creativity" that "he exploited the reproducibility of the plaster statuette, repackaging its potential for

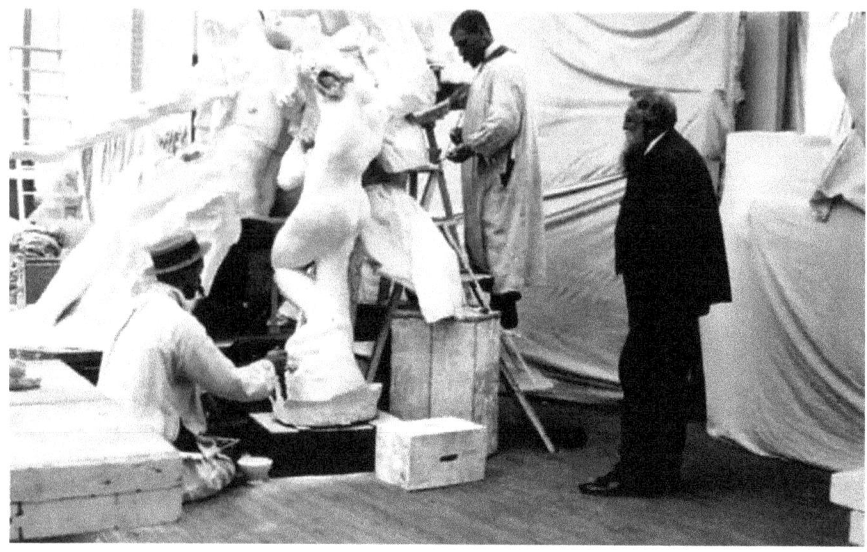

Fig. 7 — Auguste Rodin supervising work on his Monument to Victor Hugo *(original version) in the studio of his principal assistant Henri Lebossé, 1896.*

Like some of his other works (such as his formidable, brooding statue of Balzac consigned to stand in an island of the Boulevard Raspail off the Boulevard Montparnasse), the monument turned out to be too avant-garde for those who commissioned it, even after he had submitted to their demands and pared it down to the final version. But, since that version still depicted Hugo as an old man, naked, and in kind of a dark mood, it was deemed unsuitable as a monument to honor the famed author in the Paris Pantheon. Eventually, the work found its way to the Rodin Museum.

mass production."[9] So popular and available would his artworks become that some, such as *The Thinker* and *The Lovers*—for which he even sold the reproduction rights—have become practically household artifacts.

Understandably, this reproductive vagueness of "original artwork" has presented challenges to copyright and intellectual property law. The Rodin Museum in Paris attests to this, since, in effect, it holds a collection of reproductions, for that is what Rodin created. It is therefore no surprise that the museum has stringent rules discriminating between what it labels "original editions" of Rodin's reproductions and later reproductions by other hands. As the museum's "Warning . . . about the Notion of Authenticity" states: "editions of sculptures limited to twelve numbered casts, including artist's copies, are considered to be original works of art." The museum displays many bronze statues that are "original" in that sense.

In any case, Rodin's distinctive artistry lies no more in the "original editions" of his creations than in the other reproductions. It resides in the artistic ideas they embody and convey. I leave the ontological puzzles there to philosophers. But it is worth noting that Rodin's "originals" are rather like the manuscripts of books intended to be printed many times, and his "original editions," like the first editions of books, are valued mainly for their economic worth as the unique first set of reproductions. In the modern artworld, the claws of economic interest grasp for "originality" even when an artist disregarded it.

When Rodin died in 1917, an innovative young Italian painter named Giorgio de Chirico was nearly ten years into a career that would become much affected by that economic reality. In 1918 he painted a picture named *The Disquieting Muses* (see Fig. 8), which typified many of the later works in an epochal period (1910–1919) characterized by what de Chirico labeled "metaphysical" paintings. These later metaphysical works differed from those earlier by departing from mysterious, shadowy, nearly empty piazzas (like the painting on the cover of this book—see the Appendix for more on it and de Chirico) and featuring instead large, faceless, dehumanized mannequins dominating the piazzas where they stand, or presenting "metaphysical interiors" with a jumble of images. A few years after painting *The Disquieting Muses*, de Chirico made a copy of it for his surrealist friend Paul Éluard (prudently getting the consent of the owner of the original, who had declined to sell it). That would be the first of the copies or replicas of his works that de Chirico would produce from time to time over the years. But he did not proceed to make replicas of his works simply for friends or, like Rodin, from an artistic commitment to reproduction. He seems to have done it mainly because, while his style evolved away from the metaphysical paintings, critics and the art market did not follow. Resenting that neglect, he painted replicas—not exact copies—of his metaphysical works and sometimes post-dated them to both exploit and defy the market.

Later in his career de Chirico started making multiple replicas of some metaphysical paintings, or creating new ones on metaphysical themes, dating them to the past or randomly or not at all, in order both to taunt

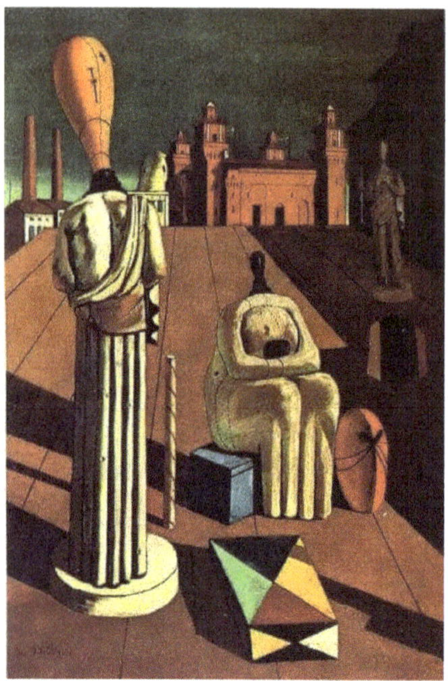

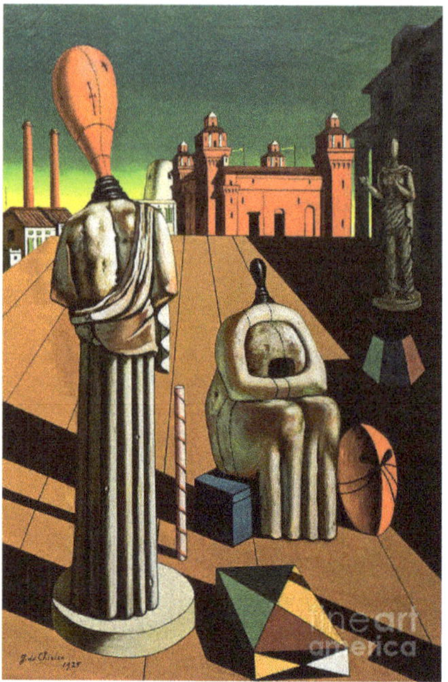

Fig. 8 — Giorgio de Chirico, The Disquieting Muses *(left, undated, but authorities say the original was painted in 1918; right, a copy dated 1925).*

Painted in the Italian city of Ferrara, where de Chirico was stationed during World War I, The Disquieting Muses *nods to that location with the rust-colored castle and factory in the background, which are more "realistic" than the structures in the mysterious plazas of his earlier metaphysical works. But their realism conflicts with their position below the plane of the piazza-like space in front of them and especially with the two weird figures in the foreground of that space. These are the muses. One stands close to us, with a dehumanized mannequin's head, facing away; the other is seated and has not even much of a mannequin's head (evidently inspired by a similarly seated, now-headless ancient Greek statue of Artemis). In the shadows behind, a third mannequin figure stands. In a poem named for the painting, Sylvia Plath wrote of three muses here, who "stand their vigil in gowns of stone / Faces blank as the day I was born." And the longer one thinks about them, the more disquieting they and the picture may become. After all, as noted in the Appendix, de Chirico's metaphysical paintings cannot be interpreted like other paintings because, essentially, they represent the enigmatic metaphysics, the inner reality, of an "atmosphere." The atmosphere here? Call it enigmatically disquieting.*

The second version of The Disquieting Muses *above (right) is dated "1925" on the canvas, but that date is unreliable since de Chirico often back-dated his many copies of this and other paintings. It differs from the undated one on the left only in small details hard to find.*

the art market and to display the artistry of repetition or variations on a theme—almost like Monet's numerous versions of chosen scenes. He was also scoffing at the cult of originality that possessed the artworld, and possibly suggesting the inherent timelessness of art and of the "Eternal Return" proposed by his philosophical mentor, Friedrich Nietzsche. Among these replicated works are renderings of some metaphysical piazzas, such as *Piazza d'Italia* (see Fig. 9 A, B). The leading authority on de Chirico today, Fabio Benzi, observes in *Giorgio de Chirico: Life and Paintings* (2019) that de Chirico's unapologetic practice of replicating his works during the 1940s and 1950s presaged the Pop Art movement.

Not surprisingly, the American Pop artist Andy Warhol, just beginning his career in the late 1950s, became a fan of de Chirico's replicas. Warhol remembered fondly meeting the Italian artist regularly at the Venice Biennial, and when the Museum of Modern Art held a retrospective of de Chirico's works in 1982—six years after de Chirico's death—including a few of the replicas, Warhol was so taken by the paintings that he produced silkscreen grids of several, such as *Italian Square* and *The Disquieting Muses* (see Figs. 10, 11) and held a gallery show of them the same year under the title "Andy Warhol (After de Chirico)." Warhol told an interviewer that he had been drawn to the Italian painter mainly because de Chirico "repeated the same images throughout his life." That was an overstatement, but it worked for Warhol. "I believe," Warhol went on, "he did it not only because people and dealers asked him to do it, but also because he liked it and viewed repetition as a way of expressing himself. This is probably what we have in common."[10]

And this brings us to Andy Warhol himself. He took the idea of artistic replication and reproduction toward its logical, if whimsical, conclusion. From an early stint in the 1950s illustrating advertisements, Warhol parlayed his commercial experience and savvy into a sensational career in art as reproduction, imitation, and commerce, and turned his life into artifice. He created and reproduced his famous *Campbell's Soup Cans* and constructed his *Brillo Boxes* identical in appearance to the commercial packaging. He also adopted the silkscreen printing process to produce manifold versions of images by applying several layers of paint to, most prominently, commercial photographs of well-known

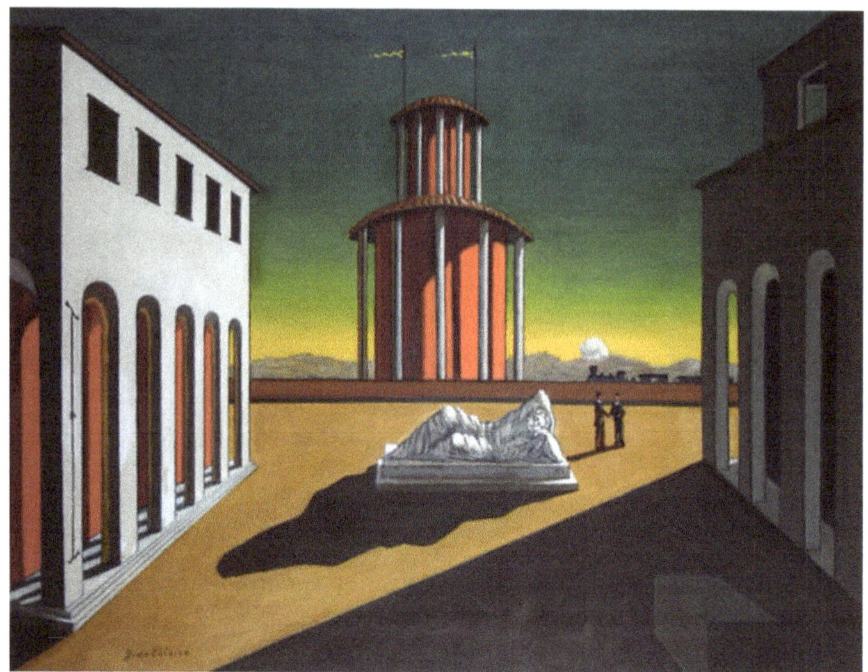

Fig. 9 A

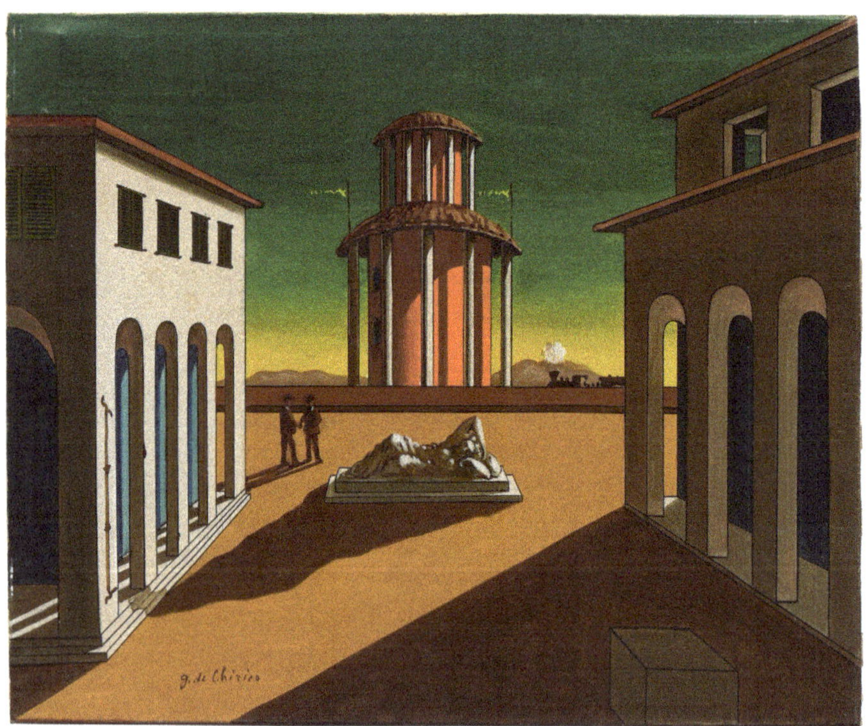

Fig. 9 B

Fig. 9 A, B, facing — Giorgio de Chirico, Piazza d'Italia.

De Chirico painted so many versions of Piazza d'Italia *that they cannot be dated with assurance. A few have been improbably dated 1913 (like Fig. 9 A), but most, if not all, were almost certainly done in the 1940s and 1950s (like Fig. 9 B, dated to 1955–56) when de Chirico was vigorously crusading against his enemies and developing a deftness at replicas that anticipated the practices of Pop Art. He used the prominent features we see here—the arcaded buildings on the sides, the exaggerated perspective, the sharp shadows, the red tower, the locomotive, and the statue—with variations in a number of metaphysical paintings given other names. And it can require a second or third look to detect the variations in his versions of* Piazza d'Italia. *But whatever their dates or differences, de Chirico created in these piazza scenes the same atmosphere of strangeness, melancholy, nostalgia, and enigma of his earliest metaphysical paintings. (I might add that de Chirico thought the train puffing along in the distance contributed a particularly melancholy and enigmatic quality to that atmosphere.) And we should not forget that in de Chirico's metaphysical paintings, atmosphere was everything.*

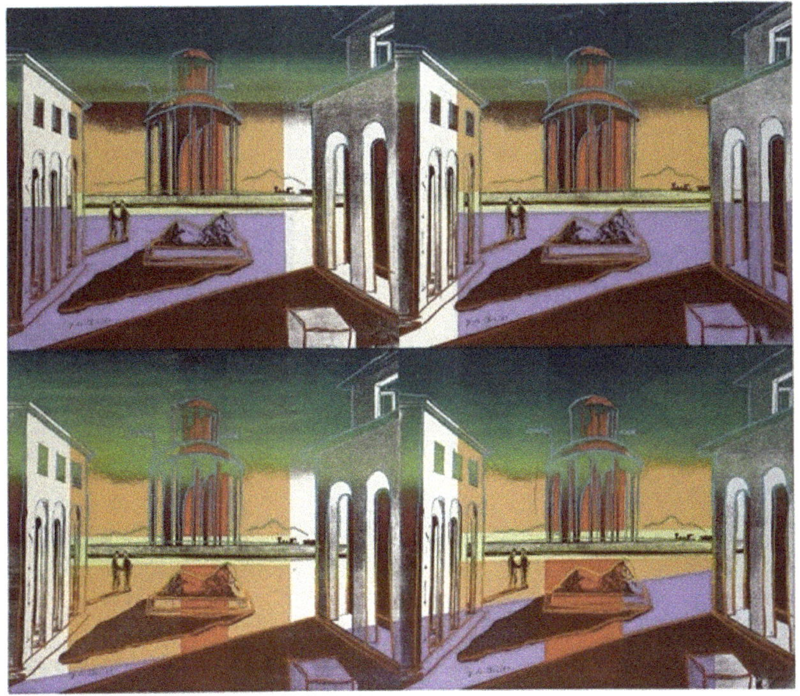

Fig. 10 — Andy Warhol, Italian Square with Ariadne (After de Chirico). *Acrylic and silkscreen on canvas, 1982. (One of three.)*

Warhol obviously modeled this artwork on a version of de Chirico's Piazza d'Italia *with the two men standing to the left of the sculpture, even though the version (dated "c. 1950") included in the exhibition catalogue, "Andy Warhol (After de Chirico)," lacks the two figures.*

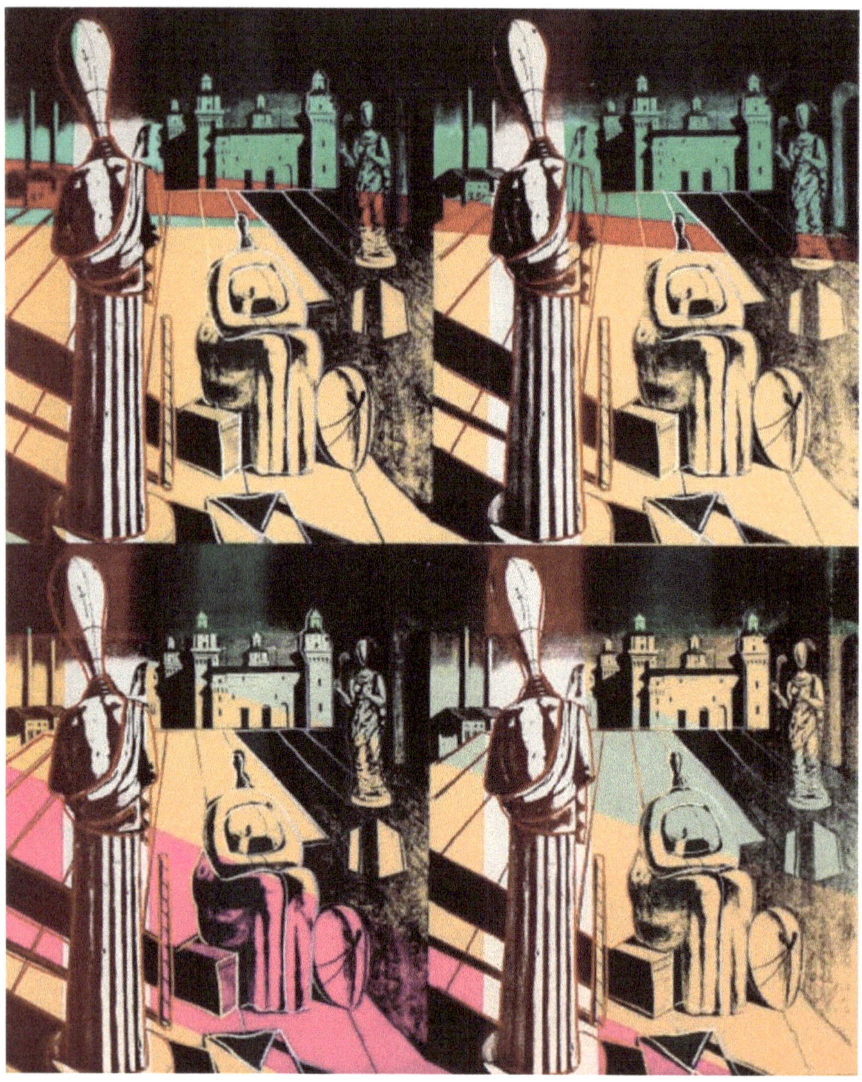

Fig. 11 — Andy Warhol, The Disquieting Muses, *acrylic and silkscreen on canvas.*

Warhol modeled this artwork on a de Chirico Le muse inquietanti *dated 1960, included in the catalogue of the exhibit, "Andy Warhol (After de Chirico)," 1982. This 1960 version is one of possibly nineteen of de Chirico's replicas of the painting known to exist.*

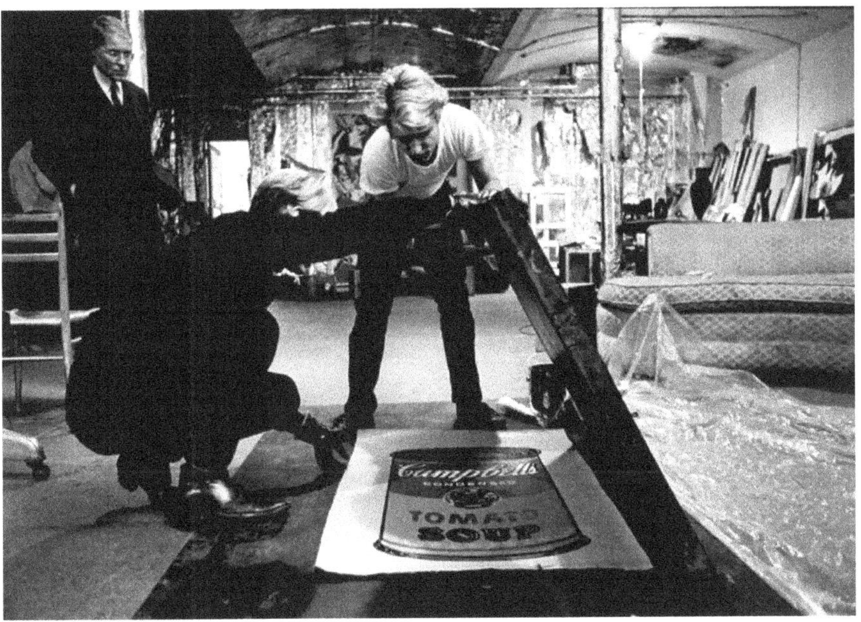

Fig. 12 — Andy Warhol in his Factory making a silkscreen of a Campbell's Tomato Soup Can, *1968.*

After painting by hand his epochal first series of thirty-two Campbell's Soup Cans *in 1962, Warhol later (1968, 1969) made another series by the silkscreen method he had adopted for its many artistic possibilities suited to his technological and commercial imagination.*

figures such as Mao Tse-tung and numerous movie stars, as well as the *Soup Cans* (see Fig. 12). These imitative reproductions mocked the sanctity of the "original" artwork and earned Warhol scorn as a charlatan, as well as fame for his own insouciant artistic novelty. They also raised new legal questions about artistic originality that culminated in a decision by the U.S. Supreme Court in 2023 ruling his silkscreen photograph/portraits of the pop star Prince had infringed on the copyright of the original photographs. Dissenters in the case held that the ruling failed to understand Warhol's work, which, Justice Elena Kagan wrote, "turned something not his into something all his own," or as an art historian pithily wrote in an amicus brief for the defense, Warhol "was concerned not with copyright but with the right to copy." "Warhol was most original," wrote the same author, "in the way he dismantled the idea of originality."[11] Warhol stamped his peculiar "originality" on

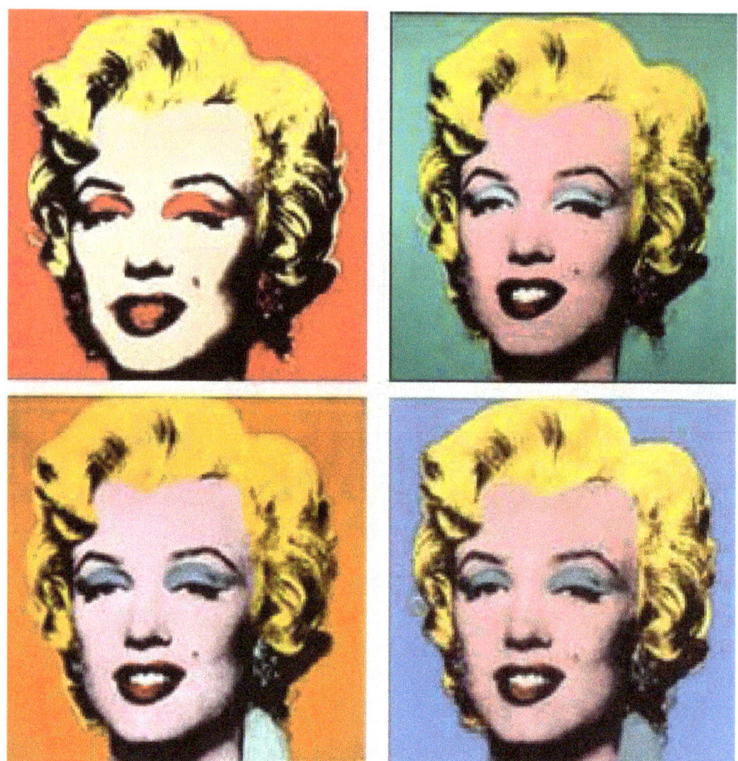

Fig. 13 — Andy Warhol, four silkscreen Shot Marilyns.

"Shot" because, while they were stacked together, the four silkscreens of Marilyn Monroe (with backgrounds and facial tints in red, orange, turquoise, and blue), were hit by a bullet from the pistol of a visitor to Warhol's Factory engaged in an unexpected act of, so she explained, "performance art." Warhol was not amused, but, in his instinctive show-business style, he put the incident to commercial use, making the "shot" a feature, not a flaw, of the four works.

anything he chose, turning it into a "Warhol"; and to lend individual "originality" to each of the silkscreens in his many series, he varied the colors, a clever marketing ploy, if nothing else. That his silkscreens now elicit many millions at auction—the $195 million paid in 2022 for his *Shot Blue Marilyn* (see Fig. 13) set a new record price for an artwork by an American—demonstrates that Warhol's fame has long since vanquished the scorn, and that, notwithstanding the Supreme Court decision, reproduction has become "art" or, as Warhol would prefer, "business art," just as commerce has come to dominate the artworld. Warhol's ingenious artistic exploits also made him the face of what got named Pop Art, which overturned traditional standards of art by celebrating—and appropriating—commercial and popular culture as "art," or, rather, virtually banishing the idea of "art" itself. We will revisit Warhol for his role in the Culture of Entertainment.

Let us now return to the question of what the created artwork tells us about what "art" is, or at least how to think about this question. It should be clear that the reproduction of artworks clouds the idea not only of the original artwork but of art itself. For when no aesthetic difference exists between an original artwork and a reproduction of it, or when a reproduction on its own is considered an artwork, we must conclude either that aesthetics is no measure of art or that the standard of what art is should be widened. Or both. When Walter Benjamin wrote about such things in "The Work of Art in the Age of Mechanical Reproduction," he thought the "aura" and aesthetic value of original artworks were getting quite lost in this age of mechanical reproduction. He feared the political implications of this loss more than the artistic consequences because he saw the Nazi regime so effectively exploiting film—to which he devoted much of the essay—for evil political purposes. But politics aside, as Benjamin was probably the first to articulate, the multiplying technologies of reproduction can readily undermine traditional ideas of what art is while expanding the terrain of what can be deemed "art." That rendered the idea of art ambiguous to say the least. And this ambiguity gave the mind games we play, in deciding what is "art" and what is not, more to do than ever.

The ambiguities that now beset the idea of art especially absorbed the philosopher Arthur Danto. He thought Marcel Duchamp's urinal, infamously displayed upside-down as an artwork labeled *Fountain*, signed "R. Mutt, 1917" (see Fig. 14), and, above all, Andy Warhol's *Campbell's Soup Cans* and *Brillo Boxes* had pulled the rug out from under all traditional conceptions of what art is, or what can be "art." Danto concluded from Warhol's reproductive fabrications that now, as he wrote in a book entitled *After the End of Art* (published in 1997,

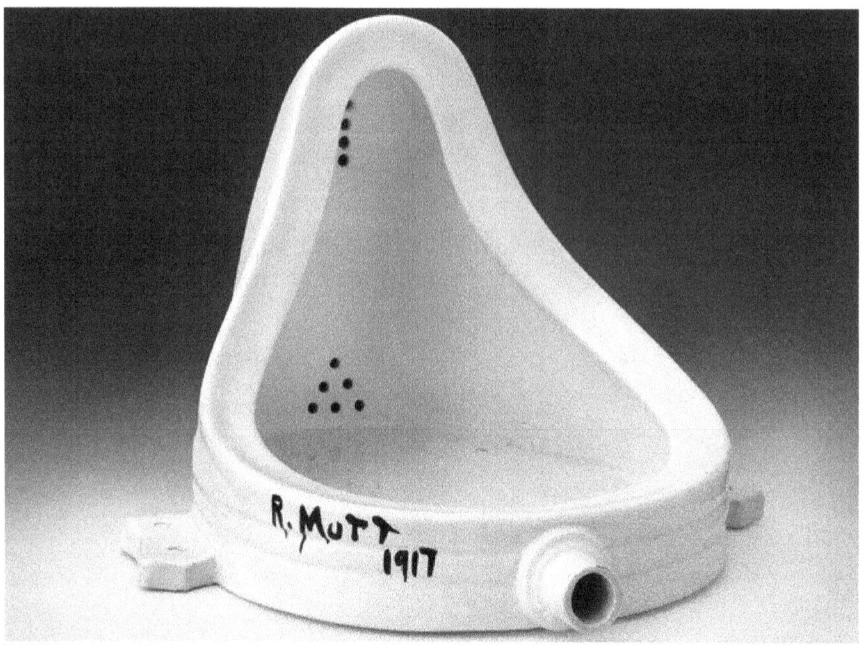

Fig. 14 — Marcel Duchamp, "'Fountain.' R. Mutt. 1917."
This was an early instance of Duchamp's "readymade" artworks, which he said were "everyday objects raised to the dignity of a work of art by the artist's act of choice."

almost exactly one hundred years after Tolstoy's *What Is Art?*), "Anything can be a work of art."[12] But that is not the same as saying *everything is* a work of art. And so he asked: What turns something into a work of "art"?

Danto's answer passed through subtle changes, but he began by asserting in 1964—the year of Warhol's first *Brillo Box*—that something becomes "art" when the "artworld" of artists, philosophers, and philosophically minded critics accept it as "art."[13] The idea struck a chord with a number of thinkers interested in the strange paths art was taking. One of them, philosopher George Dickie, elaborated on Danto's notion (Danto later said Dickie had distorted it) with what came to be known as the "institutional theory of art." This theory said that art is anything that a society's arts institutions and other authorities designate as "art." Hence anything placed on display in a museum is art. Anything performed in a theater or concert hall is art. And so on. This definition has its practical uses and takes more complicated definitions off the hook.

And nowadays, in the post-Pop Art, postmodern era, most people probably rely on it implicitly, saying to themselves something like: "If this painting is in the museum [or this piece of music is played by serious musicians] it must be art, whether I would say it is or not." But it can give art-lovers some trouble.

For instance, walking down a street in New York or any other large city these days we might run across some large, abstract, geometrical, colored object at an intersection or in front of a building or on a lawn and we are tempted to stop and ask: What's that? Why is it there? Could it be . . . art? How do we know? We come closer and look for some kind of identification. We see a small sign reading, *Green Trapeziod, 2020, Jo Doe.* What do we make of that? Experience has probably taught us to conclude, not from the appearance of the thing but from the sign, that it is a work of art by Jo Doe, and that someone with appropriate authority had arranged to put it there. We might pause and try to grasp the artistic import of the huge trapezoid. Then we go on our way, possibly questioning why anyone would think that object is art and that it belongs where it is.

Or we go to a museum where in one of the galleries we come upon an object that looks like, say, a trash can, and we wonder: Is it a trash can, or is it art? Do we dare deposit trash in it, or should we stand back and "appreciate" it as "art"? The art will not reveal itself right away. Aesthetic form is irrelevant to the decision. If there is a label identifying it as an artwork, we can feel at ease and will look at it not as a trash can but as art—or we will at least try to do that. The trash can is "art" because the authority of the museum says it is. But suppose a prankster has put the label on it. We will still see it as art until a museum official comes along and removes the label (see Fig. 15). So the label itself does not make it "art." Only someone with suitable authority to attach the label can do that. Acknowledging this, we will have learned a lesson in the "institutional theory of art"—and in the mind games that art in our times calls upon us to play.

That theory might be commonly accepted as the definition of what makes something "art" nowadays—which is not to say many people don't recoil at what experts label "art." But it prompts critics, like Danto,

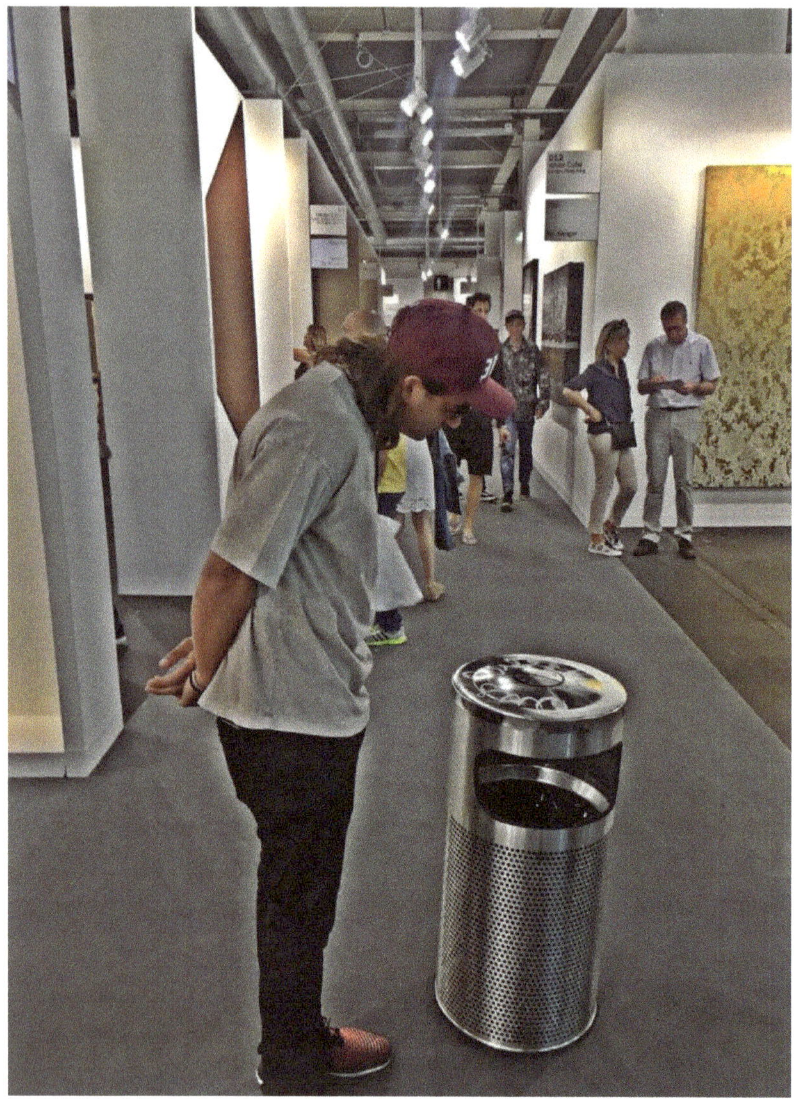

Fig. 15 — The artist Massimo Agostinelli inspecting a trash can in museum.

Agostinelli had moved the trash can from its normal discreet location at the art fair in Basel, Switzerland, hastily scrawled "La plus belle" on it, and placed it conspicuously for art-lovers to see. Watching their reactions, he was not surprised to see puzzlement then acceptance of the object as "art." No one treated it as a mere trash can—until, hours later, maintenance staff removed it. But the prank went on. Agostinelli purchased the can and put it on display in an exhibition called "Neo Pop Pop Neo" at the Zurich gallery that represents him. La plus belle *(a play on the French term for "garbage bin"* poubelle*) had become a recognized object d'art. ("How a Roguish Artist Set Out to Prank the Art World . . . ," Eileen Kinsella,* artnet news, *September 5, 2017.)*

to ask: If we allow art to be whatever the experts choose to anoint as "art," whether paintings, garbage cans, blank canvases or blank walls, we still want to know why they made that choice. They must have reasons to choose one thing over another as worthy to be called "art." Otherwise the choice is purely arbitrary and vacuous. Danto himself went on to argue that designating something as "art" depends not on "experts" or institutional authority but on finding philosophically significant artistic meaning in it—"embedded meaning" he called it in his last book, *What Art Is* (2013). In other words, if one can think philosophically about a thing and find the "embedded meaning" or art in it, then it is "art," no matter what the thing is, a urinal, a box of soap pads, or a trash can. That is why anything can be "art," and anyone of a suitably philosophical turn of mind can find the art in it—which, I would say, is what the mind games of the art experience do.

This idea might not help the ordinary art-lover much in navigating these unsettled seas. But another philosopher of art who had reached a conclusion akin to Danto's added a little guidance. Nelson Goodman decided that the question to ask is not *What* is art? but *When* is art? That is, since nowadays objects of any kind can be art, we need to know *when* an object is just a thing and *when* it *becomes* "art." He concluded that an object becomes "art" when it takes on symbolic meanings of aesthetic kinds. As he puts it, a stone on the driveway is just a stone until we find the aesthetically symbolic meaning in it then it functions as art, but it returns to being a simple stone when it functions as a stone on the driveway.[14] A sensible, pragmatic variation on Danto's theory. And, again, it is among the mind games we likely play in the art experience of our times.

These provocative ideas of "art" certainly tell us about the condition of art nowadays—a condition that amounts to what Danto declared to be "the end of art," by which he meant that traditional art history ended when *anything* could become "art." But, much as Danto, Goodman, and others have illuminated the changing character and conception of the *artwork*, does any of this really tell us how to understand art itself as we experience it? I think not. Or not quite. I say "not quite" because even if we follow Danto and Goodman and let individuals, rather than institutions or other authorities, decide which objects do, and which do not, strike us as possessing sufficient philosophical or aesthetic "meaning" to be art, we are still pointing to the artwork itself. And whatever anyone says about artworks themselves, something will be missing. And this "something" is the third face of art: the human experience of art. I mean what happens to us in the moment when we see an object or hear a sound as "art," rather than as a mere object or a sound. Whether the object or sound got to be "art" because someone in authority said so, or because we found philosophical significance in it ourselves, or for any other reason doesn't bear directly on that experience. It is the subjective human experience of art and the effects on us of that experience, more than the art object itself, much less the act of artistic creation, that provide the surest clues to understanding what is art, and what it does to us, and why.

The Human Experience of Art

Like the other two faces of art, the experience of art, or how people respond to art, has stirred the curiosity of thinkers since antiquity. Plato was again the philosophical pioneer. And for the most part he was mighty negative. He did grant in the *Symposium* that seeing beauty can lead us to a vision of truth through the ideal of beauty seen with the mind's eye, and he advised in the *Republic* using moral stories to train the young. But Plato is better known for condemning artists because he believed they lead people astray. He said they do this by, for one thing, wielding their skills to fashion deceptive imitations, and, for another, by appealing to the low emotions rather than to high rationality. Artists combine these techniques to sway hearts and minds, making people believe that art is True and Good and should therefore be imitated in their own lives. That is why Plato insisted that artists be censored, if not banned altogether, and that art be confined to subjects and to a manner that would teach moral decorum and rational restraint rather than promoting emotional self-indulgence. As he wrote in the *Republic*, "The only poetry that should be allowed in a state is hymns to the gods and paeans in praise of good men," for "once you go beyond that and admit the sweet muse of lyric or epic," or any art that acts on people too emotionally—or any "innovation" in the arts, for that matter—"pleasure and pain become your rulers instead of law and the rational principles commonly accepted as best." Then "disorder" sets in, undermining "morals and manners," infecting "business dealings generally," and spreading from there "into the laws and constitution . . . until it has upset the whole of private and public life." [15] Art can do all of that? Quite an indictment of art for its effects. And that is where a tradition began.

Plato's student Aristotle was more generous to art and artists than Plato. Although Aristotle advised parents to monitor the kinds of art that children encounter, he did not fear those effects as much as his teacher did. He actually praised artists' skills at imitating things because he thought human beings learn almost everything by imitation. And with his idea of *katharsis*, he explained how even when art arouses strong emotions, it can dissipate those emotions instead of causing people to act on them. As he puts it, when we experience "pity and fear, for example, but also excitement . . . or any other emotion," even "orgiastic effect[s]" through art, we feel as if we "had undergone a curative and purifying treatment" that leaves "a sort of pleasant purgation and relief," and "an elation which is not at all harmful."[16] Aristotle says little more about *katharsis* than this, but it is nonetheless probably history's best-known idea on the emotional effects of art—and we will encounter it again later.

In all, Aristotle saw the effects of art to be rather more benign and complex than Plato did. But Aristotle shared with Plato a couple of quite reasonable judgments on the effects of art that remain with us today. One was, as mentioned earlier, a concern for art's influence on the young. The other, perhaps more controversial, separated what today we think of as high and low art. I deal with this subject and the subtle differences between Plato's and Aristotle's views of it at some length later; here I will just point out that both Plato and Aristotle thought the primary distinction between high art and low lies in this: High art makes people better and low art does not, and might make them worse. Simple as it might seem, that idea marked the beginning of a controversial moral and psychological tradition regarding the effects of art that has made its way through the centuries and has particularly animated censorious critics and official censors. A few words on official censorship will illustrate parts of this tradition, followed by some contrary ideas and some other theories of how art affects us.

In the West, official censorship gathered force after the invention of printing in the 1450s, which helped spread Luther's Reformation early in the next century and fueled a reaction of orthodoxy in the Catholic church, bringing the Counter-Reformation, Jesuit zealotry, and in 1559 the Index of Forbidden Books. Secular institutions defensively followed suit: libraries declined to stock certain titles, and postal services, from their origins in the seventeenth century, refused to deliver materials deemed sacrilegious, scurrilous, or seditious. Illustrating that moralistic spirit, in the first consequential printed novel, *Don Quixote* (1605, 1615), Cervantes has a canon of the church condemn books of chivalry, like those that had inspired—or addled—the Don, as "liars and imposters" that can lead unsuspecting readers into "new ways of life," and he would "pitch them into the fire." Quite so. Books (and artworks) can change people, and many moralists don't like that. Moralistic intellectuals through the years long after Plato, like Jean-Jacques Rousseau, John Ruskin, and Leo Tolstoy, have demonstrated this. That censorious spirit was alive and well when, for instance, officials denied publication in the U.S. of James Joyce's *Ulysses* in 1922 owing to its purportedly corrupting obscenity. And even today, under pressure from conservative moralists, numerous public schools are cleansing their shelves anew of books deemed morally corrupting.

But notwithstanding the persistence of the censor's edicts and the moralist's pronouncements, modern times also brought the rise of a contrary idea of art's moral effects. This idea was, in fact, defiantly *amoral.* An early exponent, Théophile Gautier, minced no words in the notorious Preface to his novel *Mademoiselle de Maupin* (1835). "Someone has said somewhere," he wrote, "that literature and the arts influence morals. Whover he was, he was undoubtedly a great ass." "Art", Gautier insisted, has no purpose at all except to give "pleasure." "There is nothing truly beautiful," he went on, "but that which can never be of any [moral or practical] use whatsoever." Take that Plato! Everybody knows how this doctrine of aestheticism or "art for art's sake" became a celebrated creed in the late nineteenth century at the hands of Walter Pater and Oscar Wilde, who characteristically quipped, "Even a color sense is more important than a sense of right and wrong." From there the moral indifference (or sometimes moral transcendence) of art became more an assumption than an assertion in the artworld.

But along the way the effects of art were spawning theories beyond that of "art for art's sake." Most notably, the psychology of art became a large and quite technical subject plumbing, in part, our emotional and mental experiences of art and our responses to it. John Dewey was a pioneer of this topic in America, and, although he viewed "aesthetic experience" as akin to all others in his influential book *Art as Experience* (1934), he stressed the strong dose of emotion that lends the experience of art special "meaning" for us. Other thinkers, like Rudolf Arnheim, applied Gestalt psychology to our cognitive response to form in the visual arts. And the prominent philosophical musicologist Leonard B. Meyer drew on both Gestalt theory and Dewey's ideas to set forth in *Emotion and Meaning in Music* (1954) a theory of how music affects us emotionally. These few prominent contributions to the psychology of art only hint at the intellectual, and largely academic, interest in responses to art that surfaced in the twentieth century. And while some of that interest brushes up against the theme of this book, none that I have seen has done more than that, and it has also tended to be more technical or theoretical than I have found useful. Not that the psychology of art has lacked practical applications. Arts therapy proves that. Turning the salutary effects of art—albeit usually the effects of *doing* the arts of painting or performance rather than just *responding* to them—to medicinal uses, arts therapy became a widely popular method of ministering to the psychologically and physically impaired.

Outside of psychology, "reader response criticism" became a category of literary theory that switched the focus of criticism from the artwork to the reader. But this theory really concerned mainly how the meaning of the "text" depends on the reader, not on how the text affects the reader, leaving those effects largely unexamined.

In sum, thinking about the human experience of art I must say that, appealing as aestheticism might be, and as thought-provoking as theories of responses to art can be, none of this leads to where I want to go or how I plan to get there. For this concise book offers a fairly commonsense explanation of the human experience of art and therefore of what art is; and of why we experience art, high and low, as we do; and of what we have to gain or fear from both high art and low, especially as a Culture of Entertainment engulfs us. That explanation starts and ends with, and will tip its hat to throughout, what I label the "art experience" and the "mind games" peculiar to that experience.

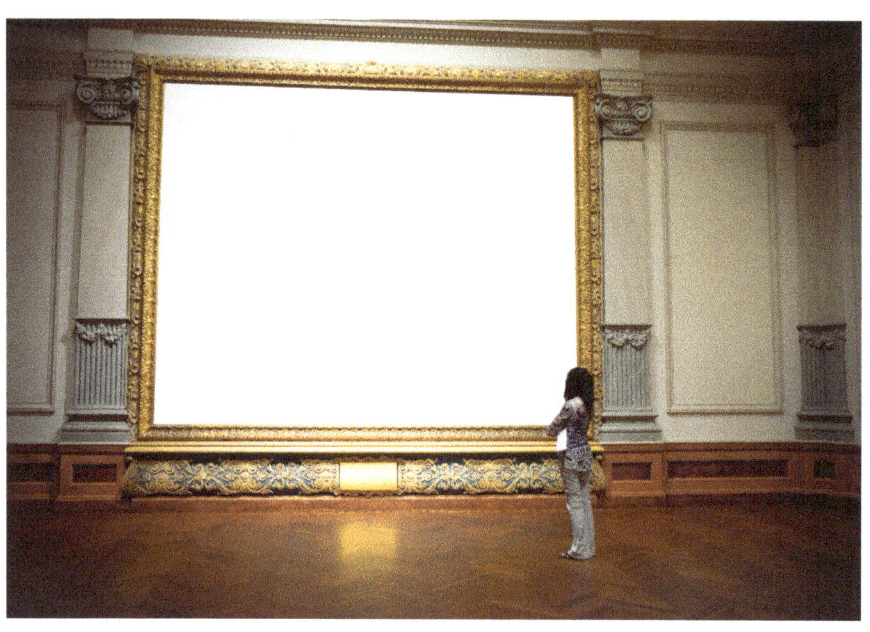

Fig. 16— Photograph of woman looking at a large, traditionally framed, blank canvas.

The artwork, the photographer, and the gallery are unidentified. But what we see invites us to play the mind games that one could play, and would have to play, to have an art experience within the frame of such a blank "artwork."

II
The Art Experience: Frames, Fantasy, Mind Games

"We love 'the unreal.'
We love everything that reminds us of our life,
but 'is not our life.'"
—Giorgio de Chirico

Frames and Mind Games

To be plain and simple about it, we have an "art experience" when we encounter something as "art," not as "reality." And we encounter something as "art"—which is to say, something *becomes* "art" for us—when we put a mental frame around it that removes it from the real world in ways particular to "art." The art experience therefore shows us what art is by contrast to things that are not art—at least for us as individuals. That might seem to be a highly relativistic assertion, but it is not as bad as it seems.

Here is also where the mind games of the art experience begin. Those mind games let us enter a psychological frame that we can step in and out of, changing our perceptions and our consciousness as we do, playing the mind games of the art experience. And within this frame, those mind games free us from the demands and constraints of the real world and from judging what is within the frame as we do real-world experience. That frame might also be similar to what critics have called "aesthetic distance" or "psychical distance," a state of mind that detaches art from life. At all events, what happens within this frame are mind games of the art experience.

We might think of mind games with two meanings. One is that we play mind games with ourselves whenever we withdraw our thoughts and attention from the constricted outer world of everyday life to the spacious inner world of our minds and imaginations. And we do this whenever we enter the frame of the art experience. The second meaning is more technical, complicated, and yet probably more familiar. It takes two forms. We can use mind games (a) to change the way we ourselves think and act, or (b) to affect how someone else thinks and acts. Pop psychology promotes mind games (a) to help us improve our own lives by thinking anew about ourselves. More cynically, we can use mind games (b) to "get inside the head" of someone else by saying or doing things that will distract or confuse them—fierce competitors sometimes do this to distract rivals from concentrating on their competition. The art experience does something like both (a) and (b) to us when we enter its frame and mentally go outside the real world. For when we do that, while we play the mind games (a) of the art experience with ourselves outside the constraints of the real world, the art experience can play mind games (b) with us, consciously or unconsciously affecting us in ways that we then might take back into the world with us when the art experience ends. I do not wish to imply that the mind games (b) of the art experience entail trickery or deception, only that they can have effects on us that we do not consciously or entirely intend. Nor do I wish to be technical about the idea of mind games itself or to push it too far but rather to let it serve, more or less, as a metaphor for what happens in us when we enter the frame of the art experience.

Samuel Taylor Coleridge described a version of this experience and its mind games in his *Biographia Literaria* as the "willing suspension of disbelief that constitutes poetic faith." He was thinking of how we can mentally accept things as "real" in art that we would not accept in life. In other words, we often play the mind game of suspending disbelief with whatever we encounter in the art experience, freed from real-world expectations, demands, and judgments.

Another, and more expansive, version of this idea comes from Sigmund Freud. He did not confine his observation to the experience of art but put that experience into the realm of what he called "psychic reality." That realm was of course Freud's bailiwick, and he thought it held the key to human nature and behavior. Say what you want about Freud's theories of psychoanalysis overall, his central ideas about psychic or psychological reality do illuminate life, and the art experience in particular, and so I will dwell on those ideas a little.

Freud explained that in the realm of psychological reality we can satisfy needs and desires internally without having to meet the demands of the real world outside—or to change that world to meet our needs and desires. Psychological reality is off-limits to real-world demands because the rules of what is possible in the real world do not altogether apply there. Within psychological reality, almost anything is truly possible, or at any rate believable, for nothing from the outside can or should intrude, or if it does it causes the freedom of psychological reality to dissolve into the maw of reality. Such are the mind games of psychological reality. I should note here that this psychological freedom and its mind games can also go bad, besetting us with paranoid fears and other imagined horrors, or bewitching us with the easy satisfactions of fantasy that can impair our ability to live in the real world, a topic to which I will return in the next chapter. Freud saw these kinds of consequences all too well. And he developed psychoanalysis to deal with them. But for the purpose of understanding the art experience, I will stick with the more common and positive features of psychological reality and the mind games it lets us play.

The freedom we get in psychological reality also liberates us from the need to act on what happens to us there. Instead of acting on it, we can just passively enjoy the states of mind, emotion, and imagination that psychological reality makes possible. There we can immediately satisfy desires (albeit within the mind) without the necessity of real-world exertions and frustrations. We can savor food, enjoy sex, win prizes, create art, change the world, sprout wings and soar—even endure artificial terrors. And pay no price. This is the stuff of daydreams, to be sure, which, akin to the mind games of the art experience, give license for nearly anything to be possible, and for nothing to depend on any of it in real life. So, just as children build castles in the sand inhabited by imaginary characters—or by imaginary versions of themselves—adults build castles in the air of mind games that they live in for a time as imaginary escapes from a world whose realities are all too demanding, more demanding than children playing with their castles in the sand can imagine.

Psychological reality permits us gratifications under what Freud called the Pleasure Principle, by contrast to the Reality Principle. Generally speaking, he explained, the Pleasure Principle governs us as children when we expect immediate gratifications all the time, deferring none. But as we grow up, we must live ever more of our lives under the Reality Principle, which teaches us to defer gratifications through discipline, restraint, and acquiring the skills of minimizing pain as we traverse the treacherous terrain of the real world. However, because, as Freud noted, "life is too hard for us," we often resort to the Pleasure Principle in the ready enticements of psychological reality and the mind games that let us get what we want, or a semblance of it, immediately without the trials of the external world, or to simply relish the freedom from those trials for its own sake. Hence, the appeal of fantasy and those castles in the air. And art.

Freud was actually rather ungenerous to artists. He tended to equate artistic creation with daydreaming as an escape from the real world. As he said in "Creative Writers and Day-Dreaming," "only unhappy people make fantasies, not happy ones," and he thought artistic creation belongs more to such escapist fantasies than it does to an affirming way of life in the world—which put him at odds with his erstwhile disciple and colleague Carl Jung, who viewed artists and the creative imagination more warmly. To be fair, Freud did grant (in his *A General Introduction to Psychoanalysis*) that by escaping into the fantasy world of art, artists can produce works that paradoxically turn out to bring them the very things in the real world that they, and most human beings, fantasize about sometimes precisely because the real world makes those things so difficult to get, namely: fame, fortune, and love. For the artist's fantasies can yield artworks that feed the fantasies of ordinary people through the art experience, winning the artist esteem, riches, even love. That paradoxical upshot might be incidental to the artist's psychological and aesthetic intent, but it is nonetheless a happy one and significant. For it points to a bridge between the Pleasure and the Reality Principles.

That bridge is *sublimation*. Sublimation—a word derived from the Latin *sublimis*, meaning "lifted above"—names what we do when we substitute mental and imaginative activities and satisfactions for physical activities and pleasures. That might be a simplistic definition, but it says enough here. Freud believed those sublimated activities and satisfactions (the mind games of sublimation) had increased with civilization, and it is easy enough to see how that is true. For high civilization depends ever more on sublimated energies as it restrains our animal instincts and increasingly supplants necessary physical activity with education, intellectual skills, and "culture." Sublimation therefore bridges the Pleasure and Reality Principles by providing satisfactions in psychological reality that also contribute good things to the real world, like scholarship, science, and art. We might even say that sublimation can allow us to combine the childlike gratifications of the Pleasure Principle with the prudent adult satisfactions of the Reality Principle. We surely get that reward of sublimation from the art experience.

As Freud remarked, artistic creation supplies these sublimated satisfactions to artists, who use their imaginations both to escape from the world and to live in it—if they are lucky. The art experience supplies sublimated satisfactions to non-artists by taking them out of the real world for a time into a realm where they can get the immediate gratifications of fantasy, building castles in the air of psychological reality. But I must add that before we can enjoy the psychological pleasures of an art experience, we must use the judgments of the Reality Principle—deliberately or spontaneously—to decide whether or not something is "art" so that we can willingly play the mind games of entering the frame, suspending disbelief, and letting ourselves go, free of real-world dangers. And here we return to the mind games of the art experience itself.

Most of us have moments when we find ourselves switching from everyday experience to the art experience. For instance, you might be walking down a city street and hear gunshots fired and see mayhem erupt. Immediately your body tenses, your heart races, and you run for cover. Then you see the mayhem subside and, instead of people fleeing or grappling with gunmen, you see them milling around. Now you discover you have come upon not an actual shooting but the making of a film. Your muscles relax, your heart slows, and your curiosity replaces fear. You had thought you had encountered an unsettling reality, but it turned out to be a type of "art" outside reality. And, because you weren't expecting an art experience, you weren't ready to put the frame of "art" around it and feel safe. That is, you were not prepared to play the mind games of the art experience. If you stay to watch filming of another scene, you will know what is going on and be unthreatened. But you will not be having an art experience. You will instead be watching the making of art, which is not the same as entering the frame of art itself. You would have to see the finished film in the theater to have a true art experience of it. For unlike the art experience that takes us out of the real world, watching the making of an artwork like a movie is simply to observe an interesting real-world event of people at work, even if they are creating what will later provide an art experience for audiences. Nevertheless, here you will have experienced directly the psychological contrast between witnessing a real shooting and an artificially artful one. And you will have learned how playing the mind games that place the frame of "art" around an experience puts us in a different frame of mind, so to speak, from that of real life.

Take another example, which will return us briefly to where we wondered if the presence of an object like a trash can in a museum alongside a label on the wall makes that object "art." Now we will look at such an object in the light of the art experience. You go to a modern art museum and there among the paintings and sculptures you see a trash can against the wall next to a workman's ladder. You are about to drop something in the can when it dawns on you that maybe the can and the ladder are not "real" but "art." Psychologically, you don't know whether to have an art experience with them or not. You ask yourself, Where is the frame? It occurs to you that the museum itself might be the frame. But you want more guidance. If you find a sign on the wall labeling them as an artist's work, you can take that as the frame and more comfortably play the mind game that transforms a trash can and a workman's ladder into an artwork—like Marcel Duchamp's urinal, which we have remarked before and will again, that he dubbed "Fountain" as a kind of jape that set a precedent for a trash can and a workman's ladder becoming "art." Even so, you might move on still wondering if such things deserve to be art.

Next you enter another room where you see a mirror on the wall within a simple picture frame. You stand in front of it and see your reflection. You assume that this is a work of art because it is on the museum gallery wall, not in the restroom, but you are not sure what the "art" is. Is it the mirror? Or does the artist want you to see the art as your reflection in it? You examine the label on the wall beside it only to learn that it is called, "Mirror, Mirror on the Wall, #5" by Snow White. You suspect the artist is just playing a joke. You stand aside and watch how other viewers respond. Their quizzical expressions strengthen your puzzlement. How do you have an art experience with something like a mirror? Then it dawns on you that perhaps the artist did not intend either the mirror or the passive reflections themselves to be the art, but rather the reactions of viewers as they saw their reflections, paused, and wondered what the "art" is. As they puzzled over "Mirror, Mirror on the Wall, #5" they became performing artists in the mirror without knowing it. Watching them inadvertently "perform" before the mirror you then put a frame around them as well as the mirror and have an art experience with the entire scene that you could not have with the mirror itself. Through the mind games of the art experience, you had found the "art" in Snow White's "Mirror, Mirror on the Wall, #5," after all (see Fig. 17).

But wait. You might decide that the mirror and the reactions of people to it, as well as the trash can and workman's ladder, have such strong real-world associations that you cannot play the mind games of putting a frame around them and having an art experience despite the museum labels intended to make them "art." We play the mind games of the art experience when the frame of art works for us. And we cannot easily play those games and put that frame around anything that is too familiar in everyday reality for us to take it outside of that reality. Nor can we have an art experience with an artwork that intrudes too much into our own everyday lives, a topic we will examine shortly. By the same token, the artwork cannot be so far removed from our everyday reality that it is nearly incomprehensible, like, perhaps, the hypothetical "Green Trapezoid" along the street mentioned in the previous chapter or, say,

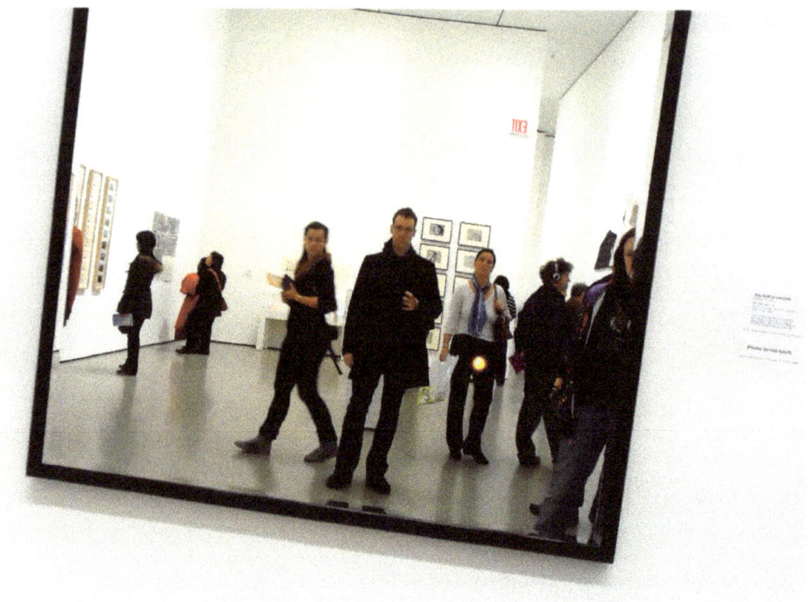

Fig. 17— Troy McCullough, self-portrait in Waltercio Caldas's Mirror of Light, *1974. This mirror on a gallery wall of the Museum of Modern Art is ordinary (if a mirror on a museum wall can be considered ordinary) but for a red dot attached to it. Just a small red dot in most views, it looks like a light in this photograph by the photographer Troy McCullough, who snapped his (off-kilter) "self-portrait" while looking in the mirror along with other curious visitors. The dot could change the very artistic meaning of the mirror. Or it could be ignored in the curiosity aroused by the mirror itself. Either way, we must play the mind games of the art experience with the mirror to see it as "art" on a museum wall.*

how most readers find James Joyce's novel *Finnegans Wake*. In short, as the Italian painter Giorgio de Chirico, whom we met earlier, put it, "We love 'the unreal.' We love everything that reminds us of our life, but 'is not our life.'"[17]

And here we encounter again the idea that the art experience tells us what is art and what is not. Namely, *anything we can have an art experience with is art; and anything we cannot have an art experience with is not art.* Simple as that. Almost. I will return to the implications of subjectivity and relativism in this definition of art later. For now I'll move on to the notion that we can *learn* to have an art experience with artworks that at first we could not.

The Art Experience vs. Life

The expectation that people should learn to appreciate challenging art has been an implicit theme, and sometimes an explicit demand, among artists in modern times. In truth, artists have long found artistic curiosity and amusement in—and have occasionally taunted—the resistance of people to entering the frame of art. They have usually done this by confusing art and life so that people could not readily tell which is which. This tradition also shows us further how the mind games of the art experience work. Consider a few historic instances of artists toying with the mind games that attempt to remove art from life—long before Duchamp's urinal and the hypothetical instances of the trash can and the mirror.

When medieval craftsmen put bawdy images among religious sculptures on cathedral facades and in the marginal designs of beautifully illustrated manuscripts, were they not winking at the viewers as if to say: Look at real life amid pious art? Who knows just how contemporaries responded, but it must have affected how they felt about art and religiosity. During the Renaissance, the invention of perspective made paintings look more like reality than viewers thought possible, which stunned many who first saw them and widened the frame—that is to say, expanded the mind games—of what viewers thought visual art could do. *Trompe-l'œil* paintings later exploited that invention by perfecting the illusion of reality in art, causing viewers to wonder if they are looking at art or at actual scenes, like saints and angels rising though the ceilings of Baroque churches (see Fig. 18). In the sixteenth century, Giuseppi Arcimboldo had taken a different tack with paintings of human heads fashioned out of fruits and vegetables that teased viewers into switching their gaze from art to life and back (see Fig. 19). Picasso brought Arcimboldo's artistic ingenuity into the twentieth century with sculptures that combined forms of everyday objects to demonstrate the interchangeability of forms in life and art—like a bicycle seat and handle bars arranged to form the shape of a bull's head with horns and a toy car as the head of gorilla (see Fig. 20). In a more radical vein, Andy Warhol would unite art and everyday commercial life with his *Brillo Boxes* and

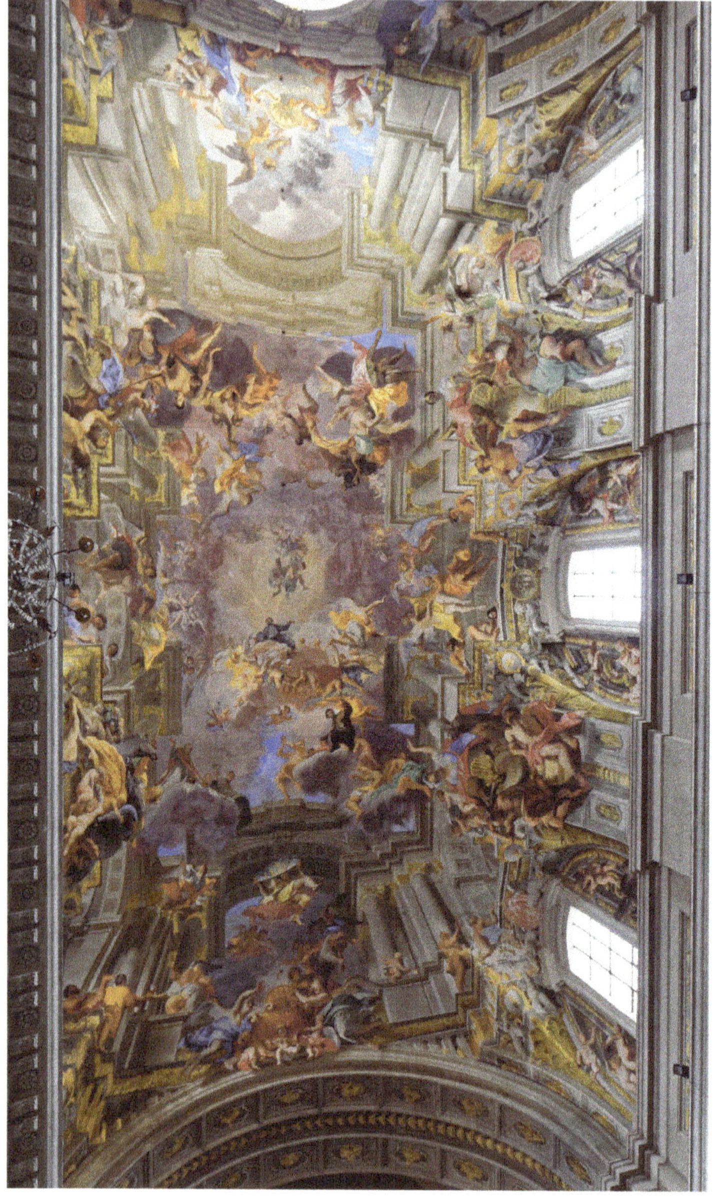

Fig. 18 — Andrea Pozzo, ceiling of St. Ignazio Church, Rome, 1685–94.

A Jesuit brother of prodigious artistic skills, Pozzo created here a trompe-l'œil Baroque masterpiece. Realistic interior architectural features, such as windows, columns, arches, and a dome (out of this picture) set the stage with exaggerated vertical perspective for countless figures to swirl in the air and float toward the heavens above, as St. Ignatius, founder of the Catholic Counter-Reformation Jesuit order, ascends in the center. Still surprising to behold, the ceiling's unreal realism must have truly astonished the church's early votaries.

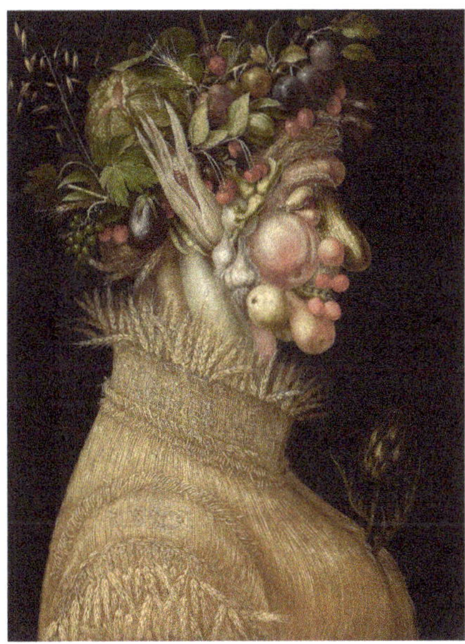

Fig. 19 — Giuseppe Arcimboldo, Summer, *1563. Kunsthistorisches Museum, Vienna.*

Arcimboldo probably deployed his artistic ingenuity in creating heads out of fruits and vegetables for the delight of the court. In any case, such creations became hallmarks of the innovative, sometimes quirky, and over-the-top Mannerist style that followed the art of the High Renaissance.

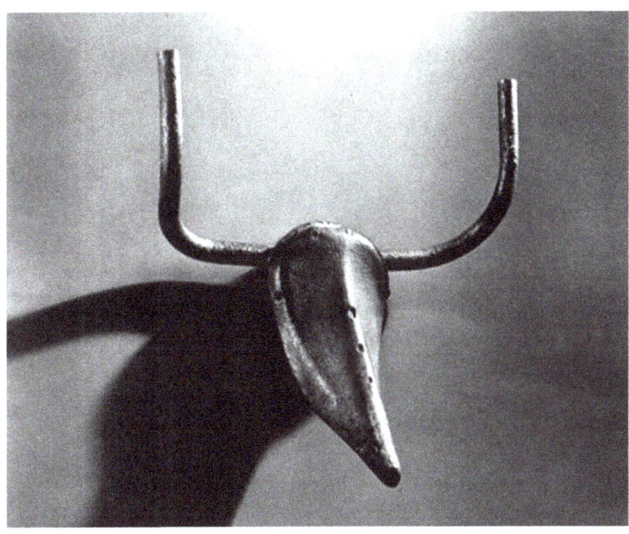

Fig. 20 — Pablo Picasso, Bull's Head, *1942. Museum of Modern Art.*

Picasso described its origin to the great photographer George Brassaï: "One day, in a pile of objects all jumbled up together, I found an old bicycle seat right next to a rusty set of handlebars. In a flash they joined together in my head." The mind games of artistic creativity at work.

practically everything else he did, including his own life. In all of these instances, artists unexpectedly merged life and art, progressively altering the rules of the mind games of the art experience.

The literary arts have also had their share of fun with the mind games of the art experience by confusing art and life, probably more than their share. What is generally deemed the first true European novel, Cervantes' *Don Quixote,* set the course by playing again and again on whether the book is fiction or fact. Soberly pretending that it was drawn from historical documents about a real person, Cervantes goes on to entangle the narrative, and the reader, in a tale where Don Quixote learns that an apocryphal version of his story has been published (which actually happened) and vows to disprove the false Don Quixote by pursuing adventures unknown to the false Don. He even meets a character from the false version. That is all good fun in a novel that today we can freely enjoy as an art experience because we understand the mind games Cervantes is playing with us, but whose early readers were not so sure about.

Playwrights have made much of this theme at least since Shakespeare. Remember the play Hamlet staged for his uncle/step-father Claudius. Claudius had attended the play expecting a diverting theatrical art experience. But Hamlet had planned to use that expectation against him. He contrived an existing play, *The Murder of Gonzago*, to have the murder take place exactly as Claudius had killed Hamlet's father, the king, in order to get both the crown and the queen for himself. "I have heard," Hamlet muses, "that guilty creatures sitting at a play / Have by the very cunning of the scene / Been struck so to the soul that presently / They have proclaimed their malefactions." Therefore, he thinks, "I'll observe his looks" for telltale signs of guilt. He asked his friend Horatio to do the same. "And after we will both our judgments join / In censure of his seeming." Yes, Hamlet is sure, "The play is the thing / Wherein I'll catch the conscience of the king." (Act II, scene ii; Act III, scene ii). Hamlet was not, of course, just having fun with mind games here. He would watch genuine guilt reveal itself on Claudius's face as the mind games of the art experience dissolved for Claudius into real life with recognition of his own foul deed being portrayed on stage. The ploy worked even better than Hamlet had anticipated. When the art experience collapsed for Claudius, he abruptly stopped the play and stormed out. The art experience, in clashing with life, had indeed caught the conscience of the king (see Fig. 21).

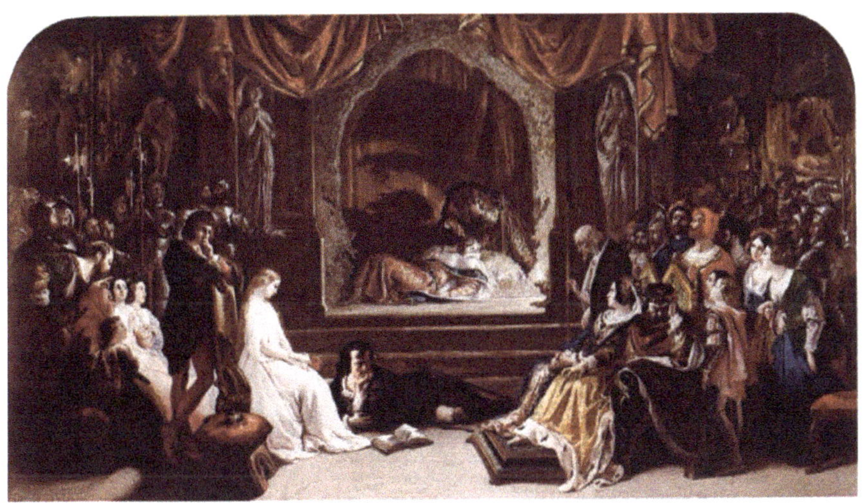

Fig. 21 — Daniel Maclise, The Play Scene in "Hamlet," *1842.*

This popular nineteenth-century rendering of the scene differs from the play in having Claudius (near right) avert his eyes and bury his head in his hand (instead of stopping the play and fleeing the room) as the murder on stage mimics his own murder of Hamlet's father. Hamlet, lying on the floor at Ophelia's feet, intently studies Claudius's reaction, as does Horatio, standing behind the chair. Hamlet knew: the mind games of the art experience had caught the conscience of a king.

The doyen of playing tricks with the mind games of the art experience in the theater was Luigi Pirandello. He made a career of it. His classic play *Six Characters in Search of an Author* piles layer on layer of those tricks, seeming to baffle even the performers as well as the audience. The tricks began when the audience filed into the theater for the first performance in 1921. They were perplexed to find the frame of the theatrical art experience missing, namely, the curtain was already up, and the stage was empty but for a few chairs and a couple of small tables. Was there no performance tonight? Then, as a few people wandered from the wings onto the stage aimlessly chatting, the perplexity deepened. This was not "art" within a frame outside the real world. These were real people not doing much of anything. When another person appears, recognized by those on stage as the Manager/Director, he puts some order into the proceedings as he prepares to rehearse with them, of all things, a play by (who else but?) Pirandello, about which he complains that "nobody understands anything and the author plays the fool with us all." This confused the audience more, now thinking they had come on the wrong day and found only the rehearsal of a different Pirandello drama that the director didn't even like. They still could not play Pirandello's theatrical mind games. But all of this merely set the stage for more bewildering tricks to come.

No sooner has the "rehearsal" begun than six more figures enter from the rear. Interrupting the "rehearsal," they tell the director that they are not actually "real people" but only "characters" (*personaggi*) in a drama of their own, and a dysfunctional family drama at that, and they need a performance of that drama to give them life, theatrical life. The director wants nothing to do with these oddities. How can people standing before him not be "real," or not even be actors playing characters, but "characters" as such? He appears as confused by the tangle of art and life here as is the audience. But, intrigued despite himself, he agrees to hear their story, and then he agrees to perform it. After a few false starts with the actors, the six characters announce that professional actors cannot perform for them, they must play themselves, for they alone know exactly who they are and how to perform their roles. The director grudgingly consents to this too. But the performance does not go smoothly.

The family drama the six characters (The Father, The Mother, their child The Son, and three of The Mother's children by a previous husband—called The Stepdaughter, The Boy, and The Child) (see Fig. 22) perform unfolds in a muddle of misperceptions and uncertain identities, infidelities and lies, betrayals and denials, rage and mourning. And when it ends with the drowning of The Child, the suicide of The Son, and the flight from the theater of The Stepdaughter, things have gone too far. Do the deaths really occur or not? "He's dead!" cry some of the "actors" who have been watching the "characters'" performance from the side. "No, no, it's only make believe, it's only pretense," cry others. The chief "character," who is The Father of the group, shouts: "Pretense? Reality, sir, reality." At this, the director stops everything in exasperation. "Pretense? Reality? To hell with it all. . . . I've lost a whole day over these people, a

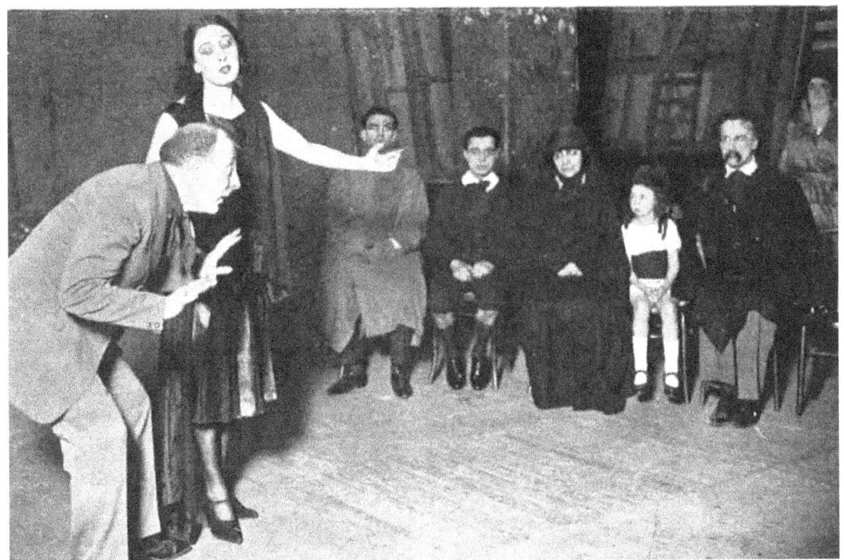

Fig. 22 — Luigi Pirandello, Six Characters in Search of an Author, *from performance in London, 1925.*

Here The Stepdaughter, a flirtatious young lady and sometime prostitute—who had had an embarrassing encounter with The Father in her line of work, an incident that figures prominently into the family drama of the six characters—explains part of that drama to the Manager/Director as the rest of the family sits waiting to perform.

whole day!" And the curtain—which had not descended at the end of Act I, when everyone on stage had simply wandered off into the wings, and had descended at the end of Act II only over the director's histrionic protests that it shouldn't have—falls for good on Act III.

By this time, Pirandello's theatrical tricks and mind games, confusing art and life, truth and illusion, had so taxed many of the audience that they had impatiently departed. Expecting a predictable art experience in the theater, they had encountered instead a bunch of deceptions taunting that expectation. Only those in the audience who could play Pirandello's mind games and widen the frame of "art" to include everything that happened on stage could have an art experience with Pirandello's play.

Pirandello was so pleased with the *success de scandal* of this and a couple of his subsequent plays that he wrote another, *Each in His Own Way*, on the very theme of audiences' reactions to his works. Like *Six Characters*, this is a play about the performance of a play. Pirandello based this one on a sensational authentic case of adultery and suicide. In his own way, to be sure, Pirandello weaves facts in the case together with doubts about their reality. Act I pieces together an argument, through rambling chatter on truth, falsehood, and human nature, about the scandalous story of an alluring lady who was said to have caused the suicides of two lovers, and who also shows up, thanks her defender in the argument, and pronounces truth to be ultimately unknowable. By the time the curtain comes down, the partisans in the argument have switched sides and vowed to fight a duel, leaving the baffled question hanging in the air, "What is true?" But the curtain immediately rises again on a scene set in a section of the theater lobby, where members of the "audience" (played by actors) come out discussing the play, some of them tearing it apart as merely "one trick after another" in "just a jumble of words," others defending Pirandello for his insights into human life, and professional critics equally divided in the fray. The squabbling goes on until a bell rings signaling the beginning of Act II. As the "lobby" empties, a woman enters who claims to be the real-life lady in the scandal and who has clandestinely attended the performance with friends. Visibly upset, she demands to go "behind the scenes" to berate the actors for portraying her life on stage. Friends urge her to go home, but she resists and returns to the hall for the rest of the performance. The curtain comes down again, with one of those friends announcing: "This evening, there's going to be a rumpus, no mistake."

Act II takes place the next day and centers on whether the duel is to be held and why, with excursions into mysteries of self-knowledge, ambiguities of reality, and quarrels over the suicides. When the curtain descends, presumably at the end of the act, it again rises immediately on the same "lobby" scene as before. This time the "lobby" stands empty except for a couple of ticket takers, ushers, and maids. They soon hear the "audience" in the hall hissing and shouting, and wonder what is going on—one of them cracks: "Isn't it Pirandello tonight? What do you expect?" Some "audience" members now wander into the "lobby" complaining that a fight seems to have erupted on stage behind the curtain. Then the stage door opens onto the "lobby," releasing the sound of clamorous voices conveying that the real lady of the scandal had gone "behind the scenes" after all and had assailed the actress playing her and the entire crew for presuming to put her life on stage. Now some of the performers come out, loudly refusing to continue in a play about a real person who has invaded the production to stop it from portraying her. That real person also enters with her illicit lover to join the protest, and "audience" members exclaim how odd it is that the play on stage has carried into the lobby. Amidst the mayhem, the stage manager throws in the towel, brings down the curtain, and steps out in front of it to announce: "In view of the unfortunate incidents which took place at the end of the second act, we will be unable to continue the performance this evening." And that is the end of Pirandello's play of a play within a play—although some of the theater audience must have been unsure of that.

Each in His Own Way and *Six Characters in Search of an Author*, along with the lesser-known third of Pirandello's Trilogy in the Theater, *Tonight We Improvise*, and, for that matter, everything else Pirandello wrote for the stage, repeatedly challenged the artistic expectations of audiences by taking them through multiple theatrical mind games, blurring truth and illusion, life and art. After his eccentric theatrics, the art experience in the theater could never be quite the same. We can no longer expect the curtain (or other traditional signs) to give us the theatrical frame, setting the rules of the mind games that distinguish "art" from what is not "art" in the theater. For Pirandello taught us to put a frame around virtually everything in the entire theater and to welcome anything that happens there with the mind games of the art experience. We sense this when, for instance, we see a workman preparing to fix something in the theater around curtain time. We study him to see if he is truly a workman or if he is part of the performance. If we decide he is a workman we can ignore him, but if we decide he is part of the performance we poise our minds and emotions to have an art experience—just as we do in a museum when a workman's ladder or a trash can become "art."

Again, to pick up a point made earlier, it should be said that sometimes, like many in the early audiences for *Six Characters*, we cannot bring ourselves to play the mind games of putting the frame of "art" around some things that artists create. Our psychological resistance to entering the frame is too great for reasons already mentioned. The composer John Cage often played on that resistance. His notorious composition "4' 30"," which consists of a performer sitting quietly at a piano on stage playing no music at all for four and a half minutes, is just too absurd for many people to experience as "art." Cage said he wanted audiences to listen to ambient sounds in the room as art, but that made the frame too amorphous, surrounding parts of experience that most people could not, or did not want to, consider "art," and they walked out. Marcel Duchamp and Andy Warhol would take Cage's side. After all, Duchamp's urinal and Warhol's *Campbell's Soup Cans* and *Brillo Boxes* were everyday objects presented as "art" to challenge and possibly change expectations of what art is. But, as I've said, this is a challenge that not all people are willing to meet.

Or take the very illuminating case of the notorious artwork *Tilted Arc* (1981) by Richard Serra. Commissioned by the General Services Administration under its Art-in-Architecture program for the spacious Foley Federal Plaza in downtown New York City, Serra created a solid, rust-colored steel wall twelve feet high and one-hundred-and-twenty feet long that cut across the plaza in a gently curving, slightly tilted arc. Seen from high above it might be an artfully abstract arcing line that added aesthetic interest to the open plaza (see Fig. 23 A). But at ground level it was an artless obstruction to everyone passing through the plaza (see Fig. 23 B). It not only compelled office workers and other pedestrians to detour around it but blocked the view across the public square and of its central fountain. It defeated the very purpose of the plaza. Office workers coming out of the Javits Federal Building no longer found open space with a bubbling fountain but an inhospitable, rusty obstruction. A friend of mine who worked nearby said it was a hostile obstacle offensive to everyone who crossed the plaza. The office workers protested and won public support. The artist and his supporters resisted. Serra sued to prevent removal of the arc on the grounds that it was a "site-specific" artwork that could not be moved and reinstalled elsewhere since it was designed for this place alone. Nearly a decade of controversy later, *Tilted Arc* was disassembled and removed. It was never reconstructed.

What had happened here was simply this: Serra had tried to put the frame of art around a real-world setting and the people in it. He had said, in effect, the only thing that matters here is "art," which he expected everyone to embrace for its own sake, even though it impinged directly on how they lived and worked. And, just as many theater-goers could not play the mind games of the art experience with Pirandello's puzzling tangles of art and life or John Cage's musical silence, most people could not play those mind games with Serra's *Tilted Arc* on the Plaza where they walked to work and where many sat for lunch. Going farther than Pirandello and Cage, Serra did not just tease theater- or concert-goers by playing with the frame of art in the theater or concert hall; he tried to impose that frame around a portion of their everyday lives. And they didn't like it. For, much as people might appreciate art for the gratifications the art experience offers, they do not—or most of them do not—want to have their lives subordinated to it. They want to keep the art experience within its identifiable frame, playing the mind games that let them enter that frame and leave it at will. Art lovers who traveled to see *Tilted Arc* as art could probably do that with it, but not the people who found it an unacceptable intrusion into their real world. Serra had failed to understand either how the art experience and its mind games work or how far an artist can go in roping people into his or her own artistic mind games—or, more likely, his arrogant ego didn't care about people's wishes and intended to teach everyone a lesson in "art." In any case, Serra's notion of art lost here. Life had won.*

It is clear, then, that not all things that come to us as "art" and invite us to play the mind games of the art experience with them can work for us that

* I might note that Serra's *Tilted Arc* violated a rule of the art experience that the works of the artist Christo, who also seemed to intrude into the real world, did not. Christo is renowned for turning large-scale real-world things into art. Like his wrapping with fabric the huge Reichstag building in Berlin and the Pont Neuf Bridge in Paris, and placing colored fabric "gates" across walkways in New York's Central Park. Presumptuous as Christo's artworks might seem, they had two decisive qualities that Serra's arc lacked: they took real-world things out of that world and put them into art where people could, if they chose, have an art experience with them; and they were temporary, lasting a few weeks until Christo disassembled the "art" and restored the real-world things to that world. Christo did not try to impose art lastingly on peoples' lives, only to show them for a short time how something familiar to them could become art. Christo respected the art experience. Serra did not.

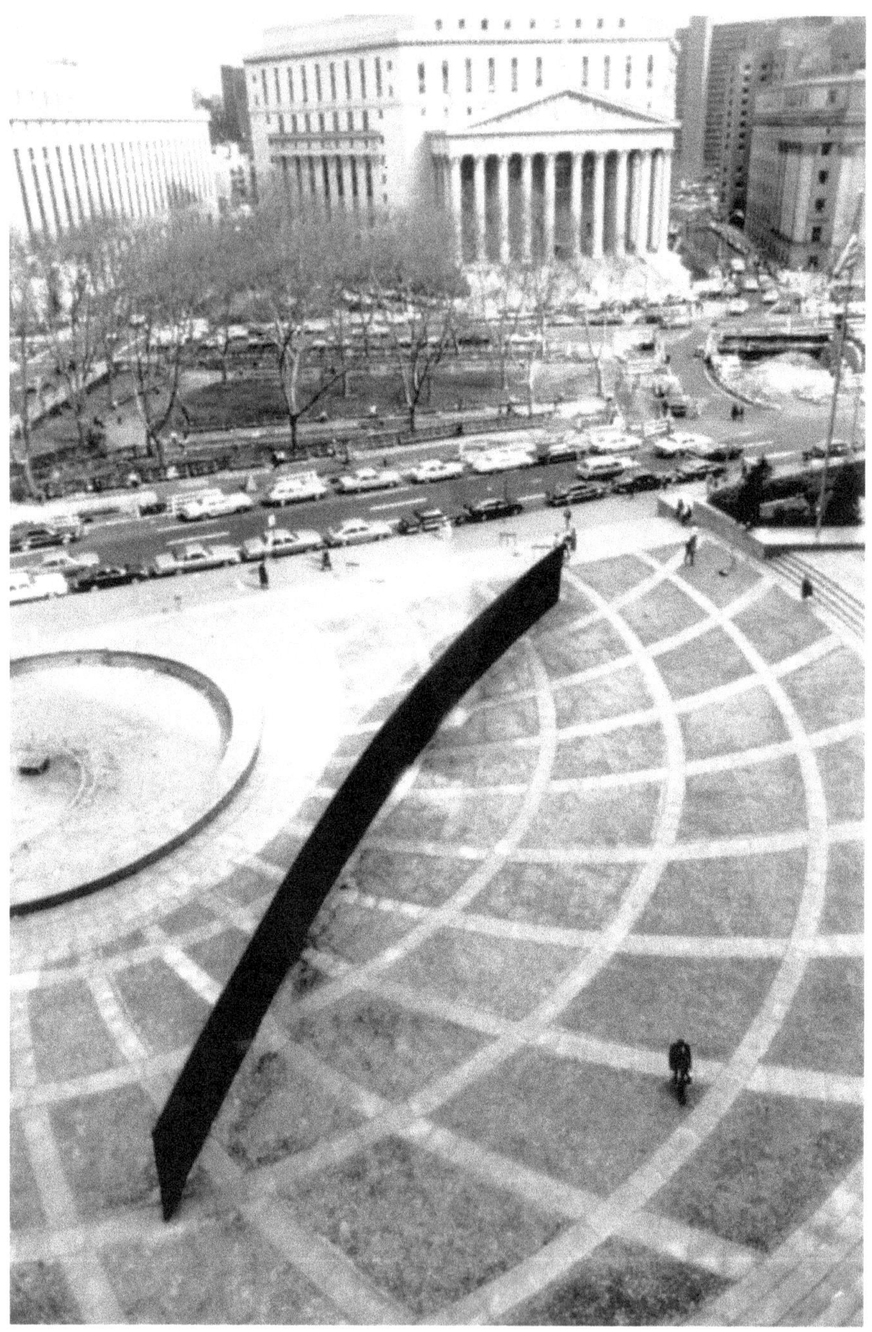

Fig. 23 A — Andrew Serra, Tilted Arc, *Federal Plaza, New York City, 1981.*

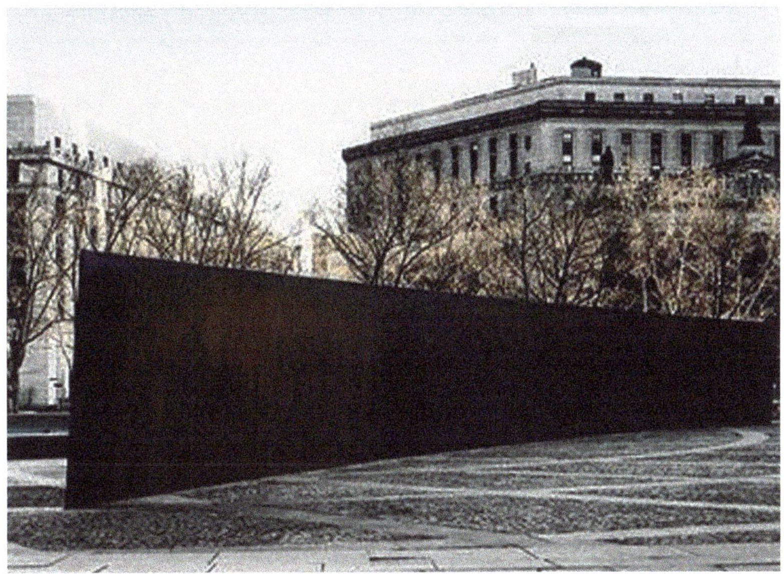

Fig. 23 B — Andrew Serra, Tilted Arc, *Federal Plaza, New York City, 1981.*

way. Our real lives won't let them. As noted earlier, this could be because an artist has attempted to turn something into art that is too familiar for us to remove it and have an art experience with it, like a trash can, or because the artwork is too far removed from our lives for us to respond to it as art, like verbal gibberish. Or, as the instances above variously illustrate, sometimes we feel a need to shield ourselves from art because it threatens to impinge upon our actual lives—a theme of movies like *Stranger than Fiction*, where a character learns to his dismay that his life is unfolding only as it is being written by a novelist, and *The Truman Show*, in which the main character discovers that his life is being filmed as a television show that others are watching. Neither of these characters wants to live in "art" for someone else's satisfaction; they want to live their own real lives.

All that said, notwithstanding situations when the art experience does not work for us, this book deals mainly with what happens when the mind games of the art experience do work for us and we can suspend disbelief to freely enter the frame of that experience and its psychological reality. But before exploring that in the coming chapters, I must visit another inhabitant of psychological reality closely akin to the art experience. That is play.

James Sloan Allen

Play and the Art Experience

As I have indicated from the beginning of this chapter, when we have an art experience we engage in a type of play, mind games. Like the art experience, the play experience is set off from the rest of life by mind games that create a frame saying: Don't confuse this experience with real life because it exists outside, and if real life comes too close the frame dissolves and the play experience ends. In his classic book on play, *Homo Ludens: A Study of the Play-Element in Culture*, the historian Johan Huizinga amusingly illustrated this truth with an anecdote about his own four-year-old son playing a game of "trains." Crawling on all fours pulling a line of chairs strapped to him, the boy was making the tooting sound of an engine. When his father bent down to greet him with an affectionate kiss, the boy shied away, protesting, "Don't kiss the engine, Daddy, or the carriages won't think it's real." For the boy, the fantasy of the game was everything, and any intrusions from outside would destroy it. And he shielded the game from reality with at least four clear rules, which are themselves mind games. First, the other players, or parts of the train, had to think the game was "real." Second, there must be no intrusions from the real world to disabuse the other players. Third, he must protect the game from such intrusions. Fourth, only he, playing the engine, could know those rules. A precocious child, perhaps, to have sensed so early the psychology (and metaphysics) of play.

As Huizinga's son understood, the rules of a game create the frame of play, and if the rules are broken the frame of the game falls away, or at least gets skewed, just as happens with the intrusion of reality into the frame of art. The overriding rule of the mind games that govern both play and the art experience is, therefore, that a game is not "real" the way things are in the real world—despite other rules of a game that might preserve an illusion for the players that it is "real," like the cars in young Huizinga's train.

I might note here that Pirandello changed the rules of the mind games of theatrical "plays" by seemingly intruding "realities" into the frame that traditional theatrical rules had prohibited. That was, however, within the rules of the mind games Pirandello was playing. He just hadn't informed the audience of those rules. In time, people came to the theater knowing his rules, which widened the frame of the theatrical art experience so audiences could play his mind games and expect anything in the theater to be part of the "play," the game, the art experience.

To be sure, real life itself has several characteristics of play. That is the very subject of Huizinga's book, as the subtitle indicates: *The Play-Element in Culture.* Huizinga had in mind the game-like rules that cultures, like his son's game, depend on. He found these in elaborate rituals, social manners, traditional practices, and so on. Although he drew chiefly on medieval European culture, when such rules dominated life more than later, the idea can still apply. For, like a child's game, the rules of culture govern how cultures function—often arbitrarily—and those rules vary as cultures do. We even have "game theory," invented in mathematics but adopted in the social sciences as a technique for explaining how people make calculated decisions within implicit rules in many social, economic, and political contexts. Or consider the "war games" "played" by the military.

"War games" involve "real" training of soldiers, sailors, pilots, and others for "real" military action, but everyone playing the game must follow the overarching rule that they are indeed engaged in a "game" and not a "real" war. If anyone were to violate that rule, very bad things could happen. The Hollywood movie *War Games* "played" on this possibility by having the computer system managing the game break that rule and start to operate as though the game itself is real, setting off a real-world drama in the film to prevent a potential nuclear catastrophe caused by the computer's rogue actions. As we watch that movie of a "war game" gone awry, we can relax and enjoy its fabricated "real-world" crisis within the frame and mind games of the art experience. But if we had missed that movie's frame we would get genuinely upset at a disturbing "reality"—like encountering gunfire on the street that you do not know is in a movie, or the terrified listeners to Orson Wells' sensational radio broadcast of 1938, who missed the introduction setting the frame for its dramatization of H. G. Wells' *War of the Worlds*, reporting an invasion from outer space and thought the events (presented as urgent breaking news with all the frightening verisimilitude Wells and his actors could muster) were actually happening.

In any case, whatever "elements" of "play" that we might identify in culture, including rules of behavior that have a game-like or play-like quality, these "elements" lack an essential ingredient of child's play: fantasy (see Fig. 24). For they still belong more to the real world than to the mind games of fantasy and true play, which take us out of the real world. And it is these mind games, taking us outside the real world, that give true play its closest affinity to the art experience.

But I must add a few words on how, even while the mind games of true play take us outside the real world, play can also become entangled in that world. It commonly, perhaps necessarily, does this for professional performers and athletes who are said to "play" at what they do. In truth, the only genuine "players" on stage or in sports and so on are children or amateurs. For once a "player" becomes a professional, she or he is not only *playing* but is *working*. And, however playful it might be, work belongs chiefly to the real world, because its purpose is to produce real world effects. These days, those effects can be huge for professional performers and athletes. Fortunes depend on how well they "play" the "game," literally and figuratively. Therefore, much as they might enjoy "playing," it is no mere game, much less a mind game, for them since their very livelihoods depend on their performance—on the athletic field or on the stage or in films or in the concert hall. (We will return to professional sports in the last chapter regarding "serious" play.)

A final note on play. If professional "players" do not really have a true play experience in their "games," we could say their spectators do. For spectators can enjoy watching the game as passive observers free of concern for the real-world consequences of the game that weigh on professional "players." There is, however, the exception of sports fans who get so involved in the game, especially its outcome, that they go kind of bonkers. Although they are observers, not players, they treat the game as a real-world contest between rival tribes, as it were, and feel such intense, almost war-like, passions about winning and losing that they sometimes take into the streets, doing battle with fans from the opposing tribe.

Such rabid effects of the spectator experience might actually be analogous to what can happen to us within the frame of the art experience. That is because the mind games we play within that frame can bestir us deeply enough that we carry the effects with us when we leave the frame of art and return to our real lives. To good or bad ends.

Conclusion

We will now take up how the mind games of the art experience—enabling us to enter the frame and go outside the real world, suspend disbelief, leave the demands and judgments of reality behind, and feel that there is nothing more at stake here than in children's play—can indeed influence our real lives. For, those mind games can tell us, consciously or unconsciously, how to live within the real world, even when we think of ourselves as playing mind games with no real-world consequences. That is how the art experience can bring both joy and sadness; how it can enlarge our lives or derail them; how it can both heal and kill.

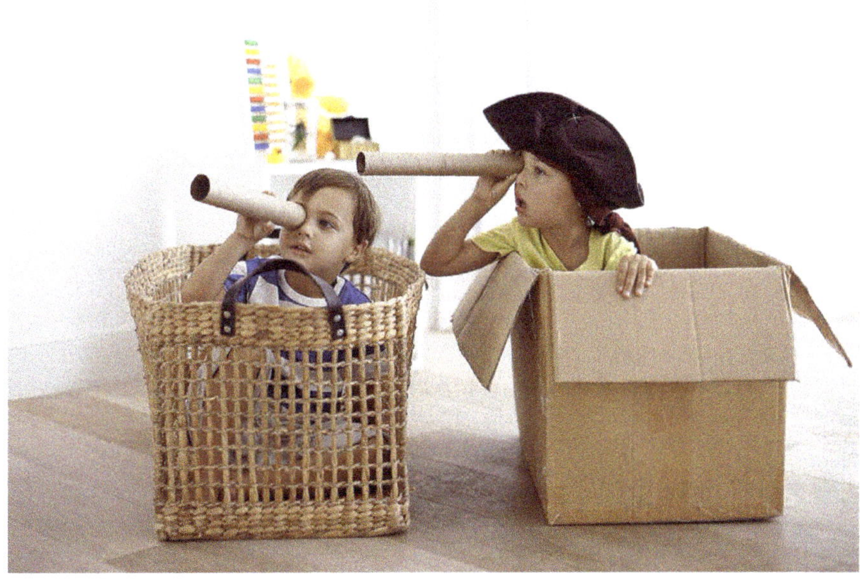

Fig. 24 — Children playing a fantasy game of pirates, sailing prosaic containers as pirate ships, peering out to sea with telescopes fashioned from the cardboard tubes in paper towels, and one child wearing a three-cornered hat, to boot. The fantasy mind games of child's play at work, or, rather, at play.

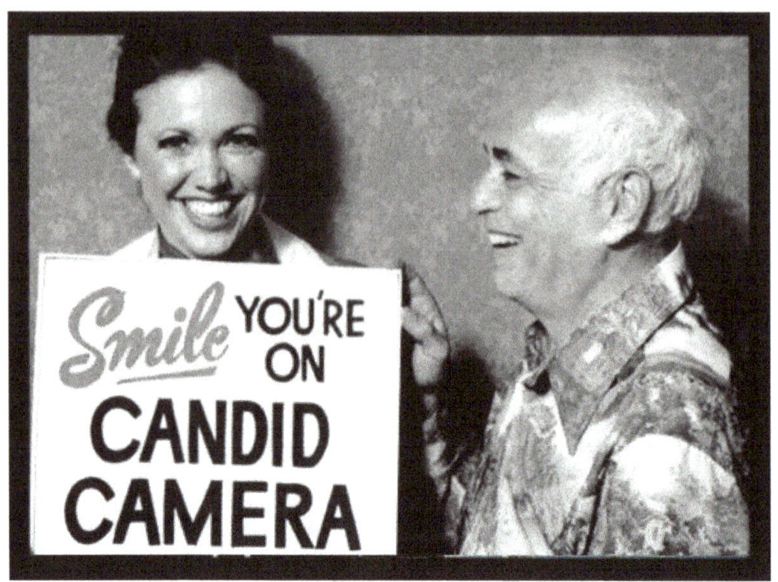

Fig. 25 — Allen Funt and staff member of the Candid Camera *show sharing a salutary laugh as they display the show's tagline.*

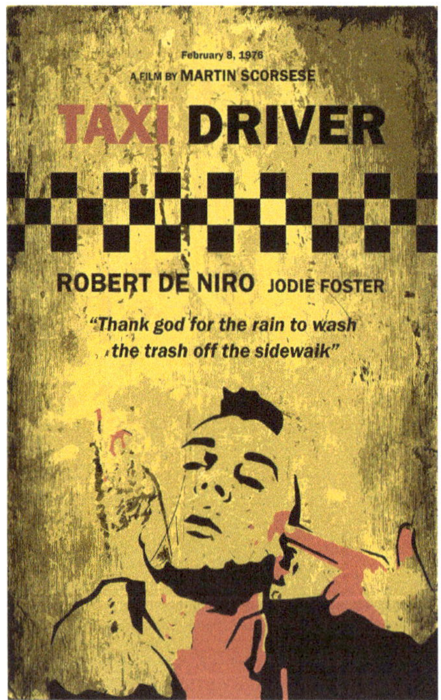

Fig. 26 — Poster for the violent, perversely idealistic film Taxi Driver, *which inspired John Hinckley to shoot President Reagan.*

III
The Art Experience: Healer and Killer

"But then why was life so inadequate?"
—Emma Bovary,
Gustave Flaubert, Madame Bovary

Everyone has been affected by the art experience at some time—emotionally, sensorily, imaginatively, even intellectually. That is indisputable. It is also indisputable that sometimes, whether we choose this or not, the effects can be strong enough to last outside that experience. To say that the art experience has the power to both heal and kill might be a bit melodramatic. But those two possible effects will serve to mark the range of what the art experience and its mind games can do to us, literally and metaphorically, for good and ill, in the real world.

Take music, the most emotional of the arts. When we give ourselves over to music it can move us in diverse ways. It can frighten or pacify us, cause sadness or elation, set the feet to dancing or to marching, make us shed sentimental tears or fall in love. What would young love be without it? As Shakespeare said, "Music is the food of love." Metaphorically he was not wrong (although that might be more true of the past than the present, since the music of the young is now mainly noise with largely unintelligible, and far from loving, lyrics). Remember Flaubert's Emma Bovary. Bewitched by the mind games of fantasy in romantic novels, she attends a performance of Donizetti's opera *Lucia di Lammermoor* (set to a novel of Walter Scott, one of Emma's favorite authors). And there, although she had cautioned herself against "the petty passions that art exaggerated," as the music swells, she grows so absorbed in it and the story the music conveys that she fantasizes about the opera's hero, Edgar, yearning to "run into his arms" and "cry out: 'Take me away, take me with you, let us go! I am yours, yours, all my passion and all my dreams are yours.'" The music and the drama have fed her fantasies of love and heated her passions to where she cannot leave them behind in the opera house. She takes them with her to find release for them. Within days of the performance, she begins a fateful liaison with a fellow-dreamer, Léon. The mind games of the art experience of the opera had so transported Emma Bovary that they changed her life. But this did not lead to good ends.

Or think of the anthems that move masses. Anthems like "The Star-Spangled Banner" and "La Marseillaise" not only provide stirring musical art experiences for listeners and performers, they use the mind games of that experience to unite, galvanize, and rally people emotionally to political causes. And those emotional effects are supposed to last beyond the anthem. The Nazis exploited this power of anthems for all it was worth. They adroitly employed rousing songs like the "Horst-Wessel-Lied" and "Deutschland Über Alles" to energize Germans and unify the country behind the Nazi vision of German superiority and a thousand-year Reich. Images of German crowds fervently singing such anthems haunt history. And who can forget the dueling German and French anthems that mark a dramatic turning point in the famed World War II movie *Casablanca*? There a German colonel summons other German officers at Rick's Café to break into "Die Wacht am Rhein," an inspiriting nationalistic and anti-French song that sparks a zealously anti-German hero to leave his table and lead the house band in a vigorous version of "La Marseillaise," bringing all non-Germans in the restaurant to their feet with the anthem ardently on their lips, rage in their burning hearts, and tears in their patriotic eyes (see Fig. 27). The French won this duel of anthems, silencing the Germans. But the German colonel, in humiliated musical defeat, pressured the local police chief to close the café. Even so, the musical duel awakened the patriotic spirit slumbering in some of the French café-goers and converted to the anti-German cause the cynical and professedly neutral Rick himself, leading to the film's unexpected and poignant climax where Rick and the previously compliant and self-serving local police chief, now also converted, proudly go off together to fight Germans. The art experience and mind games of the French anthem had done their job, long after the music had stopped.

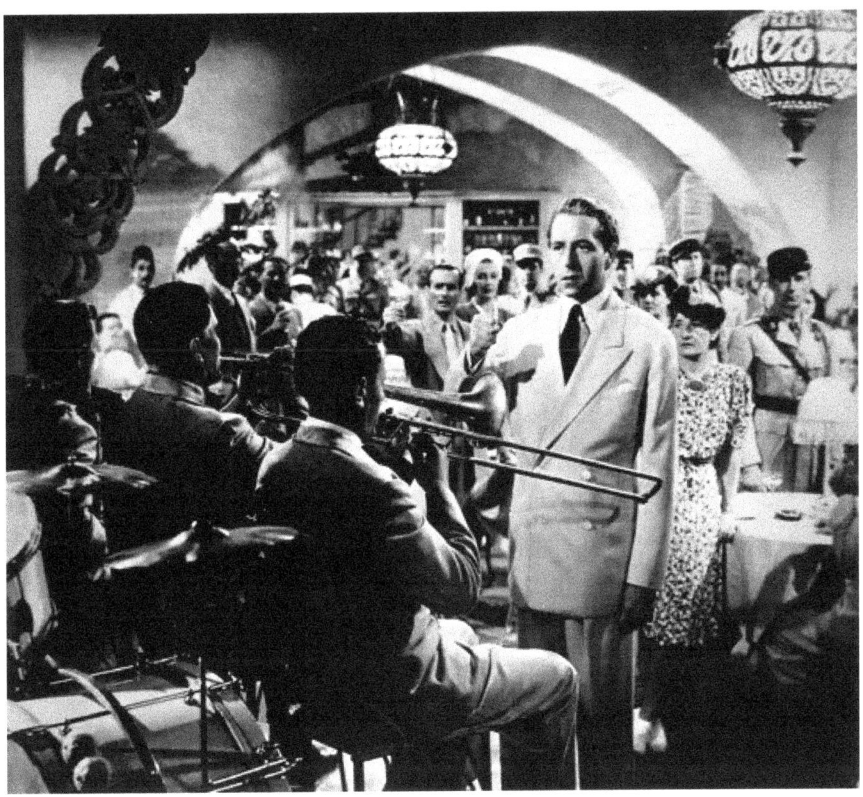

Fig. 27 — Casablanca, *1943.*

The anti-Nazi hero Victor Laszlo (Paul Henreid) conducts the house band at Rick's in a spontaneous, stirring rendition of "La Marseillaise" that silences the Germans there and rouses all French patrons to their feet.

From romance to politics, the art experience of music can stimulate emotions and fantasies (beyond the physiological effects of music as sheer sensation) that lastingly affect hearts and minds. So can the art experience of literature. For literature can carry us away on wings of words to worlds of all kinds in our minds, or mind games—that is what

Coleridge meant when he wrote of "the suspension of disbelief that constitutes poetic faith." Sometimes to good ends, sometimes to bad—as we have already had a hint of with Emma Bovary.

Look, for example, at what is arguably the world's first novel, the classic Japanese *Tale of Genji* (c. 1020) by Murasaki Shikibu. Its story of the "Shining Prince" Genji, rapturous lover, consummate artist, and tearful, sensitive soul, has enthralled Japanese readers for centuries. One of its early readers, an author in her own right known as Lady Sarashina, wrote in her memoir (*Sarashina Diary*, c. 1060, *As I Crossed a Bridge of Dreams*, trans. Ivan Morris) that she had so steeped herself in the book that she fell in love with its hero and "lived forever in a dream world" imagining that "someone like the Shining Genji in the Tale" would carry her off in loving devotion. The art experience of the *Tale* had become her dreamworld—until she eventually awakened from the dreams, concluding dejectedly, "How could anyone as wonderful as Shining Genji exist in this world of ours?" Quite so. The mind games of the art experience are not real life, however much we might want them to be. A lesson Flaubert's Emma Bovary never learns. We will return to Emma's sad case below—and take up other cases that show the damage these mind games can wreak when confused with reality—but for now let us look at a few instances of how the art experience and its mind games can work to more positive ends.

Positive Effects of the Art Experience

Start with Cervantes' *Don Quixote*. There is no more memorable instance in literature of the power of art to change lives mainly for the better than this tale of the "gentleman of La Mancha" who became the fabled knight-errant Don Quixote. This gentleman had become so absorbed in the mind games of reading books about medieval chivalry, mingling history and fiction, that he started living in a new world. Not only in his mind but in his life. He left his old existence behind and adopted the knightly identity of Don Quixote de La Mancha. With this new identity, he set out to right wrongs in the world, equipped with the regalia of knighthood, including a seemly (to him; ramshackle to others) steed, a suit of armor (with a makeshift helmet held together by green ribbons), a lady fair (actually a coarse serving woman and occasional prostitute), Dulcinea, for whom he would perform every noble act, and then a loyal squire, the sage peasant Sancho Panza. That Don Quixote's adventures are often bumbling, usually comic, and lead other characters in the book to think he's nuts, does not detract from his high-minded idealism. And, although he drubs many a head in his misadventures, he always has honorable intentions and a good heart. The cranky cleric who condemned his books for their pernicious influence proved correct to this extent: they had indeed given the "gentleman of La Mancha" a "new way of life." For the art experience of reading those books had freed him from his everyday world and inspired him to become a new and, to most readers, better man. The mind games of the art experience can perhaps yield no higher reward than that.

As Don Quixote lives out his life of knight-errantry, spawned by the mind games of fiction and of embellished history, most readers get drawn into his story and never forget it, and some are changed by it too. For just as Don Quixote was inspired by tales of chivalry to become a noble knight-errant, his fictional life has inspired readers through the years to emulate him and live for ideals instead of succumbing to a lesser existence—even several characters in the book who had at first thought him mad come to love and admire him as a gallant and honorable knight-errant after all and don't want him to abandon that identity at the end. The great Spanish philosopher Miguel de Unamuno became such a disciple of Don Quixote that he wrote a book entitled *The Life of Don Quixote and Sancho* (1905) in which he equated the knight-errant with Jesus, as fellow idealists willing to live for their ideals however much ridicule and contempt they suffered. Here the mind games of the art experience had given birth to a moral philosophy.

The art experience and philosophy actually have affinities going back to Plato. We could think of Plato as a philosopher/artist whose idealistic creations changed lives rather like *Don Quixote* did. Although Plato criticized artists for seducing people with misleading imitations and perniciously irresistible stories, he was quite a storyteller himself. His artful dialogues, featuring Socrates as the "hero" and an array of other characters, are, in effect, "stories" or philosophical fiction—making Plato the father of the literature of ideas. For these dialogues take readers into a wonderful world of ideas and eloquently portray the virtues of a life lived for ideals; and they do this through imaginary conversations and vivid, even poetic, images—like that of the cave in the *Republic*, where shadows on the wall represent the wiles of illusion, and the Myth of Er at the end of the same book metaphorically demonstrating how we choose our lives, and how the lives we've chosen to live shape our characters and our eternal souls.

Unlike Don Quixote, Plato and Socrates were historical figures. But no less, or not much less, than Cervantes' great novel, most of Plato's dialogues invite us to suspend disbelief and have an art experience with a hero, Socrates, as he lives a life devoted to his ideals, and then dies for them (while never writing a word). And thereby these dialogues can change lives. Notwithstanding his hostility to artists, Plato knew that people can often be enlightened, even philosophically enlightened, more effectively through the mind games of the art experience than through direct instruction (the more pragmatic Aristotle would give his own version of this in speaking of the "universal truths" that poetry alone can reveal, and he would imply similar powers of art in his idea of *katharsis*, as we have seen and will see again).

Plato, Socrates, and Don Quixote are, therefore, not only companions in idealism, living for the ideals that animate them, regardless of what anyone says. They are idealists who thrive on the art experience and how its mind games can, if played right, make an idealist of practically anyone. That is one way the art experience can change us mainly for the better.

Or consider the public response to *Uncle Tom's Cabin* (1852). That novel's bittersweet melodrama of slavery and goodness caused a flood of sentimental tears to flow. Yet the book also lent force to the abolitionists' cries to end slavery. For the injustices it depicted—instigating numerous factual and fictional "slave narratives"—not only brought tears, they roused anger and stirred action. "So this is the little woman who wrote the book that made this great war," Abraham Lincoln is said to have remarked upon meeting its author, Harriet Beecher Stowe. Apocryphal possibly. True or not, those words illustrated how the book's fictional portrayal of slavery gave readers an art experience of the subject that excited emotions they would not otherwise have had and then, for many readers, channeled those emotions from self-indulgent sentimentality into active support of the anti-slavery cause. A moral victory that helped vanquish slavery in America. No single anti-slavery tract, however impassioned, could have done as much as this novel.

The Art Experience as Healer

Another historic case in the nineteenth century of the art experience changing someone for the better comes from the life of the philosopher John Stuart Mill. This case demonstrates the power of art, quite literally, to heal. After spending his precocious youth and early adulthood consumed by learning and writing about improving the material conditions of humankind, he began wondering how he would feel if his labors paid off and fulfilled his ambitions. To his surprise and dismay, instead of the pride and elation he expected, he saw only emptiness in a dawning awareness that his efforts could never truly bring the happiness into the world he had thought possible. He stopped working and collapsed into apathy and despair. Then he read Wordsworth and other poets. And poetry gave him a cure. "What made Wordsworth's poems a medicine for my state of mind," Mill wrote in a chapter on "My Mental Crisis" in his autobiography, "was that they expressed not mere outward beauty, but states of feeling. . . . They seemed to be the very culture of the feelings . . . In them I seemed to draw from a source of inward joy, of sympathetic and imaginative pleasure, which could be shared by all human beings." This joy came from seeing "that there was real, permanent happiness in tranquil contemplation" and in "thought coloured by feeling under the excitement of beauty." Mill changed his life, embracing emotions, beauty, and individuality as never before. He also married a good woman, who helped steer him toward the liberating ideas of his classic book *On Liberty*, and, well, lived happily ever after. Allowing himself to enter the art experience of Wordsworth's poetry and play the mind games of suspending the rational judgments that had ruled his life lastingly affected him in ways that no theoretical treatise ever could have. The art experience had cured him of his "mental crisis," and he was much the better for that (see Fig. 28).

As if taking a cue from Mill and from Wordsworth's healing powers of poetry, art therapy emerged in the twentieth century as a technique for helping afflicted people recover by freely experiencing art. Art therapy might deal primarily with the emotional benefits of creating art rather than responding to it, but the essential features of the art experience are there in the freedom that art can give from the constraints of the real world. In that spirit, the "Healing Arts" programs that now exist in some hospitals focus directly on how, by entering into the nonthreatening and potentially salutary mind games of the art experience, patients and their loved ones can leave behind the emotional anxieties, and even some physical pains, of hospitalization. Some hospitals also provide "Poetry in the Waiting Room" with copies of poems chosen for their literary beauty, soulful delights, and inspiriting hope to help family members allay their anxieties about hospitalized loved-ones. Hospitals can even adopt a television comedy channel offering a beneficial alternative to the standard television fare that often feeds anxieties and intensifies stress. In fact, laughter itself can exercise healing powers. If anyone were to question that, the curious case of the author Norman Cousins should dissipate the doubts—while demonstrating how laughter and the art experience work together.

Stricken in middle age by a mysterious degenerative disease portending death, Cousins found his own cure. And he found it in laughter. For, as he reports in his book *Anatomy of an Illness* (1979), he discovered that the onset of the disease coincided with the decline of a certain enzyme, and that this enzyme could be produced by the physiology of laughter and large doses of vitamin C. An offbeat curative idea came to him. He called his friend Allen Funt, producer of the television comedy show *Candid Camera*, and asked him to bring films of the program to Cousins' hospital room. That show filmed ordinary people (unbeknownst to them) confronted by unanticipated, odd, and amusing situations contrived by Funt, who eventually reveals the truth to them. Over the next few months, Cousins watched many hours of *Candid*

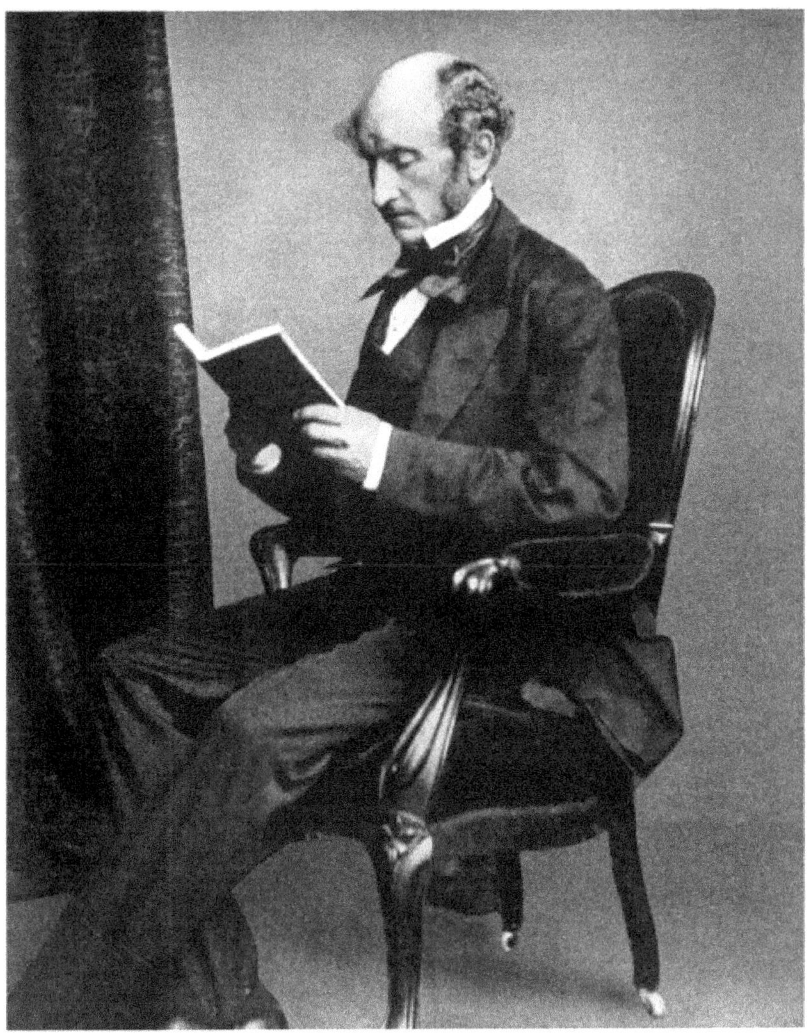

Fig. 28 — Thin-lipped, earnest Victorian John Stuart Mill, who seems to have been born old, reading a book.

Precociously intelligent and industrious beyond his years, he accomplished a lifetime of intellectual work at an early age, but that took a psychological toll, and finally he collapsed in exhaustion and disillusionment. He said that reading Wordsworth's poetry then healed his sick soul and changed his life by teaching him how to feel. Although Mill appears to have his emotions well under control in this picture, whether he's reading Wordsworth or not, his story attests to the healing powers that the mind games of the art experience can wield.

Camera and laughed himself back to health (aided by vitamin C). He had given himself over to the liberating art experience of a television comedy show that got its laughs from none other than watching real people, without knowing it, become performers in the art experience of other people. The show gave Cousins a humorous and curative art experience in watching laughable meetings of art and life. He laughed at the unwitting performers' reactions to the comical situations they find themselves in as well as to their astonished responses upon learning the truth. If any of these unintentional "performers" reacted with anger at being deceptively lured into becoming comic entertainment for a television audience, Funt did not say so. The show's catch phrase, "Smile, you're on *Candid Camera*," became a commonplace jest in American society for a generation, bespeaking wide recognition of how funny it can be to inadvertently play into someone else's art experience—and how no one would likely choose to do it (see Fig. 25).

Laughter itself is, to be sure, a complicated subject that has exercised many thinkers. Sigmund Freud speculated in *Jokes and Their Relation to the Unconscious*, that successful jokes make people laugh by deflating authority or expectations of one kind or another, thereby releasing psychic and emotional energies from restraints. That rings quite true. We could think of laughter in this sense as a spark of the art experience that ignites when we suddenly feel free from constraints to laugh at something—like the inadvertent reactions of people on *Candid Camera*. But we do not laugh at situations that immediately threaten us or those too close to us. Even gallows humor works only when we allow ourselves to feel removed from impending doom. Oscar Wilde's crack about the interminable death scene of the perfect child, little Nell, in Dickens' novel *The Old Curiosity Shop* proves the point. "One must have a heart of stone," he jeered (in a letter), "to read the death of little Nell without laughing." Wilde could laugh at her dying while reading about it, and we can laugh at his amusingly paradoxical phrase, but no one around Nell in the novel could laugh, nor could any reader who identified themselves with those fictional characters. To those characters and those readers, Nell's death was "real." But it must be said that for those characters the death was "more real" than for readers since, in the book, the death of little Nell was a genuine loss of life, and the tears they shed were authentic (if fictional) tears of sorrow over that loss. By contrast, for the readers little Nell died in an art experience that removed them for the reality of death, and the tears shed arose within that experience, which gave safe release to their sentimental feelings over a death scene in art, not in life. Wilde also read Dickens' teary-eyed account of little Nell dying as an art experience, but for him it did not release sentimental tears; instead, it freed him to play with the paradox of laughing at death. This was gallows humor of the art experience.

Wilde's laughter over something one would not normally, or should not, laugh at calls to mind the ingenious novel by Umberto Eco, *The Name of the Rose*. It tells of a pious but scholarly medieval monk who so fears the irreverence of laughter and how it can devalue godliness that he poisons the pages of the sole existing copy of a purported treatise by Aristotle on comedy (held in the monastery library, and which the monk, as a scholar, cannot bring himself to destroy) so that anyone who reads it will die from reading its evil message. Comedy and piety easily clash because they are antithetical attitudes, one elevating, the other deflating, making piety a juicy target for laughter. The comic novelist and eccentric clergyman Laurence Sterne made much of this in his novel *The Life and Opinions of Tristram Shandy, Gentleman* (1759) and other writings, including his sermons. For he judged piety and orthodoxy to be for the most part Pharisaic hypocrisy, and he deemed hearty—but never cruel—laughter to be a life-serving and humanizing gift of God. As he said, "Every time a man smiles . . . but much more when he laughs, it adds something to this Fragment of Life." And he wrote his great novel to teach people the humanity of laughter through the art experience of comedy, often at the expense of religious piety and intellectual orthodoxy.

Sterne knew, as Eco's fictional monk did not, that even if irreverent, the art experience of comedy and laughter can improve life and people too. For without the emotional release of laughter our lives would be severely constrained, awfully gray, and pitifully dull. If the release of constraints that laughter brings tends to deflate piety, authority, and the like, that simply says we probably need it the more lest we lose our individuality, our zest, our joy in life, and our humanity.

Adverse Effects of the Art Experience

Those are some of the ways that the art experience and its mind games can improve our lives and even heal afflictions. Now we turn to the other side. For just as the art experience can heal and help us live, it can, in a manner of speaking, kill. If that is, as mentioned earlier, a melodramatic way to put it, it is not wrong. We have seen that the harm art can do has been a source of worry since Plato. Following that tradition, Thomas Mann wrote, in the story *Tonio Kröger* (1903), "What more pitiable sight is there than a life led astray by art?" Mann had in mind chiefly the artists led astray by their absorption in art (a favorite theme of his) rather than those affected by the art of others. But the phrase could still fit. Here I will touch on a few notable instances not so much of artists but of non-artists, fictional and actual, who let the mind games of the art experience undo their very lives.

Consider an artist first: Oscar Wilde and his shocking novel *The Picture of Dorian Gray*. As any reader knows, Dorian Gray is a dashing young man who sees a portrait of himself painted by a friend and wishes to stay forever young like the portrait while the portrait, instead of him, betrays the ravages of time. He gets his wish, remaining in appearance like a timeless work of art, despite his dissolute and wicked life, while the portrait deteriorates not only with his every year but with his every selfish act. But in the end, life and art switch places again. After murdering the painter, Dorian slashes what has become a hideous picture then dies and the portrait resumes its original appearance as his own features take on its dreadful signs of age and depravity. Dorian Gray could not live as art after all.

Neither could Oscar Wilde himself. He had gained fame as a flamboyant dandy and irreverent wit poking fun at all conventions. His comedies, crowned by his last, *The Importance of Being Earnest* (1895), charmed audiences with Wilde's wit debunking seriousness and exalting triviality. Wilde came to think he was living in that very art experience and its mind games, where his verbal cleverness permitted him to say anything and do anything and pay no real-world price. But he went too far. Much as audiences enjoyed the comic art experience of Wilde's witty plays, late-Victorian English society was not itself an art experience outside the world. It was very much in the world. And Wilde's flippant attitudes toward his brazen homosexuality, and toward the legal charges leveled against him for "indecency" (after he had, with the same airily unserious disregard for consequences he did almost everything, sued his accuser, the Marquise of Queensbury, father of Wilde's young lover, for sexual slander and then lost), finally got him imprisoned, crushing his spirit and leading to his early death. Like Dorian Gray, Wilde had thought he could live his life as an art experience, outside the demands of the real world. Then he discovered he had been living in that world all the time, and paid the ultimate price for confusing art with life.

Long before Oscar Wilde, the dangers of wholly submitting to the art experience had poignantly showed up in Dante's *Inferno*. There in the Second Circle, near the beginning of his journey through hell, Dante meets Francesca da Rimini, who tells him her tragic story of literature-incited passion. One day, while she and her husband's brother, Paolo, were innocently reading together the story of the fabled lovers Lancelot and Guinevere, the wife of king Arthur, "more than once," she says, "that reading made our eyes meet." And then, she goes on, "when we read how the longed-for smile was kissed by so renowned a lover," Paolo, "trembling all over, kissed me on my mouth." When her husband happened upon them in passionate embrace, he swiftly slew them both. Blame it on the book? The vengeful husband didn't. And the book itself was not to blame. Blame should go to the art experience. For, as Paolo and Francesca read the tale of irresistible illicit romance, they had let the mind games of the art experience take them out of the real world into a realm of boundless romantic bliss. But Franccesca's husband had stayed behind in the real world.

Another fictional character who fell victim to the art experience of reading romantic stories was the very personification of how that experience can ruin one's life. This is Flaubert's Emma Bovary. We met her earlier when she was at the opera succumbing to the emotional seductions of music. But she has more to teach us. She grew up reading the likes of Walter Scott, Chateaubriand, and Lamartine, their writings all infused with idealized romance and often tinged by sentimental religiosity (see Fig. 29). Such writings led her into an intense fantasy life and to despise "the mediocrity of existence." "I hate everyday heroes and restrained emotions," she cries, "like the ones in real life." No wonder she was enthralled by the hero of Donizetti's opera. In time, the mind games of the art experience so possess her with "ideal ambitions and fantastic dreams" outside the real world that she loses all ability to live in that world. She demanded "the immediate gratifications of her heart" because that is what the mind games of reading romantic literature had given her through its fantasies. And yet she wants more than the gratifications of fantasy in mind games alone. She wants those gratifications in her life. She yearns for the "'happiness,' 'passion,' and 'intoxication'"

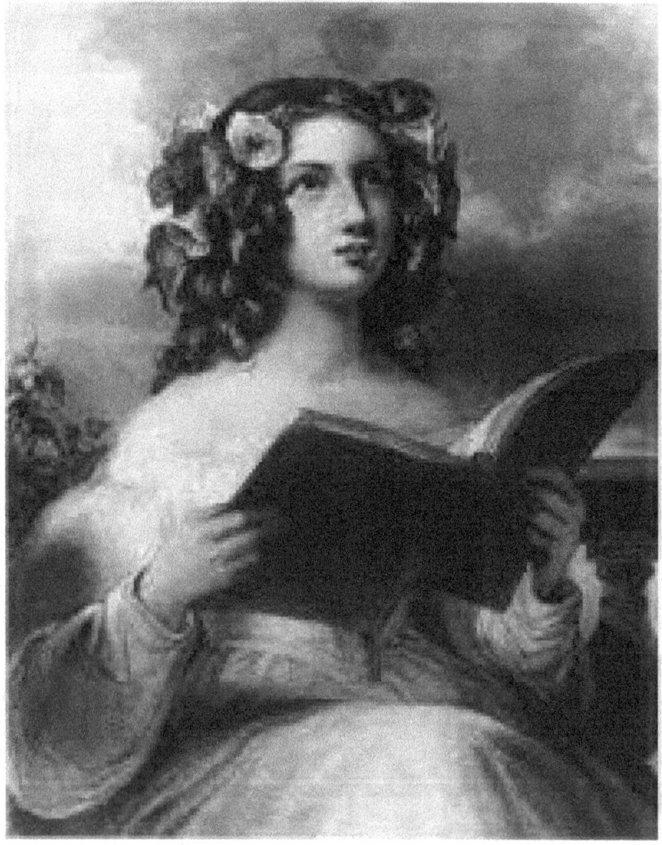

Fig. 29 — A nineteenth-century print of Emma Bovary reading, or rather daydreaming with a book in her hands, playing the mind games of romantic fiction as she did—obsessively and to her detriment.

that "had seemed so beautiful to her in books." And she cannot understand why even her voracious love affairs fail to deliver the satisfactions of her desires, the fulfilment of her fantasies. "Why then was life so inadequate?" she asks in blind bewilderment. Unable to see why she could never find the delectable fantasies of the art experience in real life, she finally turns resentfully against a world where "nothing was worth living for," and she kills herself.

Emma Bovary might be an extreme case, and in fiction at that, but she gave the name to a malady not hers alone: *Bovarysme*, which amounts to being so captivated by fantasies and ideals—usually, but not always, born of the art experience—that one cannot truly live in the real world. Flaubert actually saw a lot of this in himself. As he reportedly confessed, *"Emma Bovary c'est moi," Emma Bovary, that's me.* Detesting, as he wrote in a letter of 1854 (to Louise Colet), the "mediocrity . . . pretense, affectation, humbug everywhere," he declared, "we must take flight into the ideal . . . Oh! Our ivory towers! Let us climb them in our dreams." But unlike Emma, as a gifted artist, he used his dreams to write novels, pouring his own fantasies, ideals, and disillusionments into art experiences for others to enter, and possibly to learn from.

The Art Experience as Killer

We could class Dorian Gray, Paolo and Francesca, and Emma Bovary among literary cases that exhibit the power of the art experience to kill, at least indirectly. Now we take up a few cases in both literature and life that show the art experience and its mind games leading quite directly to murder.

First comes Tolstoy's famous story *The Kreutzer Sonata* (1889). There, a man named Pozdnyshev murders his wife because of that Beethoven sonata. He has been suspicious of her, a pianist, having a love affair with the violinist who performs with her at social gatherings (see Fig. 30). One night while they perform the "Kreutzer" sonata, Pozdnyshev listens to the music with mounting agitation. He does not understand his feelings, but he later reports that music has often had a strange effect on him. It makes him "feel what I do not really feel," and "understand what

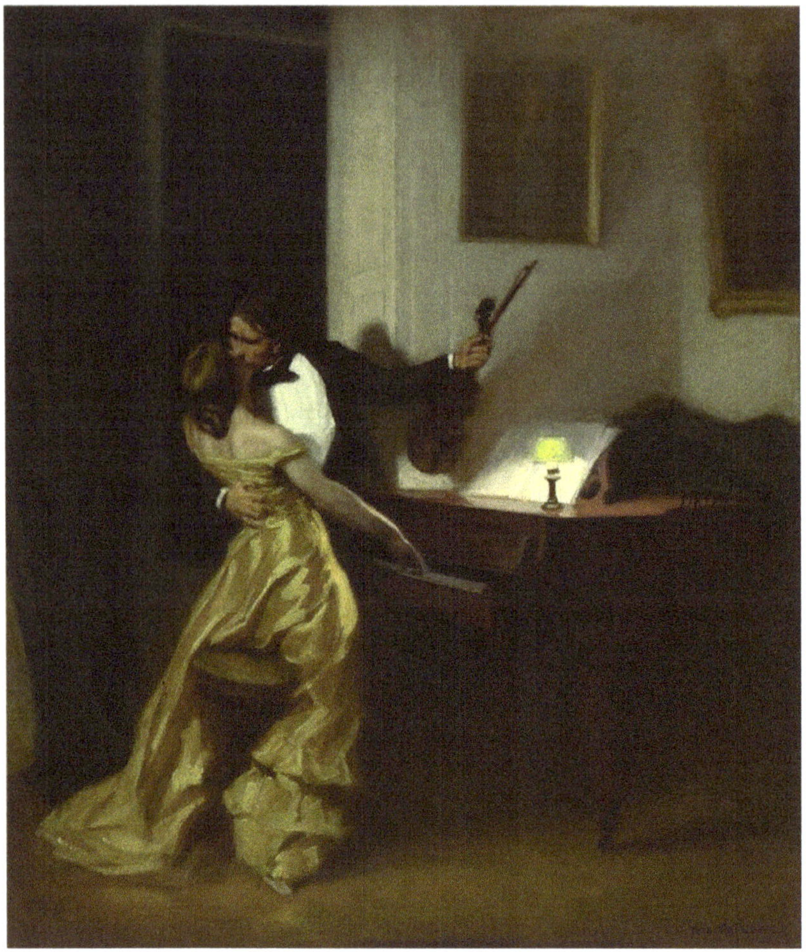

Fig. 30 — René-Xavier Prinet, Kreutzer Sonata, *c. 1891.*

Inspired by Tolstoy's story of that name, Prinet here rapturously captured Pozdynyshev's fantasy of his pianist wife's amour with the violinist who played the wicked sonata with her.

I do not understand," and to think "I can do what I cannot do." The "Kreutzer" sonata did that and more. "That piece had a terrible effect on me," he explains, "it was as if quite new feelings, new possibilities . . . had been revealed to me." What they were he could not say. Such are the mind games we can play in the art experience. But, he continues, the "consciousness of this new condition was very joyous" and put everything "in a new light." It turns out that what those mind games had done to him was first to agitate his emotions and enflame his visions of betrayal, and then to give him, albeit unconsciously, a way of releasing the agitation—a kind of delayed *katharsis*. And it would be violent. Later, when he finds his wife and the violinist together at his home where, as the violinist naïvely tells him, they have been, "having some music," the release takes place. Pozdnyshev runs her through with a knife while the terrified violist scampers away.

Pozdnyshev had let the art experience and its mind games arouse intense emotions, entangled with fantasies of jealousy, and then show him a way to satisfy those emotions and the fantasies in the real world. Acting out the mind games of that experience, he murdered his wife, blaming the music as much as her suspected infidelity. "The 'Kreutzer' sonata made me do it," he might have claimed. But he would have been wrong. It wasn't the sonata itself that made him do it. It was the mind games of the art experience he played while listening to the sonata, combined with his penchant for jealousy. At all events, the story perversely illustrates how the art experience can kill.

Pozdnyshev is a mighty sick and misogynistic fictional character, just as many of Tolstoy's ideas of art were mighty peculiar. But there have been instances of actual killings induced, or arguably so, by the art experience. Probably the most celebrated of these is that of Mark David Chapman, who murdered the famed singer/songwriter John Lennon.

Chapman committed the murder because of an art experience that had taken over his life. It is true that plenty of people doubt that crimes can ever be caused by an experience of art. But if ever there was a crime clearly connected to an art experience, the Chapman case is it. Bewitched by the mind games of that experience, he had allowed himself to identify so thoroughly with a character in fiction that he saw the world through that character's eyes. This was Holden Caulfield in J. D. Salinger's novel, *The Catcher in the Rye*. Caulfield is a young idealist who derides the adult world for its "phoniness" and thinks of himself as a champion of authenticity, innocence, and goodness. Moved by this self-image, Caulfield imagines himself with a crowd of children frolicking in a field of rye near a cliff where he poises himself to catch any of them at risk of falling off. Chapman evidently fantasized that he too was a catcher in the rye, the enemy of phoniness, defender of integrity, and protector of the innocent. And he now saw Lennon, a onetime hero of his, as a sell-out to commerce and a hypocrite, writing and singing songs extoling the authentic life while living high at the posh Dakota apartments in New York City. In Chapman's moral fantasy, Lennon had to die to punish him for betraying his professed ideals and to save the innocent from being seduced by Lennon's disingenuous art. After the shooting in December 1980, while Lennon lay dying on the sidewalk in front of the Dakota, Chapman drew from a pocket his ever-present copy of *The Catcher in the Rye* and waited calmly rereading it until the police arrived (see Fig. 31).

Not surprisingly, Chapman's actions struck many people as insane. After all, anyone who commits murder to live out the ideals of a fictional character must be nuts. It appears that, unable to become a rock star himself or to find any satisfying place for himself in the real world, Chapman had in fact become a very unbalanced guy—just as Holden Caulfield turns out to be living in an asylum. A kind of religious conversion seems to have intensified his delusions. But whatever the web of motives behind Chapman's lethal act, they were surely woven around

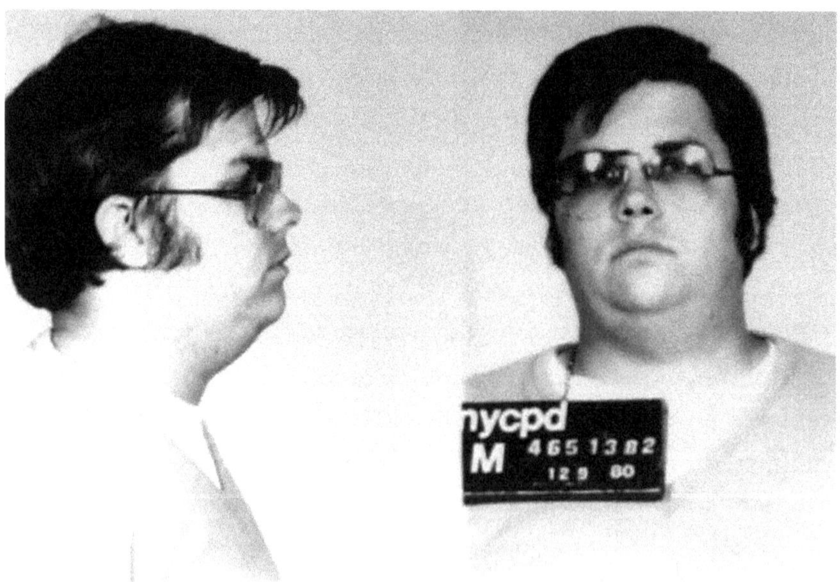

Fig. 31 — Mark David Chapman, in police photograph after shooting John Lennon, December 8, 1980.

the art experience of reading *The Catcher in the Rye* and trying to live out Holden Caulfield's moral ideals. A court sentenced him to twenty-years-to-life in prison with periodic psychiatric evaluations. He was denied parole for the eleventh time in 2020.

A little shy of four months after that shooting, another frustrated young man tried to assassinate the American president, and for reasons akin to those behind Chapman's murder of John Lennon. But it was not a novel that had put him on that course. It was a movie.

John Hinckley, Jr., had grown up in an affluent home, but, not unlike Chapman, he had lived a pretty dodgy life since then as an aspiring musician who could not make the grade in music, or anything else. Then he saw the Martin Scorsese movie *Taxi Driver* and had an epiphany (see Fig. 26). Its unsettling tale of an emotionally wounded Vietnam War vet who becomes a taxi driver in Manhattan—and who plots to kill the president in rage over romantic rejection by one of the president's female workers, and who also befriends a very young prostitute to save her from her profession, and who later winds up shooting a bunch of bad guys who exploit that profession—changed Hinckley's life. The mind games of the art experience Hinckley played in watching the movie freed him from a reality he felt crushed by and opened to him a fantasy world he could live in, and that he could then turn into his real world. He not only identified himself with the taxi driver but became obsessed with the actress, Jodie Foster, who had played the young prostitute. He even imagined he could win Ms. Foster's affection, in real life, and sent her effusive letters and rhapsodic poems. He also stalked her wherever she went. When nothing availed, he decided he must do something dramatic to impress her. Like the taxi driver in the movie, he decided to shoot the president. At the end of March 1981, he pumped five shots from a 22-gauge pistol at President Ronald Reagan, striking him with a ricochet and hitting several other people directly. What Hinckley afterwards called "the greatest love offering in the history of the world" had certainly won him notice. But it didn't get him the girl, as they say in movies. His fantasies turned out not to work in the real world (see Fig. 32). A court ruled him not guilty by reason of insanity and confined him to a mental hospital, where he remained until 2016, when he was released under stringent constraints that ended

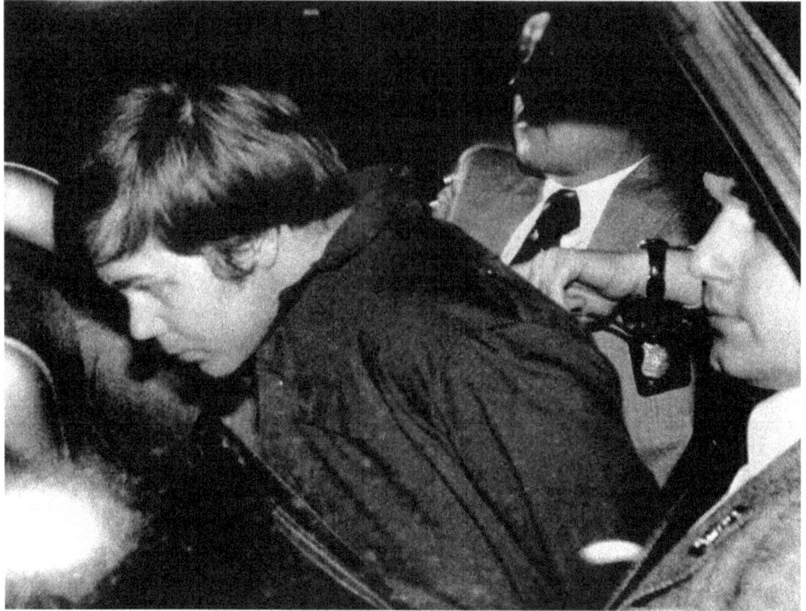

Fig. 32 — John Hinckley in police car after shooting President Reagan and others, March 30, 1981.

in 2022 after he was judged at last capable of living in this world again.

Both Chapman and Hinckley let the mind games of the art experience become their reality. It goes without saying that many villains do bad things without the art experience. But here are two historic cases demonstrating quite convincingly how those mind games can ignite or fuel fantasies that shape lives outside that experience. And to very bad ends indeed: killing people, or trying to.[18]

I should add a note here on the numerous young males of recent times who, like Chapman and Hinckley, translated frustrated yearnings and resentments into acts of homicide. But they chose to make their mark not by killing prominent public figures; instead, they committed mass shootings. Scholars have examined scores of these characters—including the few shooters who survived their attacks and some would-be shooters who stopped short of consummating the killings—and have found several distinct commonalities among them, shared with Chapman and Hinckley.[19] Among those commonalities, besides bitter frustrations and consuming resentments, these mass killers fantasize about dramatically avenging their grievances through a "quest for fame and notoriety," and they "study other mass shooters" whose acts get widely publicized in the media. In other words, to a significant extent, they view themselves as performers and their violent acts as performances that will immediately exalt them into the ranks of celebrated avengers. It might not have been an art-experience as such that had inspired them, like Chapman and Hinckley, but the attention given mass killings, especially on television, had focused their fantasies, melding the desire for revenge with the hunger for celebrity. Just as Chapman had modeled himself on the well-known fictional Houlden Caulfield and Hinckley had done the same with the cinematic taxi driver, they would model themselves on killers made widely known (becoming celebrities of a sort) through the mass media. Their motives and fantasies, therefore, belonged more or less to the mind games of the art experience, freeing the frustrated young men from constraints of the real world and then emboldening them to take those fantasies into that world, to tragic effect. I would venture that those kinds of mind games play a greater role in our world, increasingly influenced as it is by the cult of celebrity and by what I will later describe as the Culture of Entertainment, than most folks would think. In that light, it should be no surprise that mass shootings have increased for the reasons they have.

Conclusion

The few anecdotal instances from art and life in these pages illustrate how playing the mind games of the art experience can affect people in ways that they carry back with them into the real world for good and ill—unto healing and killing. I have presented those effects rather simplistically in attitudes and behavior. But many such effects are subtler than that, more nuanced and ambiguous. We will now move toward some of those subtleties by taking up a subject that has been lurking in the background from the outset here. Namely, the difference within the art experience between high art and low art, or entertainment. And the difference that difference can make when we go from the mind games of the art experience back into the real world.

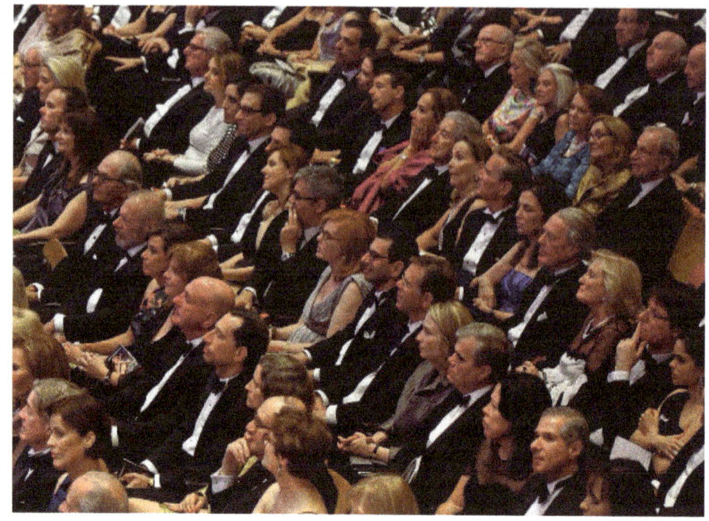

Fig. 33 — An elegantly attired and emotionally restrained audience at a classical music concert, calmly rising inside themselves to the collective high-art experience. That the audience members are all white and of certain age also says something about high art in contrast to low art.

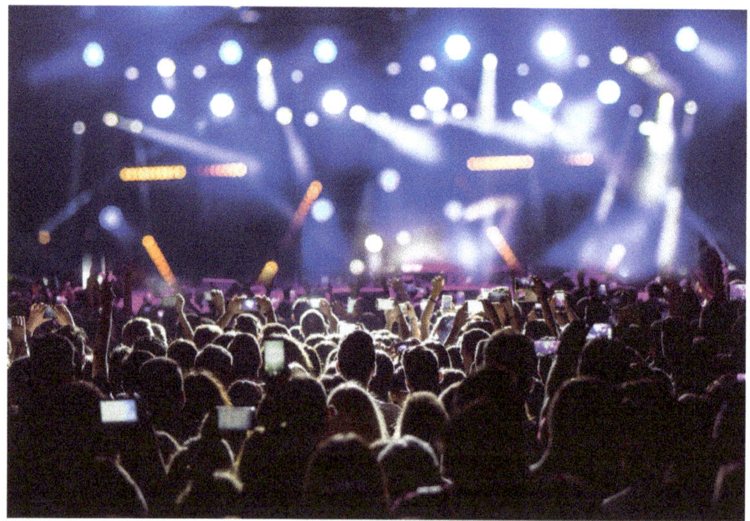

Fig. 34 — Twenty-first-century pop music concert: strobe lights working the crowd, colored lights playing through the air, the wildly amplified sounds from the stage no doubt deafening, and the audience of animated young people jammed together in communal enthusiasm, waving their arms and, of course, photographing the event with ubiquitous cell phones. Here the low-art experience is almost primitive: entirely sensory and socially bonding en masse. *But the cell phones add a technological stimulus to the event, turning the raucous scene into sharable experiences. The whole thing is kind of a collective mind game played by hordes of youths who have left the real world together to enter a place of exciting sensations where nothing matters but being part of the throbbing moment—and "sharing" it by cell phone.*

IV
The Art Experience: High and Low

"High art makes us better, low art doesn't, and might make us worse."
—Plato (paraphrase)

Now that we have seen how the mind games of the art experience take us outside the real world, and how that experience can affect us in lasting ways, to both good and bad ends, we can look into what I will call the high-art experience and the low-art experience. That means again considering artworks not for themselves but for the response of people to them.

One might think that high art and low differ primarily in their aesthetic properties. And to some extent they do, if not *primarily*. Anyone today would say, for instance, that a Mozart symphony belongs to high art and rap music to low art, that the tragedies of Shakespeare belong to high art while action movies are low art, and so on. But, since the same artwork can change status from high to low or from low to high over time and across cultures, aesthetics alone cannot tell us all we need to know here, any more than aesthetics can tell us what art is. So, we must ask: Why do we distinguish between high and low art as we do? The answer lies in what happens to us when we experience one or the other. And what happens follows from the mind games of the art experience.

First, I want to point out that the mind games of the art experience are essentially the same in both high art and low, or entertainment (which I equate with low art). That is, those mind games take us out of the real world by letting us enter the frame of art where we can suspend the mental demands and constraints of ordinary life in that world. But the effects of doing this can differ in the experiences of high art and low. For while we play those mind games with art and ourselves, those games can play us, in a manner of speaking. High art and low just play them a little differently. And the diverging effects of that difference show how best, or perhaps I should say how pragmatically, to distinguish between high art and low.

The Moral Tradition

Tradition has, of course, put its own stamp on the distinction between high and low art. And it is the stamp of moral consequences. Namely: high art makes us better; low art doesn't, and might even make us worse. For high art asks us to rise to it with a kind of reverence or appreciation of its lofty purpose and complex qualities, whereas low art demands nothing of us and just draws us, sometimes irresistibly, into the diversions and pleasures it provides.* Platitude though this idea now might be, it was the heart of Plato's philosophy of art that launched the moral tradition of distinguishing high art from low.

Plato was quite straight-forward about how high art makes people "better" and low art can make them "worse." He did not use the terms "better" and "worse" or "high art" and "low art," but he made the point clear enough. "Better" meant to him what encourages rationality and restraint, reverence and respect, honor and obedience. "Worse" meant the opposite. "On what part of the human being," Plato asked, should art "exercise its power?" He answered that it should be the "highest part of us," the realm of "reason . . . restraint" and "the direction of princi-

---

* I grant that high art might attract some art lovers in a similar way, but I would say that even if the attraction of high art feels irresistible, it depends on the art lover having a measure of preparation for the artwork, or at least a sensibility alive to its high-art attractions. And more, the attractions of high art, however keen, are not as blatantly contrived to grab attention as are the attractions of low art—even when we can experience both high-art and low-art attractions in the same work.

ple." That is the realm of high art. By contrast, low art—which for him, as we have seen, included most art—appeals to the lowest, "irrational" part of us, leading us to be "recalcitrant . . . lazy and inclined to cowardice." Consequently, Plato proposed beginning the education of the young with stories that "aim at encouraging the highest excellence of character." For that matter, he thought all the arts must do that, too, or be prohibited. He would, therefore, prevent visual artists from "portraying bad character, ill-discipline, meanness, or ugliness in . . . any work of art." As for poets, he said, "the only poetry [or literature] that should be allowed in the state is hymns to gods and paeans in praise of famous men." Plato was concerned not only about the effects of art on individuals either. Far from it. As already noted (and quoted), he believed the experience of art profoundly influenced the welfare of the state. For "once you go beyond" art that teaches rationality, restraint, and "the highest excellence of character," he insisted, "and admit" any art that acts on people too emotionally, "disorder" sets in, undermining "morals and manners" and spreading "into the laws and constitution. . . until it has upset private and public life."[20] No wonder Plato worried so much about art and devoted so many pages to it in the *Republic* and other writings.

That was Plato's theory anyway. Obviously, it had nothing to do with the Christian virtues of selflessness, kindness, piety, preparations for life in heaven, and so on. Plato was a philosophical idealist and conservative humanist more concerned with how human beings can cultivate good character and organize society in this world—even if he also had notions of an afterlife. And Plato's most renowned pupil, Aristotle, also a committed humanist, if not a Platonic idealist, accepted his teacher's basic premise that the power of art, high and low, deeply affects character. But Aristotle viewed that power more subtly and added some important nuances to Plato's ideas on the effects of high art and low. Less of an idealist and moralist than Plato, and more practical-minded, Aristotle did not care as much about art's power to do harm as its ability to do good, affecting individuals and society for the better (see Fig. 35). His thoughts on this are worth dwelling on.

Just as Plato had given art a central place in his great political dialogue,

Republic, Aristotle concluded his *Politics* with a chapter on art, explaining its vital role in the lives of individuals and of the state. There, he echoed Plato's conviction that art should shape "a certain kind of character" and that young people should not be exposed to art that would do otherwise, like "debased paintings," "unseemly" stories, and "tunes and modes" that have "orgiastic and emotional" effects. But from there, Aristotle went his own way.

For one thing, Aristotle divided high art, or high culture, from low along less moralistic lines than Plato had done. Very pragmatic about the roles art can play—as he was about most things—he believed that educated adults experience art unlike children and the uneducated do and are therefore less susceptible to art's dangers and more able to gain from the good art can deliver. That gain occurs above all, he said, by providing "civilized pursuits [or "noble activities"] during leisure." For these "civilized pursuits" bring the "best kind of enjoyment" since they require "a certain amount of learning and education" to appreciate and to engage in them, thereby elevating us while providing enjoyment. That is high art and high culture.

Aristotle also thought that a person who is properly educated will find that such high-minded activities complete a well-lived and truly civilized life. And he contended that everyone (at least in the upper caste) should be educated in the appreciation and practice of all the arts as civilizing activities. But he cautioned that this art education not become professional training, because then the arts would lose their civilizing purposes and sink into mere mechanical activities pursued for money, making "the mind preoccupied and unable to rise above lowly things." And he was not wrong in principle. For the professionalization of art can change the role art plays not only in the lives of artists but in the lives of those who turn to the arts for "the best kinds of enjoyment." That is, professional artists can become narrow career-minded technicians, and the artworks they produce (or perform) for money can descend into merely social diversions or degenerate into cheap entertainment.

Not that Aristotle opposed entertainment in itself. He was a subtler thinker than that. He simply extolled high culture and art for their ele-

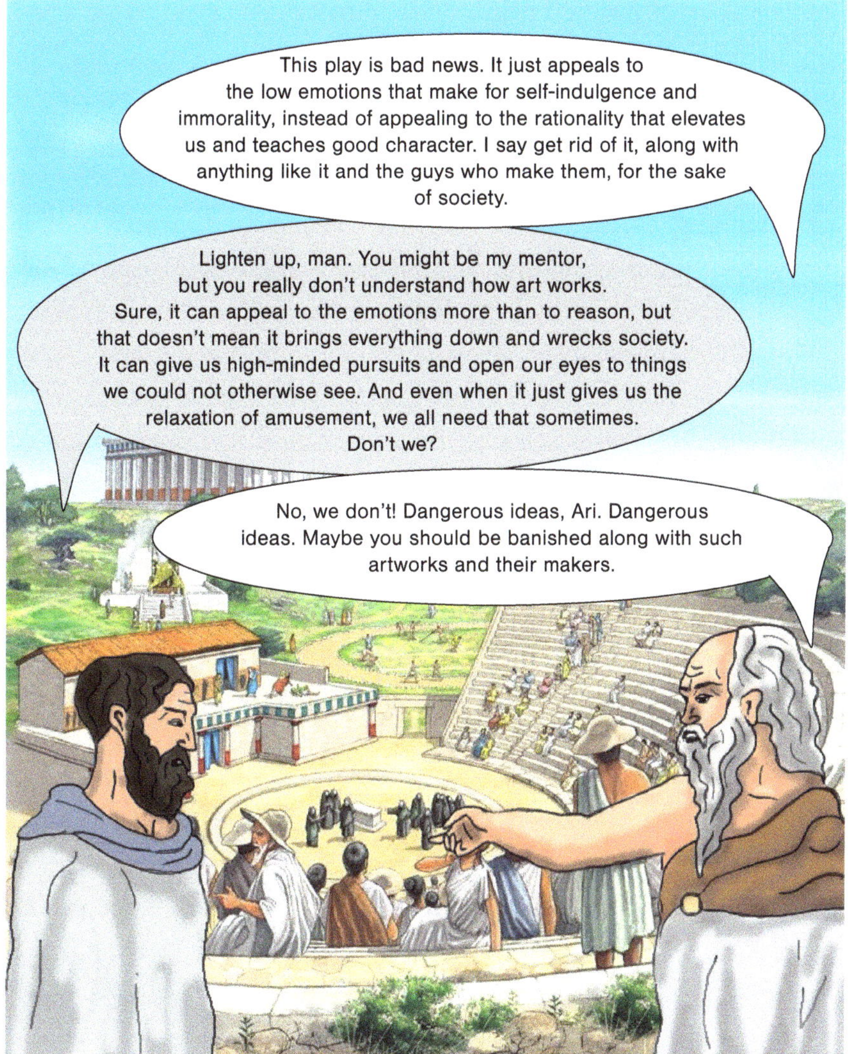

Fig. 35 — Illustration of Plato and Aristotle at the Greek Theatre. Foreground cartoon by Rachel Davis Mariano.

vating benefits in the civilized life, and gave entertainment, or low art, a lesser role to play. Even so, he judged this to be a necessary role at that. Again, no stringent moralist like Plato, who would banish all art that did not teach rationality and restraint, Aristotle recognized an actual human need for the low art of what he called "amusement." Everybody needs "amusement," Aristotle said, as "a kind of cure for the ills we suffer in working hard" because it provides "refreshment" or "relaxation" like "taking a nap or having a drink."* Nonetheless, Aristotle added a warning: useful as they are for recuperating from toil, we should not "make amusements an end in themselves," for that would be like making rest the purpose of life.[21] And doing this would make a mockery of living.

Pragmatic as he was, Aristotle saw that human life embraces many activities, but he also saw that these must be managed properly to enable people to fulfill their natures. Amusement is certainly one of the activities that needs wise managing. Many modern critics have complained that the blandishments of amusement, or entertainment, have become so prevalent that, as Neil Postman put it in the title of a book, we are "Amusing Ourselves to Death." Aristotle would have understood. We will return to this complaint in the next chapter when taking up the pervasive influence of entertainment in our world.

Although Aristotle shunned Plato's moralism in recognizing the uses of "amusement," he still had no doubt that high culture and art make us better, and that low culture and art, however necessary within limits, do not. Aristotle was not finished with art though. And another of his ideas added more nuance to understanding the effects of art, both high and low. This was his idea of *katharsis*.

Katharsis was Aristotle's answer to Plato's claim that whatever people encounter in art they will instinctively, and adversely for the most part, imitate in their own lives. Aristotle acknowledged that people learn much through imitation, but he did not think they were bound to imitate in their lives everything they encounter in art. That is because he thought a proper education would render adults "completely immune to any harm that might come to them from" the imitations or even the emotionality of art. And, more important, he understood that emotions themselves function somewhat differently in the art experience than in real life. Emotions do not necessarily spill over from that experience directly into real life. Instead, the art experience itself gives us, as Aristotle said, "a way of working off the emotions." That is *katharsis*.

---

* Aristotle used two Greek words commonly translated into English as "amusement" or "play." One is *paidia*, which indicates "child's play or fun games" (not to be confused with *paideia* , the Greek word for education). The other is *anapausis*, which denotes recreation, relaxation cessation, rest.

Katharsis—a term Aristotle borrowed from medicine and mentioned in the *Poetics* but said more about in the *Politics*—occurs during the art experience after we freely give ourselves over to emotions without fear of real-world consequences. Then, no matter how emotionally whipped up we let ourselves become, those emotions get innocently expended right there. As Aristotle explains (noted earlier), when we experience "pity and fear, for example, but also excitement . . . or any other emotion," even "orgiastic effect[s]," through art, we will suddenly feel as if we "had undergone a curative and purifying treatment" that leaves "a sort of pleasant purgation and relief," and "an elation which is not at all harmful."[22] *Katharsis* names this emotional purgation. But we still might wonder why and how *katharsis* happens. Does it occur automatically and mysteriously? Or does *katharsis* come from a discernable sequence of mental and emotional events? Aristotle judged it to be the latter. And his account, fragmentary though it may be, illustrates a telling quality of the art experience and its mind games.

When we feel intense emotions in real life, they usually have consequences that we can anticipate and might be wary of. But when we feel these emotions in the art experience, Aristotle assures us, we can readily let them take us wherever they want to go without worry, for ultimately something inside us springs their *kathartic* release. In literature—Aristotle focused on tragedy—that spring comes from the "discovery" or "recognition" of why the drama unfolding before us has roiled our emotions and stirred "pity and fear." This recognition gives us an understanding of both the tragedy itself and our feelings about it. And that understanding lets the steam out of the pot, so to speak, causing our agitated feelings to dissipate or subside. In other words, entering the frame of the art experience allows us to play mind games that can free our emotions from restraint and culminate in a kind of epiphany about the artwork and ourselves that we could not have achieved outside that experience.

I might note that Sigmund Freud's famous "talking cure" worked somewhat like that in psychoanalysis. When he had his neurotic patients talk freely about themselves and their emotional conflicts, they would eventually discover the hidden unconscious source of those conflicts, and that revelation would relieve their psychological repression and enable them consciously to manage the conflicts and therefore abandon their unconsciously neurotic behavior. That was the intent, anyway. The talking cure would do for Freud's patients something like what the mind games of the art experience can do for anyone: free us from defenses against the demands and pains of the real world, liberate us to feel what otherwise we could not freely feel, and open our eyes to truths we could not otherwise have seen. This is akin to *katharsis*.

Some final words on Aristotle's ideas about art. Aristotle went beyond the intellectual/emotional enlightenment of *katharsis* to assert in the *Poetics* that the art experience of literature can actually open our eyes to "universal truths." "By universal truths," he explains, "are to be understood the kind of thing a certain type of person will probably or necessarily do in a given situation." Which is to say, they are truths of "possibility and probability" in "the kinds of things that might happen" in human behavior. Aristotle is pointing here to how the mind games of the art experience give us the imaginative freedom to see "possibilities" that we could not see within the constraints of ordinary life or find in history. As he says, ordinary life and history belong to the world of "particular facts" and "what has actually happened" rather than to the "universal truths" of human "possibility and probability." "For this reason," he concludes, "poetry [literature] is more philosophical and more worthy of attention than history." Historians might object, but most people have probably found that the art experience can indeed awaken us to what *might be* as nothing else quite can. And that is a principal way the mind games of the art experience can change lives, for good or ill. Aristotle would have emphasized the good, since the insights that reveal "universal truths," for instance, belong more to the betterment we get from the "civilized pursuits" of high culture than to the *relaxation* we get from the "amusements" of low culture. But, then, Aristotle was an optimist.

At all events, the Western tradition has followed Plato's and Aristotle's precedent whenever it has separated high art from low by effects that make people either better or not. This book clearly belongs to that tradition. I will briefly identify some of those contrasting effects of high art and low, not in behavior so much as in mind and psyche. Then I will look at a few of the complications that beset separating high art from low in the first place. From there, I will take up some of the historical reasons that low art has ascended to preeminence during the past couple of centuries. Then, in the next chapter, I will deal with several adverse consequences of the low-art experience becoming dominant in what I call the Culture of Entertainment.

Psychological Effects

Take high art first. Although the explicit distinction between high art and low arose only in the eighteenth century when critics formally elevated the fine arts above the crafts, tradition has always implied that we must *rise* to high art, or the likes of Aristotle's "civilized pursuits," by contrast to the ready enticements of low-art "amusements" that ask nothing much of us. Because high art is more complex and challenging than low art, the first signal of high art, therefore, is this: We expect it to make some demands of us, and in some sense we probably prepare ourselves mentally to rise to them. To truly appreciate a Beethoven symphony, for example, don't we first need to have, or at any rate don't we benefit from, some acquaintance with classical music? Then don't we also have to muster the attention to concentrate on the music and be elevated by it (see, e.g., Fig. 33)?

In that light, I might outline the demands of the high-art experience like this: 1) that experience calls for some thoughtful preparation; 2) it requires mental effort to fully experience and appreciate it; 3) that mental effort involves a discipline of attention that concentrates both the mind and the senses on the artwork; 4) meeting these demands entails an attitude of seriousness. I would also say these are, in essence, how the high-art experience makes us better. This clearly does not mean "better" in the selfless Christian sense any more than Plato and Aristotle intended with their ideas of how high art improves people. Akin to those ideas, the list above amounts to a humanistic definition of "better" that focuses on cultivating human capacities in order to live well in this world.* That is because, even though the mind games of the high-art experience liberate us from the constraints of the real world, high art, at its best, gives us a multidimensional experience engaging our emotions and imaginations, our minds and psyches, in ways that can improve our lives in the real world. For the high-art experience refines and expands the range of our emotions, imaginations, and even intellects, which not only "enriches our lives," as the cliché goes, but does many good and useful things: it intensifies feelings and opens windows of understanding; it helps instill what William James called the "habit of effort" that we can draw on in any pursuit; it teaches the discipline of attention that can awaken us to much in life we would not otherwise perceive, notice, comprehend, and appreciate; and it breeds an attitude of seriousness that can give heft to our thoughts and substance to our lives. It was for such reasons that Aristotle made high-minded arts education central to his political theory. And it is for such reasons that thoughtful citizens advocate arts education in the schools today.

The rewards of the high-art experience also lead to a significant difference between this experience and that of the low-art experience. That difference is: when we enter the frame of the high-art experience and the mind games that take us outside the real world, we do not leave that world as far behind as we do in the low-art experience. For emotional vitality, sensitive understanding, mental effort, discipline of attention, and seriousness all serve our lives in the real world. The high-art experience cannot, therefore, give us a complete escape from that world. And so much the better. Leave that escape to "amusement" and the low-art experience.

It is a commonplace to say that low art, or entertainment, or popular culture, provides an easy escape for the mind from the world. But

---

* One does not need to be a Christian moralist to recognize that an appreciation of high art can easily go with inhumane actions. The case of Nazi elites reveling in great classical music then slaughtering innocent people quickly comes to mind. But the violent history of Christianity and other religions gives plenty of reasons to say that religious ideas of goodness do not insulate anyone from inhumanity either. The best hope for insulating humanity from inhumanity lies in a humanistic commitment to helping all human beings live well in this world, whatever other ideas—secular or religious—of goodness and of making people "better" one might embrace. But that is another book.

fundamentally it is just that. In the first place—to elaborate on a point made above—we do not expect low art to ask much of us. Instead of requiring preparation, effort, attention, and seriousness, it attracts us, lures us, grabs us quite instinctively with its promise of effortless, ephemeral diversions (see, e.g., Fig. 34). Consequently, when we enter the frame of the low-art experience, we give ourselves more fully to the mind games that liberate us from the mental demands of the real world than we do when we enter the frame of the high-art experience. In the words of the emblematic Beatles' song "Strawberry Fields Forever," in the low-art experience "Nothing is real. And nothing to get hung [up] about . . . Living is easy with eyes closed." That is why, although the mind games of the art experience are essentially the same in high art and low, they can affect us somewhat differently.

So it is that the high-art experience can encourage effort, discipline, concentration, and seriousness, whereas the low art experience can induce habits of effortlessness, emotional self-indulgence, lapses of concentration, and an attitude of unseriousness. And these effects are among the reasons the high-art experience can benefit us in the real world, whereas the low-art experience can impair our lives in that world.

Now that low art, or entertainment, has become the prevailing art experience in our times, widely infecting modern culture as a whole, we should expect the consequences to do some harm. And they do, a topic we will explore in the next chapter. But before getting to that, we must consider some of the complexities and complications that beset all distinctions between high art and low art, and that might throw doubt on the value of making those distinctions. For the mind games of the art experience do not always play out predictably.

Separating High Art from Low Art

The first of these complexities and complications lies in the fact that works deemed high art at one time or place can become low art at another time or place and vice versa.

Think of religious art. The oldest artworks or art objects in history—e.g., cave paintings of animals in Indonesia c. 45,000 BCE, and fertility figurines c. 30,000 BCE—probably had religious or ritualistic purposes. And all traditional societies have valued such objects for those same reasons. That means these objects would elicit a kind of reverence among believers. But the same objects would elicit a lesser response among nonbelievers and tourists viewing them simply as historical artifacts. Then, if those objects were removed to a museum and labeled "art," they would encourage a high-art response analogous to the reverence among the religious votaries, while small copies of them in the museum curio shop would bring more of a low-art response, or less. The same thing is true of the great religious paintings that adorn the walls and ceilings of European churches and cathedrals. Painted to glorify Jesus Christ and Christian saints and to stir reverence among believers, they now elicit little to none of that reverence, and offer not even much of a high-art experience, among the hordes of tourists who gawk at them as merely "sights" to see on holiday (see, e.g., Fig. 18). People must *learn* to have a high-art experience with such creations, an instruction that museums facilitate by earnestly exhibiting similar works as "art" and publishing catalogues meticulously "explaining" them, otherwise, such artworks would remain in the realm of low art or of historical curiosity.

History shows us, then, that identifying artworks as high or low derives from people's responses to them, and those responses have much to do with historical and cultural context. And that just as artworks deemed high art at one time and place can become low at another time or place, artworks judged low at one time or place can become high.

Plato damned Homer's poetry, for instance, because it released low-art emotions and disrespected the gods, whom Homer depicted as an unruly lot. Nowadays, no one would accuse Homer of having such low-art effects, for he is read in college, if at all, as high art. Or look at the ribaldly bawdy writings of Boccaccio and Rabelais. Hardly the stuff of high art in their day, they are now studied as "literature" by students and scholars in a context of high art. I might also mention the movies originally made as low-art entertainments that have become venerated by many film aficionados as serious high art (or close to it)—although moviegoers can still have a low-art experience with them as entertainment if they don't watch them entirely with the sober seriousness of high art.

Besides the promotion to high art, over time and place, of many originally low-art creations, the twentieth century saw deliberate efforts among artists to turn low art into high art, or at least to obscure the distinction. In music, for example, numerous composers integrated jazz and classical sonorities—going beyond "classical" composers who had, since the eighteenth century, woven folk melodies into their compositions. George Gershwin, a notable instance, had won renown with his many popular songs for the low-art musical theater, then earned new recognition with the jazzy orchestral compositions *Rhapsody in Blue, Concerto in F*, and *An American in Paris*, and with the opera *Porgy and Bess.* These compositions defied conventional categories, lending themselves to performance as both low art and high. And if they have not been wholly admitted into the canon of high art, they surely narrowed the distance between high and low and gave low art a musical stature it had not had before.

Modern visual artists had a field day with that fresh aesthetic freedom. They merged all kinds of low-art objects into high art, profusely documented in the Museum of Modern Art's large exhibit of 1991 and its hefty catalogue *High and Low: Modern Art and Popular Culture*. The entire movement of Pop Art, celebrating commercial and pop-culture imagery, at once fueled and thrived on that artistic revolution. Now, thanks largely to that revolution, as observed earlier, anything can be "art." And that means anything can provide a high-art experience, if we learn to play the mind games that make this possible.

As if distinguishing between high art and low were not complicated enough owing to the movement of artworks from high to low and from low to high over time and place, this complication introduces another. It is that artworks can have both high- and low-art effects within the same time and place. Not only, as remarked above, can we *learn* to have a high-art experience with low art, like movies or Pop Art, but we can have a low-art experience with high art, like opera. That is to say, the mind games of the art experience can play out variously according to how we play them with an artwork as well as to an artwork's time in history or place in culture.

We might think again of Emma Bovary at Donizetti's opera *Lucia di Lammermoor*. Although she had expected an elevating high-art experience in a grand theater among elegantly attired, presumably serious-minded opera lovers, she did not listen to the opera with the emotional restraint and disciplined attention of high art. Instead, the opera became for her a low-art experience feeding soaring fantasies of love, leaving her oblivious to the serious high-art performance. And she carried her low-art emotions from the theater as she pursued her romantic dreams ever more ardently in real life.

We might say something similar about Tolstoy's Pozdyshev, whom we met as an art-inspired killer. He responded to Beethoven's "Kreutzer" sonata with such unrestrained emotions, entangled with groundless suspicions of his wife's infidelity, that instead of listening to the piece in the decorous manner suited to the serious music and the sober-minded audience in the drawing room, he let his emotions and dark delusions devour him. His was a self-indulgent low-art response to what should have been a more restrained high-art experience. And, like Emma, he took his low-art emotions with him; then, acting on them, he murdered his wife.

No actual person is likely to experience the "Kreutzer" sonata as Pozdnyshev did or *Lucia di Lammermoor* as Emma did, because we likely listen to Beethoven's and Donizetti's works with the mental discipline and restraint suited to a high-art experience (if, perhaps, not as high as for the music of pre-Romantic times for reasons to come). Tolstoy actually wrote his story to show the evil consequences of all "false art," as he defined it. And he classed much of what we would consider high art in that category—including his own great novels, along with the Beethoven sonata—for failing to achieve the effects he believed all art should achieve, namely, uniting humankind through simple, universal emotions in a spiritual brotherhood. But never mind Tolstoy's theory. His story and Flaubert's novel illustrate how, just as we can learn to experience low art as high art, one might have a low-art experience with a work of high art.

A related complication deserves notice here. It is that some works of art, high and low, can reach us on both high and low levels at the same time, stirring both high-art and low-art responses. As people have been saying since the eighteenth century, it is possible to be both elevated, or *enlightened*, and *entertained* by works of high art, as well as to be both *entertained* and *enlightened* by works of low art. For instance, a symphony or a novel or a stage play might demand all the effort and seriousness of high art while also providing some of the irresistible pleasures of low art. And a movie or Broadway musical can draw us in through the irresistible pleasures of low art then lead us to a higher art experience and to ideas we ponder. Everyone who has had an art experience—and everyone has—can think of responding this way to some artworks in their own lives, whether novels like *Don Quixote, Tristram Shandy*, and most anything by Dickens, operas of Mozart, Verdi, even Wagner, or movies like *Casablanca, Citizen Kane*, and *The Godfather*. In short, our responses to many of the best works of high art and low (but I would say this probably happens more with works of high art than low) are neither altogether high or low but, in varying degrees, both at once. This is a principal reason that we deem such works Great, and that they endure over time—and that they further muddle the distinction between high art and low.

The difficulty of separating high art from low does not end with variations in how the mind games of the art experience can play out according to history, culture, personal inclinations, and how we can respond to some artworks on both high and low levels at once. It thickens when we meet another complication that besets distinctions between the effects of high art and low. This lies in the faulty assumption of Plato, and the many who have followed his lead, that because high art teaches rationality and restraint it necessarily has a stabilizing or conservative influence on society, and that because low art feeds base emotions and breeds self-indulgence it has a socially subversive influence. That might be a plausible conclusion. But to class high art as inherently conservative and socially stabilizing and low art as inherently radical and socially subversive is to miss the more complex reality.

Despite the contrasting mental effects of high and low art on individuals described earlier, the social influence is not so predictable and can be the reverse of what Plato and his tradition have assumed. For the truth is, the mind games of both the high-art and low-art experiences can perform either socially stabilizing or subversive roles. Those mind games perform a stabilizing role whenever they enable people to share a common response to an art experience, be that, say, reverence for religious hymns, admiration of a great novel, adoration of a magnificent painting, the pleasures of campfire songs, or revelry at a pop music concert (see, e.g., Fig. 34). In such situations, whether the art experience be high or low, encouraging emotional restraint or emotional release, it tends to satisfy common expectations, strengthen social bonds, sustain the social order, and reinforce the prevailing sense of what is good in life overall.

In the same vein, the mind games of high and low art play a socially subversive role through art experiences that challenge conventions and accepted standards. That is why conservatives like Plato have set their faces against innovations in the arts. "We shall have no innovations in music" (i.e., the arts,), Plato declared flatly in the *Republic*. For he was certain that innovations undo the authority of traditions and respect for authority itself. In that spirit, Pope John XXII banned polyphony and other "modern" novelties from church music, condemning them in a papal bull of 1324 for profaning the sanctity of sacred music, like Gregorian chants, and undermining the reverence that such music should inspire. Polyphonic chants subversive? One might suppose that the richer musical qualities of polyphony detracted from the chants' austere sacred purpose. But one would have had to be there to really fathom that.

In any case, opposition to the subversive influence of innovations in the arts would become a lost cause in Western history. In modern times, and especially in the era of Modernism, "Make it new," in Ezra Pound's proclamation, became the order of the day for artists, creating a cult of novelty and rolling toward the idea that *anything* can be art. Not that conservative voices have fallen silent over the perceived dangers of artistic innovations and related unconventional attitudes. Traditionalists persist in trying to protect society from a loss of high art reverence and restraint, which they fear will dissolve respect for tradition in general. And they might be right. Who can say how much these artistically subversive trends in high art contributed to the decline of traditions from religion to social manners and public morality that has occurred in modern times (which Plato had predicted and Tolstoy had seen happening all around him)? But who can deny that those trends have indisputably accompanied the decline? And plenty of irreverent artists have openly promoted it.

At the same time, low art or popular culture has not only kept up with those subversive trends in high art, it has set a faster pace while ascending to preeminence in the culture at large. We can see that happening, for instance, in the attitudes of young people. Ever since the emergence of adolescence as we know it (first described in detail by the psychologist G. Stanley Hall in his two-volume *Adolescence* [1904]) within the mushrooming commercial culture of the late nineteenth century, the low arts have often served primarily the subversive desires of the young who have sought liberation from the perceived stodginess and oppressive authority of the older generation and have yearned for "fun" and often ideal lives of their own, while living in a world to which they do not yet wholly belong. Thus did the music of youth—often dance music—from, we might say, the Charleston in the 1920s, Swing in the 1930s and 1940s to rock 'n' roll from the 1950s to the 1980s and rap and hip-hop in the late twentieth century and after, appeal to youthful restlessness and yearnings and galvanize the young against the constraints of an adult culture. And since the low-art experience draws people irresistibly into a lair of effortless diversions and self-indulgent pleasures, it readily plays to lurking resentments and idealized aspirations. That seems to be what Mark David Chapman found in *Catcher in the Rye* and what John Hinckley saw in the movie *Taxi Driver*. Plagued by failed dreams of becoming rock stars and possessed by resentments against the world, both young men identified themselves with the idealistic, frustrated, and resentful "heroes" of those works and committed violent, self-justifying, and self-promoting acts to satisfy their fantasies. This is, of course, the kind of thing conservative critics have blamed low art for doing ever since Plato. And they hadn't seen anything like the youthful upheavals of the twentieth century.

I should also stress that it is actually in a subversive role that the mind games of the art experience, both high and low, perform their most important positive purpose in human life—making us better not worse. They do this by educating the senses, the imagination, and the emotions—expanding their range, enhancing their powers, and intensifying their gratifications—and often stimulating the intellect as well. That cannot be done without challenging things as they are. Conservative critics have always been at least wary of the arts for this very reason. But if the arts do not serve us in these ways—letting us freely play the mind games of the art experience—nothing else will, and a certain stagnation of the senses, the imagination, the emotions, and the mind will set in.

That said, I must touch on a final and rather troubling complication in the effects of the art experience. Useful as are the powers of art to educate us and enlarge our lives, the strong appeal of those powers can seduce people to exalt the art experience above everything else in life. As noted earlier, yielding to this seduction in the low-art experience could bring an inertia of mindless pleasure-seeking and self-indulgent lethargy. But the seductions of high art can be nearly as hazardous. We call the exaltation of high art and beauty above everything else *aestheticism* (see Fig. 36). And we often associate it with Oscar Wilde, who turned aesthetics into ethics and could therefore glibly declare that "even a color-sense is more important in the development of an individual than a sense of right and wrong." But Wilde's blithe aestheticism led him to a sorry end. He had ignored the dark theme of his famous novel *The Picture of Dorian Gray,* the cautionary tale of a young man whose ardent love of beauty and pleasure took him into an emotionally self-indulgent, morally degenerate, and tragic life. As Oscar Wilde was sorrowfully departing the scene, the author Thomas Mann was making the exaltation of aesthetics and its dangers a lifelong preoccupation, although, unlike Wilde, he did not succumb to those dangers. "What more pitiable sight is there than a life led astray by art?" Mann asked in his early story *Tonio Kröger* (1903). Later, in his classic tale *Death in Venice* (1912) he told of a literary artist who literally dies for his obsessive love of beauty in art and life. The narrator explains there that beauty can have such effects on artists because beautiful artistic form is

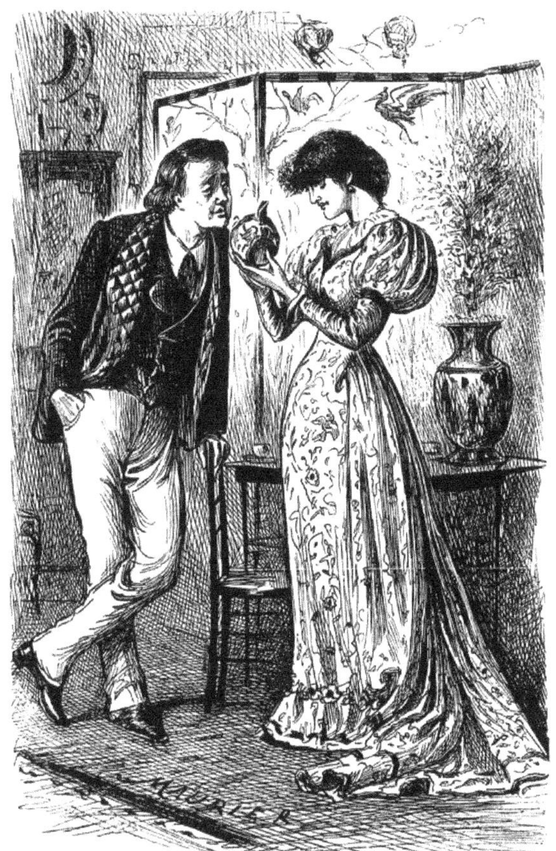

THE SIX-MARK TEA-POT.

Æsthetic Bridegroom. "It is quite consummate, is it not?"
Intense Bride. "It is, indeed! Oh, Algernon, let us live up to it!"

Fig. 36 — George du Maurier, "The Six-Mark Tea-Pot," Punch Magazine, *October 30, 1880.*

Tea-drinking aficionados know that a six-mark tea cup is of the highest quality according to the marks on the bottom of the cup. In Victorian England everyone knew that. And du Maurier had some fun with this fact and the aesthete's inclination to prize art and beauty as the standard of life.

"moral and immoral at once." It is moral in being "the expression and result of discipline," but it is "immoral—yes, actually hostile to morality" in being "indifferent to good and evil, and deliberately concerned to make the moral world stoop beneath its proud and undivided scepter." That is the moral and psychological paradox of art: the high art that elevates us can actually dehumanize us. Mann saw this more clearly than perhaps any other author has done—and in his last novel, *Doctor Faustus* (1947), he has the main character, an overwrought composer, trade his soul to the devil for the genius and exhilaration of spontaneous artistic creativity. Both Wilde and Mann memorably portrayed how the mind games of the high-art experience can take people out of the real world to a place of such transcendent aesthetic delights that they do not want to return—to their detriment. In such cases, high art, for all of its potential benefits, clearly does not make people better, it makes them worse.

So much for the idea that high art always makes us better. When we add this complication to the others mentioned here—e.g., how artworks can move from low to high and from high to low by historical and cultural context; how an artwork can elicit either a high-art or low-art response according to an individual's inclinations or personal circumstances; how some artworks can appeal on both high and low levels at once; how it can now be difficult even to identify an art object as high or low because anything can be art; how both high art and low can play conservative or subversive social roles—we see that drawing distinctions between high art and low is tricky, to say the least, and could never be unqualified.

And yet, keeping in mind those complications, I will let the general distinctions I have made between the effects of the high-art and low-art experiences guide us through the short exploration in the next chapter of the reverberations that have followed from the low-art experience becoming dominant in modern culture. For it is not too much to say that now we live in a culture of low art, or a Culture of Entertainment, with the psychological, emotional, social, and political consequences that entails. But before I get to those consequences, we will, as promised, look briefly in the rest of this chapter at some of the historical conditions or circumstances or, for simplicity, let's call them *causes* that have brought the ascendency of low art. These causes are: secularization, democracy, consumer capitalism, and communications technology. They have obviously interacted, but here I will visit the four of them separately, for the most part, if only suggestively.

Secularism and Low Art

First among those causes is surely the rise of secularity and the decline of religious authority. In fact, secularization created the historical conditions for the other principal causes—democracy, capitalism, modern technology—to arise as well. For, whereas religious beliefs of one kind or another used to pervade all cultures of the world, granting shamans, witch doctors, priests, rituals, tabus, religious institutions, and so on authority over most activities of life from birth to death, modernity progressively pushed those beliefs to the sidelines. Secular ideas gradually took over, and the secular authority of science eventually surpassed the spiritual authority of religion practically everywhere—excepting the religious life itself for the diminishing numbers who have held it fast. That secularization, the "disenchantment of the world," as the pioneering sociologist Max Weber put it, also brought the loss of religious reverence for much of what we now call "art." As previously noted, artworks once venerated in religious practices became secular art objects for Western museums, ornaments for collectors, and reproduced as souvenirs for tourists, while sacred ritual performances became secular entertainments for nonbelievers, and many of their revered settings became merely tourist sights to see (to be sure, tourism inevitably profanes and commodifies all it touches, carelessly disenchanting a once enchanted world). And since the 1960s in the West even remnants of religious reverence persisting in the high-art experience have lost some of their luster as the art world has welcomed low art into high art and has embraced the idea that *anything* can be "art." At the same time, the low-art experience, which thrives on secularity, has burgeoned. So profound and wide-ranging an influence has secularism had in Western culture that it all but goes without saying. And I will let that be all I say about secularism directly as a cause of low art's rise, leaving its influence evident enough through the other three causes I will examine.

Democracy and Low Art

As the secular disenchantment of the world proceeded on its inexorable course, the second cause of low art's rise appeared on the scene:

democracy. Democracy—not just as a political system but as a way of life suffusing all society with the spirit of equality, in the sense described by Alexis de Tocqueville in his groundbreaking *Democracy in America* (1835)—gave low art or popular culture a very nurturing home, indeed. The nurturing took several forms. For example, the rise of egalitarian democracy liberated art, and what thinkers in the eighteenth century labeled "taste," from the aristocratic elitism that was supplanting religion in Europe as the measure of artistic value, just as democracy, in league with nascent free-market capitalism, freed artists from dependence on aristocratic and ecclesiastical benefactions and brought them closer to "the people." That this freedom came with the perils of the marketplace was another matter, as we will see shortly.

The French Revolution and the rebellious spirit it fueled across Europe, along with the Romantic movement that arose in those years, propelled the spread of democratic notions. And this encouraged artworks that celebrated the common life and the ideals of democracy. The arts displayed this from, say, Wordsworth's plain poetry of ordinary feelings and his celebration of the revolution itself in *The Prelude* (1850; early versions written in 1799 and 1805) to Eugène Delacroix's rousingly populist painting *Liberty Leading the People* (1830) (see Fig. 37), and Beethoven's rousing *Ninth Symphony* with its rhapsodic paean to human brotherhood, "Ode to Joy" (1824; adapted from the poem by Friedrich Schiller), and Hector Berlioz's magnificent choral version of "La Marseillaise" (composed by Claude-Joseph Rouget de Lisle in 1792 to rally soldiers of revolutionary France, then reorchestrated by Berlioz following the revolution of 1830).

The revolutionary and romantic fervor also stimulated—as anyone can see from this abbreviated list alone, and as practically everyone knows anyway—an emancipation of the emotions in art and life. Not that the emotions had been altogether denied before. The eighteenth century had seen an efflorescence, almost a cult, of feelings and sentimentality, manifest in, for example, Samuel Richardson's weepy novel *Clarissa* (1747), the lachrymose paintings of Boucher, and in the music of what the Germans called *Empfindsamkeit*, which prescribed that every sound in a musical composition express a particular emotion, as well

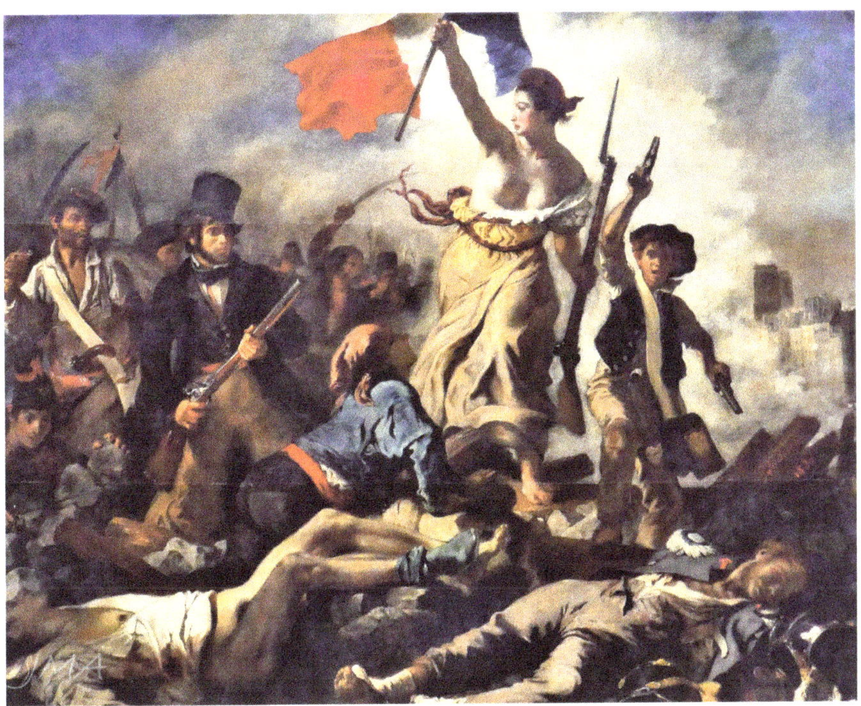

Fig. 37 — Eugène Delacroix, Liberty Leading the People, *1830.*

Delacroix (1798–1863), painted this quintessentially democratic, dramatically patriotic, and unmistakably Romantic picture in the fall of 1830 to honor the idealistic French revolution of that July. Shortly after he started applying the brushes, he wrote in a letter to his brother, Charles, that "I have undertaken a modern subject [departing from his previous historical paintings, like the sensational "Death of Sardanapalus" (1827)], A Barrricade . . . [sic] and if I have won no victories for my country at least I can paint for it." The "Barricade" became Liberty Leading the People. *It also became one of the most celebrated paintings in French history as well as a monument of Romanticism. It unforgettably shows the large symbolic figure of Liberty triumphantly barreling forward waving the French revolutionary flag as she rallies the people of France across the barricades strewn with bodies of both government soldiers and martyrs to the cause of liberty. With this painting, Delacroix achieved a kind of victory for his country after all. Meanwhile, the July Revolution proved disappointing, merely replacing a traditional king, Charles X, with a bourgeois version, Louis Philippe I. Threatened by democratic idealism, the new government pulled* Liberty Leading the People *from public view, and it was not exhibited again until after Louis Philippe I was overthrown in the revolution of 1848, and then only briefly. It was not put on permanent official display in the Louvre until after the political upheaval of 1870 ushered in the Third Republic.*

as in philosophical books on feeling or sentiment as the ground of morals, like Adam Smith's *The Theory of Moral Sentiments* (1759). But this was superficial emotionality compared to that of Romanticism.

To say Romanticism punched the emotions is to echo a cliché. But here that cliché indicates a noteworthy historical fact: how emotionality further strengthened the bond between democracy and low art. Tradition had associated high art with emotional restraint and elite tastes, and it had identified low art with emotional self-indulgence and vulgar appetites. That meant high art and emotional restraint went with aristocracy, whereas low art and emotionality went with democracy and "the people." It is no surprise, therefore, that traditionalists would spurn what they judged the artistic and emotional excesses of Romanticism. Adhering to strict rules of artistic composition as they did, traditionalists saw the artistic revolution of Romanticism as a lowering of standards, reducing high art to low, just as they thought the political revolutions were handing society over to the rabble.

And, in a sense, the traditionalists were right. The very artists named above, like most artists from that era—whom we would today surely rank among creators of high art—prove that high art was itself changing under the influence of political revolutions and Romanticism, and in ways that brought it closer to low art. Or to put it another way, the rules of the high-art experience and its mind games were changing to admit more open emotionality and more varied aesthetic sensations, and to reach more people. Compare, for instance, Beethoven's *Third Symphony* (1803–04) to any that came before it. Known as the "Eroica" (Heroic) symphony—a rubric taken from Beethoven's inspiration for it: the conqueror Napoleon, before he disillusioned the composer by crowning himself emperor, resulting in the symphony being printed with the dedication, "To the memory of a great man." It is certainly a work worthy of its rubric, pulsing with energy (a favored Romantic term) and rushing toward the future. Just listen to its third movement and then any symphonic third movement before it (including Beethoven's own): here Beethoven replaced the standard, aristocratically decorous minuet with a bouncing scherzo that makes the blood race. No wonder this composition is widely considered the first Romantic symphony.

In subsequent decades many artists would continue to plumb the emotional powers of art with abandon, yielding artworks that were aesthetically adventurous and emotionally arousing. Paintings got larger, more colorful, and evocative; novels got longer, more detailed, and dramatic; and in music, as one historian put it, the "orchestra . . . became larger . . . everyone's symphonies longer," and "huge sensations and extreme emotional intensity became necessities."[23] "At the same time, music, especially opera, was appealing to the emotions through melody more than ever. This trend had actually started in early-eighteenth-century England with the emerging contrast between the often ponderous, thickly contrapuntal operas of Handel set to historical and mythological subjects, and the lighter, more melodic "popular ballad opera" set to earthier themes and sung in English, like John Gay and J. C. Pepusch's *The Beggar's Opera*. In this "contest between pretense on a high level of artistry and truth on the level of popular simplicity," in the words of musicologist Edward Lowinsky,[24] the popular was bound to win in a country already on its way toward democracy. In less democratic, pre-revolutionary France, that same contest erupted during the 1750s in a celebrated musical brouhaha known as "The Battle of the Buffoons." This dispute pitted aristocratic partisans of French opera, as exemplified by the dense Baroque harmony and counterpoint of Lully, and populist partisans of Italian opera, as exemplified by the light and melodic rococo music of Pergolesi, championed by Jean-Jacques Rousseau. As Rousseau said in an article on melody in his *A Complete Dictionary of Music* (1768), "the pleasure in melody and song is a pleasure of interest and feeling which speaks to the heart. . . . Music, therefore, must necessarily sing in order to move, to please, to sustain interest and attention."[25] Melody prevailed everywhere. Mozart demonstrated that in Vienna. But the full triumph of melody came with the ravishingly melodic operas of the nineteenth century that blatantly sang to the heart and were composed by Italians like Rossini, Donizetti, Bellini, Verdi, and Puccini, as well as by some non-Italians like Bizet, Gounod, Weber, and Wagner. That most of these operas were set to Romantic tales of love, often ill-fated, added bittersweet juice to the emotional cocktail.

In the light of these aesthetic and emotional revisions, it would not be so very unusual for a person to have primarily an emotionally low-art experience—or close to it—with a work of high art from the Romantic era, as Emma Bovary did at a performance of Donizetti's romantic opera, *Lucia di Lammermoor*—if not with the kind of obsessive fantasies that captivated the hapless Emma. Let us also remember that, before Emma attended the opera, Flaubert had made her aware of "the petty passions that art exaggerated." Surely Flaubert was thinking of the Romantic arts that had shaped Emma's character, and not the arts of previous times. In fact, in Donizetti's homeland, Italy, opera filled the air, from opera houses to the streets, attesting that the styles of that music (particularly the glorious bel canto arias of the kind that Donizetti's and Verdi's operas exemplified) were reaching more people and on a more emotional plane than the reverence and emotional restraint typical of traditional high art and that conservative critics had commended.

As a sign of the times, the first solo musicians gained international renown, to say the least of the adoration some of them aroused. The virtuoso violinist Paganini was a pioneer in the early decades of the nineteenth century, performing his sensational fiddling techniques for awed crowds wherever he went—and in the 1830s he toured across Europe. But it was not just his musical skills that attracted audiences. It was the pyrotechnics of his performances coupled with his cadaverously demonic appearance and demeanor, his long dark locks flying as he madly bowed the strings, all conveying "extreme emotional intensity" and feeding the rumor that his astonishing artistry must have come from the devil (see Fig. 38). Paganini's success inspired the pianist and composer Franz Liszt to follow his razzle-dazzle virtuosic lead. Although not as wild as his mentor's performances, Liszt's keyboard displays of his own unimaginably challenging compositions won him frenzied fame, and "Lisztomania" erupted wherever he performed (see Fig. 39). This was just before P. T. Barnum turned Jenny Lind into an unprecedented box office attraction across America, bringing a wave of "Lindomania," a story to come.

Audiences moved by such virtuoso performers and the popular operas and concert music of the nineteenth century were surely having as much of a traditionally low-art as a high-art experience. This melding of high

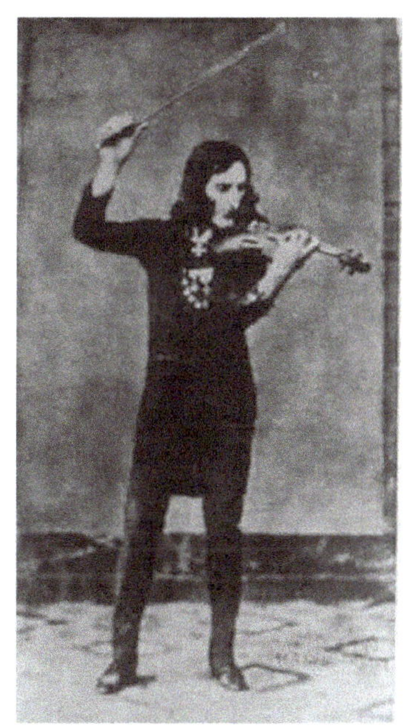

Fig. 38 — Niccolò Paganini.

This well-known daguerreotype of Paganini, ostensibly from the late 1830s (he died in 1840), has been proven to be an early-twentieth-century forgery. But—apart from the hammy hands, not at all like Paganini's long slender hands and fingers—it captures the Satanic demeanor of the eccentric virtuoso.

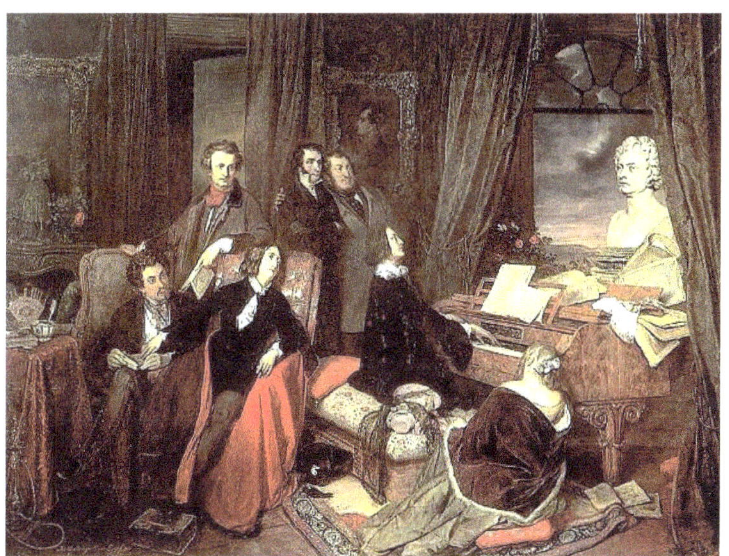

Fig. 39 — Josef Danhauser, Liszt at the Piano, *1840.*

This painting illustrates the cult of art as well as Liszt performing for a coterie of music-loving friends. They are: Liszt's mistress, Comtesse Marie d'Agoult, enraptured on the floor; the author George Sand in a swoon (seated with red cape); Alexandre Dumas, Jr. (seated next to her); and standing (left to right), Victor Hugo, Paganini, and the composer Gioachino Rossini. A bust of the musical deity of the age, Beethoven, seems to arrest the worshipful attention of Liszt at the piano.

and low art experiences clearly reflected the democratization of culture. It also foretold that the appeal to audiences through sensational artistic exhibitions and irresistible emotionality would likely drive the low-art experience ever lower. And that is what we got with the mass, commercial, technological entertainments of the twentieth century and beyond.

Perhaps this is the place to note that the lowering of some high art to accommodate the public and provide income for artists had another consequence: some artists would not compromise. Or they hadn't the talent for it. This led to the self-conscious image of the courageous and suffering artist toiling in defiance of the commercial world (we will meet a few of them later), as well as to creation of a new artistic elitism through artworks that became increasingly challenging, by contrast to the works that appealed to the public (which even included reorchestrations of existing musical works to make them more emotive and popular, as Berlioz did with "La Marseillaise"). From here came the avant-garde and a parting of high art and its devotees from low art that had never quite existed before, because even high art had previously served social purposes of the church and the court. The twentieth century saw Modernism push the boundaries of aesthetics in all the arts, leaving much of the public baffled and yearning for the more accessible high art of the nineteenth century or turning to the easy attractions of low art. The attitude of the new artistic elite toward the Philistine public was captured in the title given to an essay by the twentieth-century serial composer Milton Babbitt, "Who Cares If You Listen." Babbitt did not choose those words, but his infamous essay unapologetically praised the severely atonal "serious music" that few people can appreciate, much less love, while belittling the "traditional" and popular music that wins the public's heart but that he believed would stagnate culture.

I might add that the elevation of an elite artistic culture above traditional high culture, and far above popular low culture, also gave rise in the twentieth century to three cultural levels that critics would label: High Brow, Middle Brow, and Low Brow. The existence of the middle confirms that at least some high art had come down, alienating elite artists but pleasing a lot of people on a level above that of even lower popular art.

Meanwhile, it should be noted, the age-old folk arts that had flourished in the pre-modern world of the rural peasantry largely yielded their place to the low-art diversions of the modern urban working class and bourgeoisie. To be sure, this change in what we might call styles of low art also came with the rise of commercial capitalism. For that matter, we could say that almost every step in the ascendancy of low art from the eighteenth century onward came tangled in strings of commerce. But I leave those strings for later and move on to more about the democracy of low art.

As democracy gained steam and urban life expanded, the democratic hunger for low art found a mounting array of attractions. At the bottom of urban democratic low art, Grub Street fiction offered cheap, trashy, and sometimes pornographic tales; burlesque theaters staged goofy acts, salacious shows, and absurd melodramas; and the likes of sword swallowers, magicians, and dancing animals entertained folks in every city and town. When Alexis de Tocqueville traveled America in the early 1830s he saw the signs, often telltale, of democracy everywhere, including what he judged to be the feeble artworks he considered typical of democratic people, and he doubted that America's democratic culture would ever produce anything worthy of high art. In the long run, Tocqueville proved wrong. But the truth is, notwithstanding some notable artists and some great artworks, America's chief contribution to artistic culture is probably its low art or its popular culture in general.

Not long after Tocqueville's American travels, a character took the stage of American popular culture to become what we would now call an icon of that culture. This was P. T. Barnum. A peerless huckster by nature, Barnum embodied and promoted the alliance of democracy and popular culture more brazenly than anyone else. Barnum's first success came with his American Museum, which opened in 1841, displaying oddities of all kinds. His pitch was fervently democratic, commercially ingenious, and unapologetically geared to the low-art experience. "Come and see the strangest things in the world," he might proclaim—like a hundred-sixty-year-old woman said to have been George Washington's nurse, the skeleton of a mermaid, the jawbone of Jonah's whale, and numerous living humans with bizarre defects, like four legs—"then you

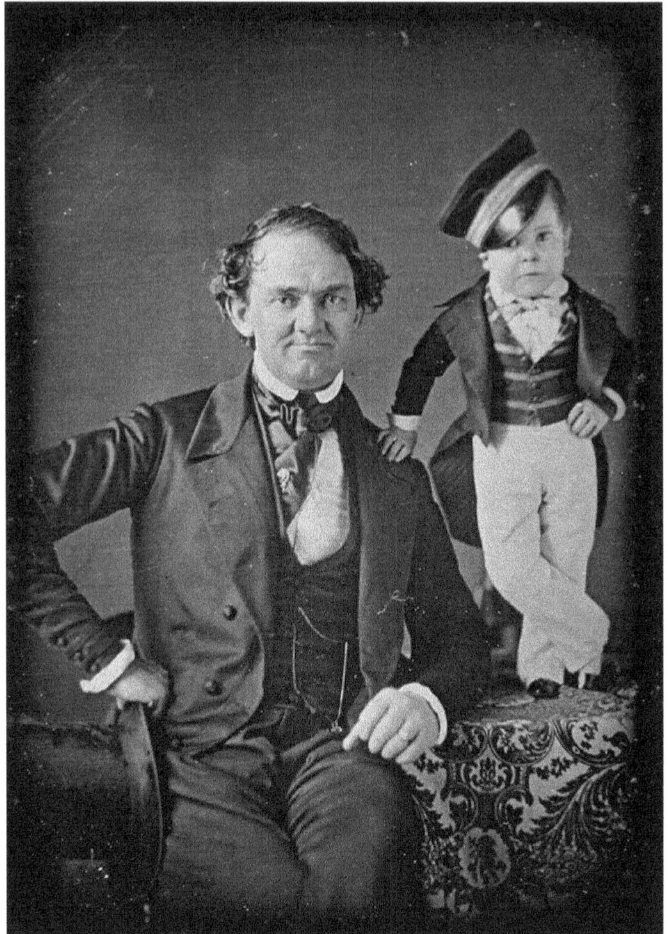

Fig. 40 — P. T. Barnum and General Tom Thumb (a.k.a., George Stratton), c. late 1840s. Barnum hired Stratton at age five to be a novelty exhibit in his museum. Stratton was then just two feet tall and never grew taller than three feet. But this little person took to the role of General Tom Thumb, first at Barnum's museum then on international tours, with alacrity and natural performing skills. At age 45, he married another diminutive member of the Barnum cast in a grand ceremony of 1863 staged by Barnum at Grace Church in New York City for the fashionable people of the city.

decide if they are what they seem." No elitist standards there. It was all very democratic and "entertaining."

From there Barnum went on to exploit the novelty of a precocious and good-natured midget standing just over two feet tall, whom he had discovered and named General Tom Thumb (from an English fairy tale) (see Fig. 40). Barnum exhibited him, beginning at just five years of age, at the museum and taught him to dance and sing and impersonate people then took him on tour in both America and Europe. Audiences loved him—as did even Queen Victoria—and General Tom Thumb quickly became the most popular low-art act of his times.

So successful was Barnum at roping curious and diversion-hungry urban crowds into his very low-art experiences that he decided to up the ante and try it with high art. He persuaded the esteemed Swedish soprano Jenny Lind to tour America under his management. Uniting the high art of her operatic vocal reputation with his low-art promotional genius, Barnum presented her as not just a great singer but as the benevolent "Swedish Nightingale," pronouncing her "simplicity, charity, and goodness personified" (see Fig. 41). He cared less about her vocal talents or character, of course, than about selling tickets. And sell them he did. The tour was a triumph. Crowds thronged to see Jenny Lind as much, and possibly more, for the saintly person they believed her to be as for her artistry, owing to Barnum's tireless promotions (she did in fact donate her substantial earnings from the tour to charity, a gesture Barnum touted in his normal manner, namely, shamelessly). In his own way, Barnum had brought European high art to American democracy. But amid all the hoopla, was it still high art? Audiences wept while Jenny Lind sang like a nightingale, but theirs were probably quite sentimental tears for the music of this paragon of "goodness." They were having a low-art experience in a high-art setting, rather like Emma Bovary did. Barnum's ingenuity saw to that.

As the low arts grew with democratic culture, critics would in time begin to speak of "mass culture." At the end of the twentieth century, the historian Michael Kammen went to pains in *American Culture, American Tastes: Social Change and the Twentieth Century* (1999) to identify phases in the evolution of popular culture culminating in "mass culture" after World War II. But long before that, the Spanish philosopher José Ortega y Gassett had already seen the emergence of a personality type he called "the mass man." In his unsettling book *The Revolt of the Masses* (1925), Ortega described "the mass man" as a creature of mass society

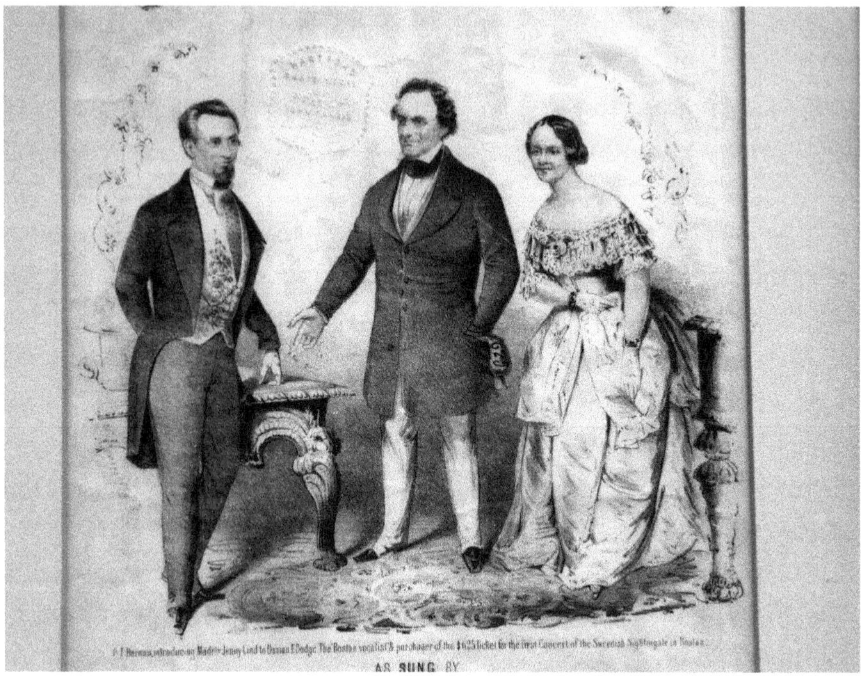

Fig. 41 — P. T. Barnum introducing Jenny Lind to Ossian E. Dodge, a "Boston vocalist," composer and performer of "fashionable entertainments," and purchaser from Barnum of an auctioned ticket for the first Jenny Lind concert in the grossly inflated amount of $625. Barnum never missed a trick in turning a buck. Among Dodge's "fashionable entertainments" was "Ossian's Serenade," which Dodge, a self-promoter in his own right, proudly advertised with this picture on the cover of the sheet music.

and its popular culture who demanded immediate gratifications like a child, who could hardly imagine anything beyond his own interests, and who would acknowledge nothing superior to his own life. "The mass man," with his myopic, self-centered vision of the world, could easily be manipulated through the self-indulgent enticements of low art. The political implications in those days of rising Fascism were obvious to Ortega and were becoming clear to other insightful thinkers as well. A decade after Ortega's book, with the Nazi's now running Germany, Walter Benjamin elucidated some of those implications in "The Work of Art in the Age of Mechanical Reproduction"—particularly, as noted earlier, how popular film can serve political propaganda.

A final quick observation on the alliance of democracy and low art or popular culture. During the great wars of the twentieth century, especially World War II, entertainers became national heroes, performing for the troops and thumping to sell war bonds, while popular songs and movies summoned all Americans to the cause—think of George M. Cohan's stirring "Over There" and Irving Berlin's moving "God Bless America," both from World War I, and from World War II, which saw patriotic themes woven more tightly into the fashions and sentiments of popular culture; the jazzy hit "Boogie Woogie Bugle Boy"; and the soldier's sentimental song "I'll Be Home for Christmas." Popular culture went to war as surely as did the ships that carried soldiers to fight in foreign fields. This was low art as propaganda, for sure. But the cause this propaganda served was to save American democracy from vicious tyrannies abroad. It should be said, though, that serving this cause would also save the American experience of popular culture itself. At the same time, the low-art experience, with all of its inviting pleasures and ready emotionality, unmistakably played the conservative role of uniting people under the flag and harnessing their energies to the common patriotic good, far from the subversive self-indulgence that conservative critics of low art have traditionally fretted about. If we can say that low art would not have arisen as it has without democracy, we might almost equally say that low art returned the favor in World War II. And now it would not be wrong to say that just as American culture is a child of democracy, America's reigning artistic culture *is* democratic popular culture, and that this is what America stands for in the eyes of the world as much as anything—along with consumer commerce and the principles and institutions of American political democracy.

In sum, the growth of democracy and of low art went hand in hand. The mind games of the low-art experience, which can give us almost unbridled fantasies of possibility, gamely collaborated with the hopeful ideals of democratic possibilities (a theme played out with other terms in Kurt Andersen's *Fantasyland: How America Went Haywire* [2017]). So, as democratic culture came to pervade American life, it brought the low-art experience with it, both of them abetted at every stage by their alliance with consumer capitalism. We now turn to that alliance and what it did for both low art and high art. We will pick up the story with how that alliance changed the economic lives of artists.

Consumer Capitalism and Low Art

As ecclesiastical and aristocratic patronage waned, artists were freed to create as they chose and yet dependent now on the public and the market to survive. That became conspicuous in the eighteenth century. The cleric and novelist Laurence Sterne, for instance, scraped together a living as a country minister, but he then so adroitly marketed his bizarre novel *Tristram Shandy* to publishers and booksellers in London that it won unprecedented popularity, and he became, he joked, "the richest man in Europe." About the same time, the precocious musician Amadeus Mozart began his remarkable career performing and composing under aristocratic patronage and for aristocratic listeners. But later he also organized concerts in private homes for wealthy Viennese who bought subscriptions; and his operas were staged in public theaters for audiences of both aristocrats, who purchased the boxes for socializing, and of ordinary ticket buyers, who herded perhaps most enthusiastically to his operas with librettos in their own language, German, crowned by *Die Zauberflöte* (*The Magic Flute*), premiered just two months before the composer's death. Mozart did well financially from these enterprises, although he let the income slip through his fingers.

It is worth noting that although the practice of charging entry fees to public performances seems to have originated in ancient Rome for the masses at popular sporting events, like chariot races, and it persisted through the centuries for some events of high popular demand, it did not become the norm with ticket sales until the era of democratic and commercial revolutions delivered the egalitarian bourgeois society of the nineteenth century. Until then, patronage by the elite was the rule. In Shakespeare's time, for instance, theaters had several levels of entry prices, from standing room in the uncovered yard to covered balcony seats and the prime seating on the side of the stage. Shakespeare himself eventually grew affluent from his earnings in the theater as actor, playwright, and partner in the acting company. Even so, he depended for years on a series of wealthy patrons, not ticket sales, just as Mozart would do.

After Mozart, Beethoven also benefitted from royal and affluent patrons, earning his keep mainly by getting commissions from them for specific compositions. Then these commissions started moving from wealthy individuals to musical organizations, such as London's Royal Philharmonic Society (founded in 1813 "to promote the performance in the most perfect manner possible of the best and most approved instrumental music"), which commissioned the *Ninth Symphony*—foreshadowing a practice still common in classical music today. But, before Beethoven could rely on commissions, he held public performances of his piano compositions and attracted ticket-buying audiences by distributing flyers door to door himself; for some years he also supplemented his income with piano lessons, which he hated doing.

In fact, Beethoven's lifetime (1770–1827) spanned the rise and heyday of Romanticism together with the passage from artistic patronage to the artist's dependency on the marketplace. And since Beethoven's times, subjection to the perils of the marketplace has marked the lives of nearly every artist—except those cushioned by their own means. The prodigious author Honoré de Balzac, for example, became a celebrated literary figure in France while nevertheless constantly grappling with financial troubles until his death in 1850, owing in part to reckless business adventures misaimed at assuring his affluence. Vexed by his economic circumstances, he made the pernicious cult of money a theme in many of his writings. Balzac's younger contemporary, the poet Charles Baudelaire was so financially distressed—after youthfully squandering an inheritance—that he cultivated the image of himself as the suffering *poèt maudit* struggling to survive on art in a crass and heartless commercial world. That set a model others would proudly follow, and it gave one of them, Paul Verlaine, the title of a book he published in 1884 honoring some of his fellows: *Poètes maudits*. At the same time, Vincent van Gogh was becoming the exemplary tormented, penniless painter, who depended for support on his brother, Theo, and who would sell only one painting in his life—for 400 Francs, two years after he had painted it and just four months before he committed suicide in 1890 at age 37. In the first decade of the twentieth century, that painting, *The Red Vineyard*, sold again to a Russian collector for about 10,000 Francs (confiscated by the revolutionary government in 1918, it now hangs in the Pushkin

State Museum in Moscow), hinting at the perverse economics of the artworld to come. Another painting from 1888, *Orchard with Cypresses*, sold in 2022 for $117 million, the record price for a van Gogh, proving this perversity had surely arrived.

Some artists in those days flourished financially, of course. We saw that with Laurence Sterne, and with celebrated performers like Paganini, Liszt, and Jenny Lind. Charles Dickens was another. He had a genius for appealing to the low-art sensibilities of the reading public—even with books that had more to them than that—as well as of theater-goers who flocked to hear him dramatically read from his works on the stage. That popularity made him a very wealthy man. Dickens' younger contemporary, the prolific author Henry James, also made a fairly comfortable living from writing. But, lacking Dickens' low-art genius, he complained that his published books never did well in the marketplace so he had to churn out serial fiction, short stories, and nonfiction for magazines. He also tried upping his income by writing for the theater, but his talents were not suited to that any more than to Dickensian popular art.

I could go on and on with lists of artists who struggled financially and some who finally succeeded from their art. In all, while a handful of artists have struck it rich in the marketplace—where low art has an advantage over high art, much to the despair of most artists committed to high art—countless others have not. As the adage goes, in the arts (literature is the model), one might make a killing, but one can't make a living.

Be that as it may, the democratic commercialization of art, high as well as low, subjecting it to money-making strategies in the marketplace, could not help but further link high art with low art, just as Barnum did in drawing hordes to adulate the beatific "Swedish Nightingale," Jenny Lind. We might even speak of an alliance of convenience in the nineteenth century among democracy, commerce, and high art, particularly in America, which had almost no high art of its own and had to get it from Europe until near the end of that century. This alliance produced some curious creations. For instance, a faux aristocracy arose in some American cities imitating European high culture with ersatz European-style mansions (like those Tocqueville described in disbelief along New

York's East River boasting wooden columns whitewashed to look like marble) and venues for high art, like the Astor Place Opera House in New York that opened in 1847 (nearly forty years before the more elitist Metropolitan Opera House first raised its curtain). And such imitative creations could yield tensions.

Just two years after the Astor Place Opera House opened, it saw a historic clash between European high culture and American low culture, or between aristocratic elitism and democratic populism. By then, high art and low had to some extent become rivals in New York, pitting sophisticated supporters of European high art and its performers, especially the British, against populist (often immigrant) supporters of American entertainment and American performers. That rivalry erupted one night when a British actor was performing Shakespeare's *Macbeth* at the opera house (which often staged plays in order to pay its bills). He and an American actor had become competitors in the public eye for the title of greatest stage actor. Heated by newspaper accounts of the competition and by handbills urging "Working Men" to protest at the "English Aristocratic Opera House," rabble-rousing partisans of the American actor and of American democratic culture gathered in Astor Place (see Fig. 42). That provoked sympathizers of upper-class British culture to rally. A riot broke out between the camps leaving some thirty rioters dead in the street and injuring many more. We cannot say that the alliance of convenience among democracy, commerce, and high art was to blame, but we might wonder if the passions would have run so hot that night without this alliance. Or, to put it another way, would the Astor Place riot have occurred without the exploitative commercialization of high art no less than low art in democratic America?

A year after the Astor Place riot, P. T. Barnum would exploit the alliance of democracy, commerce, and high art for all it was worth. That is when he launched the American tour of Jenny Lind, convinced that all "art is merchantable" (as he announced in the chapter of his autobiography candidly entitled "My Start as a Showman") "from the highest to the lowest." That promotional enterprise in high art might have been just another episode in Barnum's insatiable hunger to reap financial rewards from uniting democracy and commerce. But Barnum's promotion

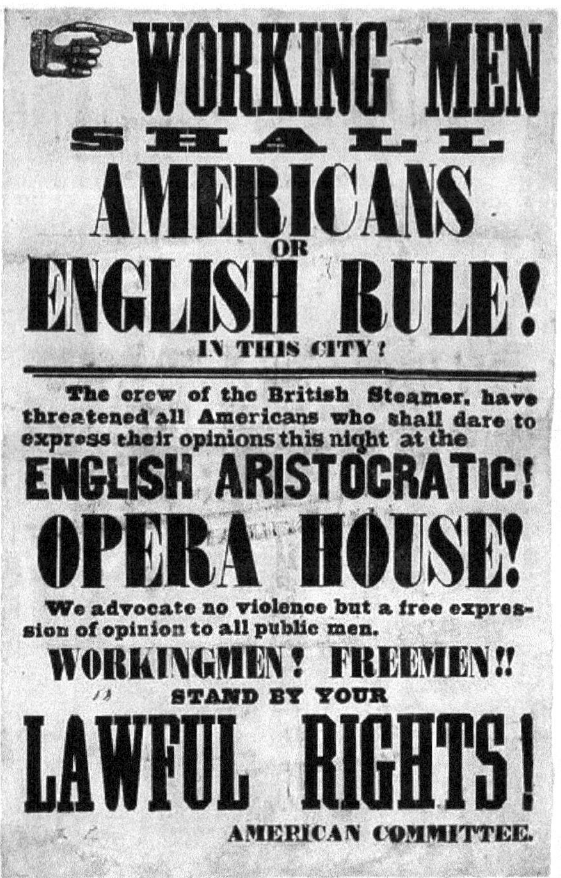

Fig. 42 — Handbill distributed to summon "Working Men" in New York to a rally at the Astor Place Opera House (May 10, 1849) to defend American "Rights" against British influence, purportedly supported by "the crew of the British Steamer" then in port and assumed to be headed for the "English Aristocratic Opera House." The handbills seemed to have done their job, since hundreds of "Working Men" came loaded for bear. But the request for nonviolence did not avail. A riot erupted that killed thirty people and injured 150 more.

of high art with the same low-art vulgarity he exploited at every opportunity invites us to dwell briefly on the topic of commercial promotion itself, or what we generally think of today as advertising, a sibling of low art, and what we now know as public relations.

In Barnum's day, the advertising of art and everything else was still very elementary. It consisted mainly of posters (see Fig. 43) and handbills simply informing potential customers of an object for sale or a performance to attend, as Beethoven did in "advertising" his concerts, or summoning people to an event, as populist partisans did for the Astor Place protest. But P. T. Barnum added his own style of brash excess that surpassed the staid presentation of facts or even the bold-faced announcements of events. Coupling conventional advertising techniques with inventive acts of public relations, he surrounded all he did with the air of a Happening not to be missed. He advertised his museum with parades through the streets, stunts like the "Brick Man" who silently and repeatedly placed and replaced bricks on the sidewalk, leading curiosity seekers to the museum, and phony news stories hyping the unique and weird things on display there; he publicized the child-midget George Stratton as "General Tom Thumb" and made up a fascinating biography for him,

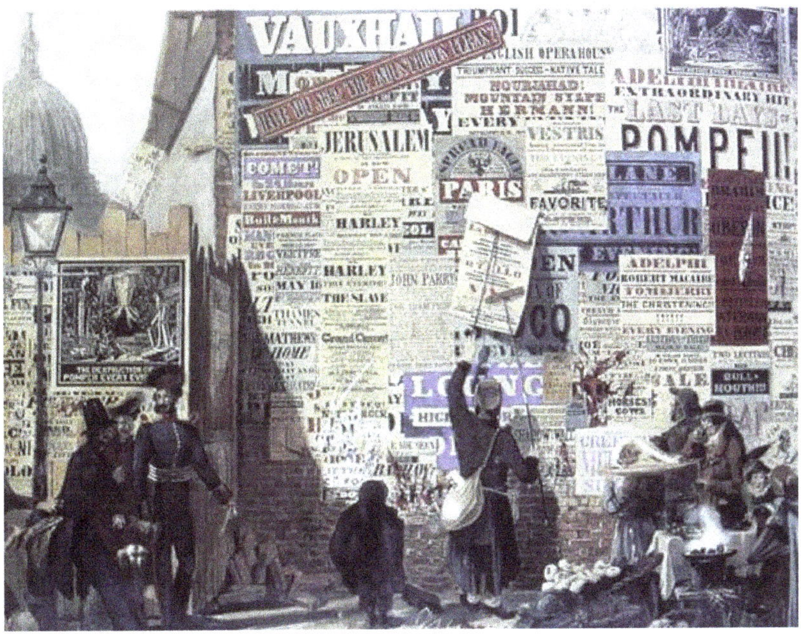

Fig. 43 — John Orlando Parry, A London Street Scene, *watercolor, 1835.*

Parry was a multitalented artist who devoted most of his artistic energies to composing songs and performing in music halls. But his few paintings also display genuine skill. This watercolor from the 1830s shows a wall of poster advertising amidst a rather Dickensian setting of London street life. The figure pasting a new poster over the others signals both the competition for advertising space and the transitory character of such advertising.

then took him on tour complete with the hoopla of a historic event; he marketed Jenny Lind with similar hyperbole as the saintly "Swedish Nightingale" and had her travel in a specially made—and therefore inviolate and "newsworthy"—railroad car, then peddled a line of commercial products in her haloed name, from clothing to pianos; and when he joined circus-owner James Bailey to form the Barnum and Bailey Circus, he did not promote it as merely an ordinary circus: it had to be "The Greatest Show on Earth," a heady slogan that became part of that circus's official name and lives on in memory to this day. As Barnum confidently declared, "Without promotion, something terrible happens: nothing!"*

Modern advertising took the cue. While consumer products proliferated, offering new conveniences and satisfactions, advertising moved in Barnum's direction. Attention-grabbing images and stirring slogans besieged the public, who were rapidly becoming "consumers." A writer in the professional advertisers' periodical *Printers' Ink* spelled out the scheme to colleagues in 1920. "Emotions must be aroused," he wrote, because "the appeal to reason doesn't contain the elements that make a man want to do the thing you want him to do." Is the advertisement true? Never mind. Just get people's attention, if fleetingly, then you can draw them in. That is, without doubt, a low-art experience, the mind games of wish-fulfilling fantasies playing with us as we play with them.

It is no surprise that advertising and low art grew up together as children of consumer capitalism, both bent on luring people into their lairs with images and enticements that seize the senses and stir the emotions. The high arts might use advertising, too, but, as seen above, the more it depends on advertising the more it is likely to be tainted by the low-art nature of advertising. Attesting to this low-art nature, the Museum of Modern Art's controversial exhibit "High and Low: Modern Art and Popular Culture" devoted the largest portion of its substantial space and its large catalogue to the low art of advertising and its influence on modernist high art, an influence that melded high and low, inevitably bringing high art down, as the innovative artists had probably intended.

---

*Even if Barnum never wrote those words, or even uttered them, he could have, for he certainly lived by them.

Leaving the effects of advertising on high art aside, we find the low arts of entertainment deploying the full arsenal of modern advertising techniques (and communications technology) to become very Big Business indeed, lifting entertainers—who, before the nineteenth century, had been ranked distinctly low in the order of society, stage actors alongside organ grinders—to the status of supreme "celebrities." And, while exploiting those advertising techniques for marketing purposes, the low arts also got a boost from advances in communications technology that not only served marketing but made the low-art experience itself almost omnipresent in American culture. This boost brings us to the last principal cause of the ascendancy of low art in our times: technology.

Technology and Low Art

Everyone knows that technology has changed the way human beings live in the world. And it has done so over and over again ever since the invention of stone tools some two-and-a-half million years ago. Innovative technologies have not just changed the ways we do things either. They have changed how we think about life and reality itself. And they have done that at an ever more rapid pace and to more expansive consequences.

The Renaissance, for instance, brought epochal technological and cultural change with the invention of the printing press (see below) and, on a lesser plane, the invention of the mechanical clock, which kept more accurate time than any clock device before it and could be made small and transportable enough to become part of everyone's life. Later, the nineteenth century saw the pace of technological and cultural change double and redouble thanks to the Industrial Revolution. The railroad, for example, whose steam-powered engines entered public service in the 1830s, not only transported people and goods faster and farther than was possible before. It altered the human sense of time and space, speeding the first and shrinking the second. In fact, railroad timetables all but created the modern imperative of "being on time," since no technological innovation before the railroad had been so dependably prompt and had yoked so many people to the clock, the mechanical clock, of course—Marcel Proust had the narrator of *In Search of Lost*

Time become so captivated by those timetables that he pored over them, probing their import for time and space. The railroad's influence on the modern experience of time widened with the formation of time zones to coordinate uniform times for travelers to meet trains speeding far across the landscape. The railroads also facilitated popularity of the performing artists by making possible their rapid movement great distances from one venue to another. In Europe, the railroad aided Franz Liszt in igniting the "Lisztomania" that swept much of the continent in the early 1840s, and (as Orlando Figes astutely demonstrated in *The Europeans*) it shaped the career of Pauline Viardot, who became Europe's most celebrated opera singer, performing to adoring audiences from Russia to Spain and Italy. In America, Jenny Lind's sensational tour would have been impossible without the railroad. As noted above, P. T. Barnum even had the first-ever private railroad car built just for her, which, as his insatiable marketing imagination intended, enhanced her fame while she chugged immaculately and glamorously from one city to another. If the railroad did not create the performer as international "celebrity," it surely enhanced that celebrity. And even though those early "celebrities" were generally performers of what we think of today as high art, thanks to rapid transportation and to Barnumesque promotion, they became the rock stars of their day, exciting audiences wherever they went. And that advanced the low art experience.

But transportation technologies had a less direct effect on the rise of low art than did technologies of communication. For these technologies shaped the cultural life itself. We could say this began way back with the arrival of the printing press.

The invention of mechanical printing in the 1450s stimulated the distribution of reading material (and, over time, the growth of literacy) more widely than ever. It also begot the phenomenon of what would, in the late nineteenth century, be denoted the "bestseller." As early as 1499 a fantasy tale printed in Italy became perhaps the first such bestseller, and it was still popular over a hundred years later when it so charmed Pope Alexander II that he had the eminent sculptor Bernini fashion a statue depicting a fanciful image from the book showing an elephant carrying an obelisk on its back (standing today on the Piazza della Minerva in

Rome). A few years after that fantasy tale was published, Martin Luther tacked his infamous theses to the Wittenberg Cathedral door, launching the Protestant Reformation, which spread on the tide of printed pamphlets and the newly published Protestant Bible. Close to a century later, the first true novel was published: *Don Quixote* (1605, 1615), in which the printing press even plays a role in Part II where a false version of Part I has already appeared (as it had) with a false Don Quixote pursuing his own quixotic adventures, duly denounced by Cervantes himself, who has his "real" Don Quixote do things to deliberately discredit the illicit imitator. The first English novel came a century after that with Daniel Defoe's wildly popular *Robinson Crusoe* (1717), about the same time that the cheesy Grub Street novels started proliferating. Within a few decades, fiction would be the rage, including the previously mentioned *Tristram Shandy*, much influenced by *Don Quixote* and adroitly marketed by its author, Laurence Sterne, in the new commercial world of low art, which is what all fiction was deemed then. In eighteenth-century France, the popular press produced countless works of populist and irreverent fiction that helped undermine established authority and fed revolutionary fervor by turning the low-art mind games of ideal possibilities against the established order. Nowadays, mass market fictions, many of them romance novels, sell in the tens of millions every year, fulfilling wishes in fantasies of love and adventure through those same kinds of mind games.

I should also remark that, as Elizabeth Eisenstein pointed out in her influential book *The Printing Revolution in Early Modern Europe* (1979, 2005), along with the dissemination of reading material, printing brought a glut of what today we call "misinformation" in books that told tall tales as fact and made crazy assertions, seeding doubts and igniting controversies over what is true and what is false on a scale previously unknown. The rise of science, also greatly aided by printing, would combat such doubts, but would not put an end to them—as we know well today, especially owing to the later invention of communications technologies outside of print. And (as Eisenstein also observes), it should not be ignored that the technology of printing also engendered the literary class, which began in the low culture of popular writing but eventually split into both low and high, thriving on publishing and, in its higher reaches, serving as arbiters of taste and the Good. In all, the technology of printing changed the very fabric of Western culture, often in subtle, indirect ways, affecting religion, politics, social relations, the intellectual life, and our understanding of the universe and of human nature (see Fig. 44).

Surely no single technological innovation had as wide an impact on the cultural life and on the growth of low art as printing did until the Industrial Revolution tapped new sources of physical energy and recast economic and social conditions. The era of that revolution also brought two early communication technologies that changed perceptions of reality, removed people a step or two from actuality, and boosted popular culture: the telegraph and photography. The telegraph, invented in the 1830s but formally demonstrated for the first time by Samuel Morse in 1844 (see Fig. 45), did for printed communications what the railroad did for transportation. As the first newspaper to receive and print a telegraphed up-to-the-minute piece of "news" exclaimed: "This is indeed the annihilation of space."[26] They could have added "time." For the telegraph made "news" and other communications available almost immediately across great distances in pithy bits—foreshadowing the electronic technologies of the late twentieth century that would hook people on fast information "bites," increasing the quantity and diminishing the substance of "information" overall. What we might call the telegraphic mentality served the rise of low art well, since low art subsists on irresistible sensations, immediate gratifications, and untaxing content.

Photography arrived about the same time as the telegraph. Louis Daguerre produced his first daguerreotypes in the late 1830s, and his invention was officially recognized in 1839 (see Fig. 46). Although the daguerreotype was not destined to become quite the technological model for modern photography because of its cumbersome and time-consuming process, it set a high aesthetic standard and opened the door for more efficient inventions to come. Like the telegraph, photography was an effective, fast, and arresting form of communication. And the more arresting for appealing to the senses with visual images rather than to the

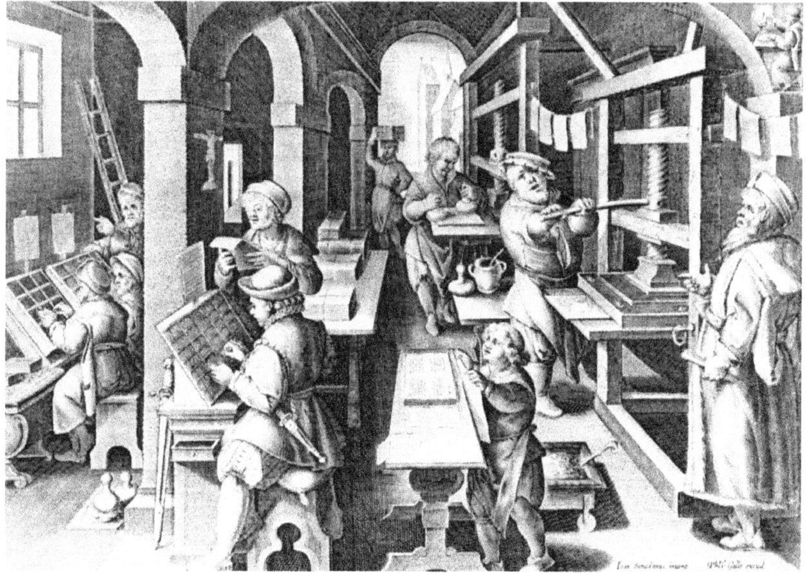

Fig. 44 — A printing press establishment displaying the several stages of the printing process from typesetting to bookbinding. Engraving, c. 1605.

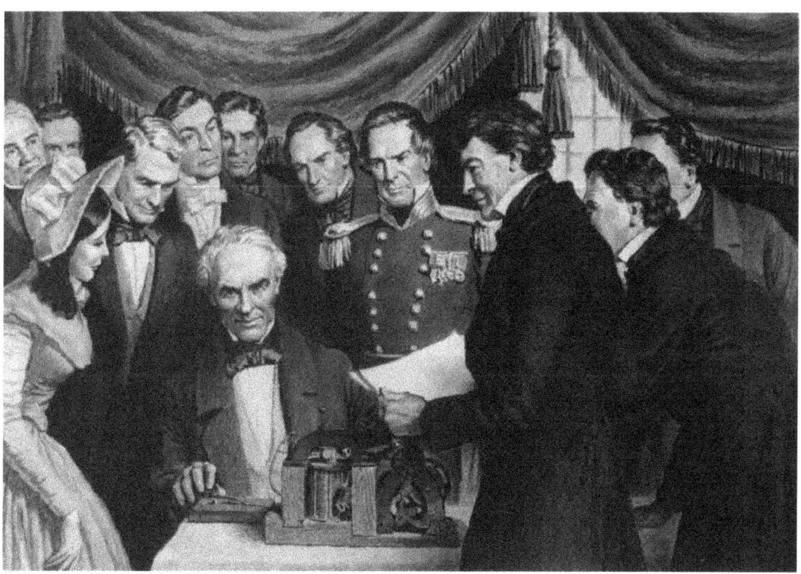

Fig. 45 — Samuel Morse sending the first official telegraph message in 1844.

Previous experimental telegraph machines had appeared in the 1830s, but Morse and his code proved most effective and influential. Sent from the Supreme Court Chamber in the Capitol, where dignitaries gathered to witness the epochal event, to Baltimore, Maryland, that first telegram sped through thirty-five miles of telegraph wires carrying Morse's message: "What hath God wrought!"

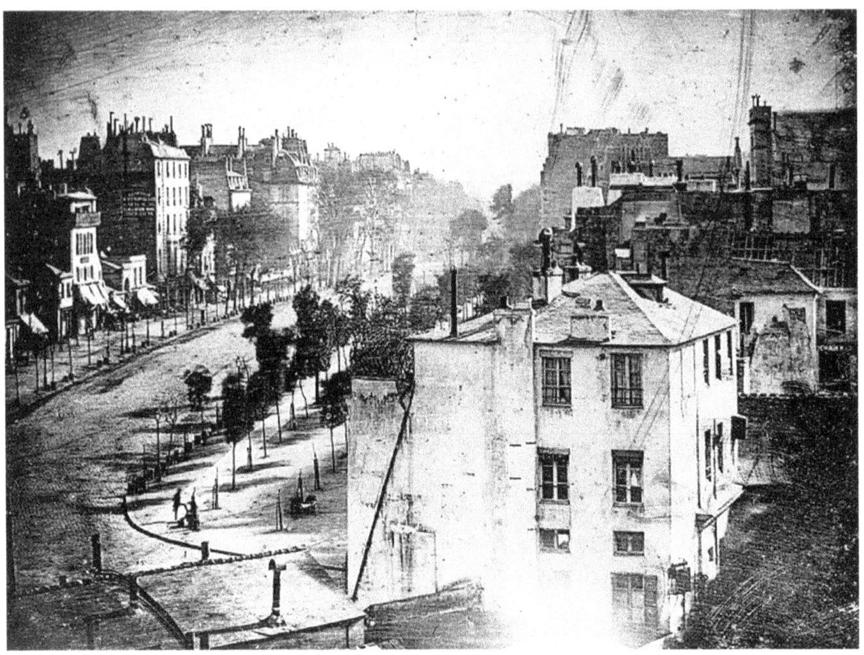

Fig. 46 — Louis-Jacques-Mandé Daguerre, Boulevard du Temple at 8 o'clock in the morning, *1838.*

One of Daguerre's first photographs, and the first known photograph with a human being, a man getting his boots shined on the corner. In January 1839, with fanfare, the French government announced Daguerre's new invention. As it happened, Samuel Morse, the principal inventor of the telegraph, was in Paris at the time, and the announcement excited him enough that he arranged to meet Daguerre. They hit it off—allaying Morse's first concerns that Daguerre's invention would eclipse his own—and Morse then enthusiastically brought to America the first widely disseminated news of the invention of photography. For a couple of decades the daguerreotype reigned in photography. But its cumbersome process—impressing a lighted image onto a silver/copper plate through the opening in a box, or "camera," which could take a while—and costly materials later yielded to more efficient and inexpensive photographic processes.

intellect with words. It also affected perceptions of nature and of painting as an art form. Pessimists thought it might put an end to painting. But some painters, notably Impressionists like Monet and Degas, happily drew on it. And yet, despite its embrace by painters, and the artistry of some early photographers such as the great Nadar, photography was also judged largely a low-art novelty not widely recognized as capable of high art until the twentieth century.

In a more prosaic vein, photography also likely inspired the maxim "A picture is worth a thousand words." First used by print advertisers in early twentieth-century America, the maxim signaled that photography and advertising had a marriage made in heaven—or, cynics might say, made in hell. After all, the written word takes time and mental effort to grasp, while pictures do not. And, whereas newspaper advertising had originally relied on words alone—American newspapers even had a rule to that effect until late in the nineteenth century—by the early twentieth century, advertisers had adopted that maxim, which suited the principle that advertising must appeal to the emotions, not to the intellect.

In time, photographs and other visual images would appear conspicuously in all newspapers. Sensationalizing tabloids led the way, and before long photographs would practically fill many publications, especially pages devoted chiefly to advertising. (The more traditional *New York Times* first put photographs on the front page in the 1890s, albeit sparingly, but declined to use color until 1997; and the even more traditional *Wall Street Journal* resisted photographs until 2014.) The proliferation of visual images in print at the expense of words has by now driven most newspapers and news magazines out of business. The invention of photography deserves a large measure of the credit, or blame, for that.

We could view what photography did to newspapers as a sign of the visual eclipsing the verbal in modern culture. Since the senses react to most stimuli more instinctively than does the intellect, we might expect sensory experience to attract us more readily than words. But there is more to the story than that. For what has occurred—or is occurring—is not just the passage from a verbal to a visual culture, but the passage from a culture of actuality to a culture of artifice. That is, to a world of technologically stimulated sensations and pseudo-realities (what Daniel Boorstin called *images* and *pseudo-events*). And this not only removes us from natural reality, it chains us to technology more than ever.

Is this not what the electronic technologies of the twentieth- and twenty-first centuries do? The motion picture film, the phonograph, the radio, television, and then, perhaps even more deeply, the computer, the Internet, smart phones, social media, and so on, remove us from everyday reality while chaining us to their arresting technologies, introducing a world where people can prefer Virtual Reality to the real thing, and where the conjurings of Artificial Intelligence will thread through all existence (both VR and AI will return at the end of the next chapter).

It is not hard to see how this culture of technologically artificial sensations serves low art more than high art. For one thing, because the mind games of the low-art experience invite compelling and irresistible sensations that spark fantasies taking us outside the world, those mind games welcome technologies that create alluringly artificial worlds. For another, because the technologies those mind games welcome lie in the hands of commercial interests that reap profits from the expansion of both such technologies and the low arts that those technologies serve, the low-art experience and its mind games become inseparable partners at once of the technologies and of the commercial interests. How could low art not flourish in such conditions? And it does flourish, as the Culture of Entertainment.

Conclusion

The Culture of Entertainment is not just a mode of cultural life. It is much more. Thanks to the deep and expansive historical causes that delivered it to us, the Culture of Entertainment has tentacles that extend everywhere. And thanks to the mind games of entertainment, or the low-art experience, those tentacles reach into everyone's life, shaping perceptions, judgments, and attitudes toward what reality is. Many of the results are not pretty.

We will now take up those results, focusing on some of the mental or psychological effects of the low-art experience, culminating in an account of the events of January 6, 2021, as a sorry and cautionary instance of what the mind games of the low-art experience can do to people, society, and politics within the Culture of Entertainment. And not at all for the better.

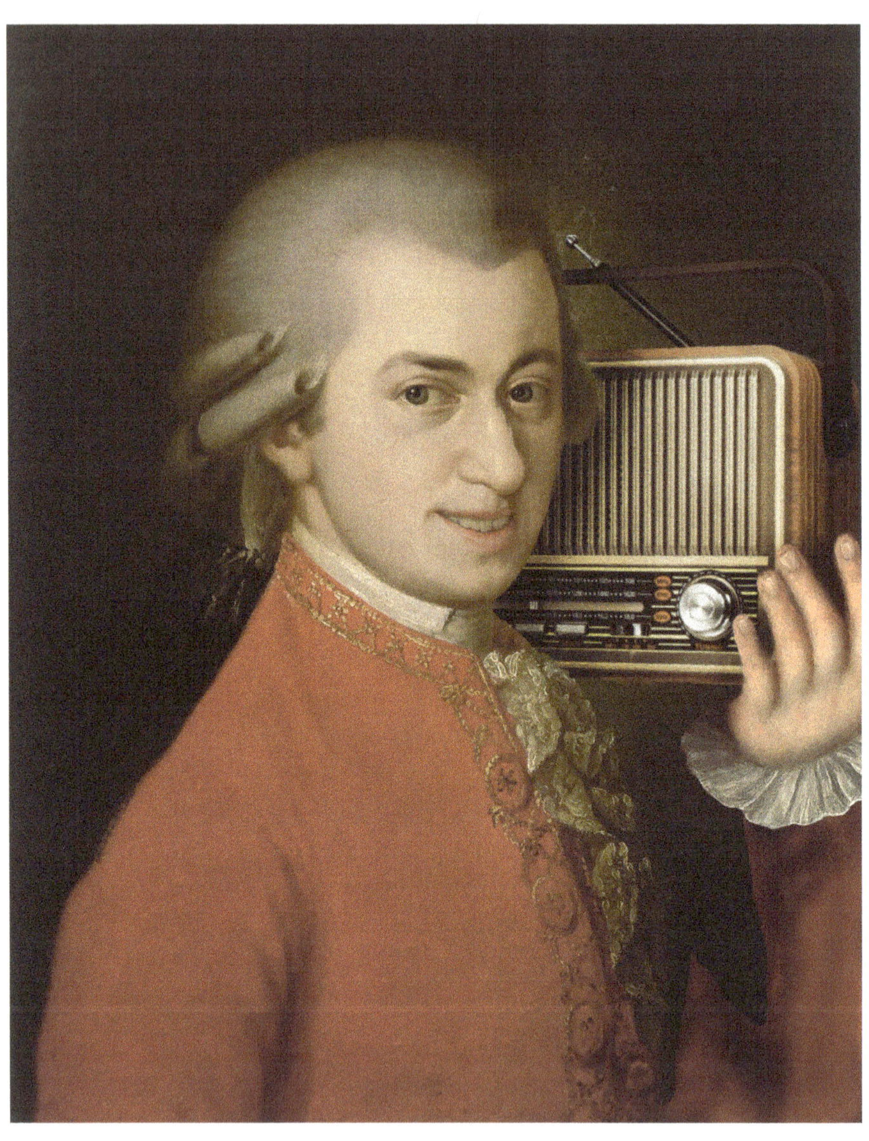

Fig. 47 — Mozart laughing at "the radio music of life" in Herman Hess's novel Steppenwolf*—see pages 160–61.*

V
The Culture of Entertainment and the Perils of *Unseriousness*

"Learn to laugh at the radio music of life."
—Mozart,
Herman Hesse, Steppenwolf

The Culture of Entertainment—if not by that name—has become a commonplace idea since the 1980s. Anyone interested in the character of contemporary culture can see entertainment laced through this culture in countless ways, from art and advertising to schooling and politics, from religion and human relations to how people think and judge reality. As previous pages have indicated, entertainment or low art, in one form or another, has always been around. But not on the scale we know in the Culture of Entertainment.

I should begin this portrait of that culture by recalling that the English term "entertain" originally meant to "maintain" or "sustain" a person, usually as an employee (derived in the late fifteenth century from Old French and Latin words for "hold" or "keep"). From this came "entertain" as a term for "to engage" or "to host" someone, and "entertainment" was the noun for being so "entertained." And from there we got the idea of "entertain" as an engaging style of hospitality offering pleasure and amusement. By the eighteenth century, although the original meanings still held, "entertainment" had also grown into a term for a public performance that would "engage" or "entertain" people pleasurably and amusingly. In his seminal English dictionary (1755), Samuel

Johnson defined "entertainment" in the traditional ways but added, "Dramatick performance; the lower comedy." And he defined "opera" rather dismissively as an "exotic and irrational entertainment," clearly ranking it as low art. Since that time, opera has gone from low art to high—if not, as remarked in the previous chapter, to the more reverential and restrained heights of "classical" music before Romanticism popularized it and brought intense emotionality to the surface. And while we still use the verb "to entertain" for a kind of engaging hospitality, as in "to entertain guests," and for a kind of mental engagement, as in "to entertain an idea," we also generally think of the noun "entertainment" close to Samuel Johnson's last definition, as a diversion or amusement of low art. The essence of "entertainment" in this sense is, therefore, an artistic creation that reaches us effortlessly through its almost irresistible aesthetic and emotional appeal, and to be "entertained" in this way is the verb for having that low-art experience—which, as observed earlier, can occur to some degree even with certain works of high art. And it is through the low-art experience of entertainment that the Culture of Entertainment engulfs us.*

Entertainment and Its Critics

In recent decades, articles and books galore have described and analyzed the intrusion of entertainment into every corner of our lives. A small sampling will do here. We could well begin with the landmark book, mentioned earlier, by the historian Daniel Boorstin, *The Image: A Guide to Pseudo-Events in America* (1959). Boorstin focused not on entertainment itself but on a society that was supplanting the substance of human

* This is especially true of American culture, the primary subject of this book, but it is also evident elsewhere in an amalgam of American commercialism and entertainment, from the glittery advertising of Tokyo and the malls of Singapore to the pop music of London and the Americanized popular culture of Paris. The distinguished French author Annie Ernaux records an unhappy awareness of this amalgam in her memoir/novel *The Years*. There she recalls celebrating the idealistic social upheaval in Paris of spring 1968 as marking "the first year of the world," only to then report sadly that within a decade, "Advertising provided models for how to live," and "The ideals of May, '68 were being transformed into objects and entertainment."

life with a shadow world of images and what he dubbed "pseudo-events." He detected this trend emerging in the nineteenth century with the invention of the telegraph and photography, and he saw it flower in the twentieth with the rise of public relations and many practices exalting appearances over reality, or rather, *turning appearances into reality.* For example, as "news" coverage proliferated, beginning with the telegraph, it increasingly granted mere statements, and even the "press releases," of officials and other public figures the same "newsworthy" status as actual events (by the twenty-first century the news media would dignify as "newsworthy" every daily rant, however brief and idiotic, of an American president who knew that the more outrageous his words the more notice they would get—an exemplary "pseudo-event"). Radio and then television made politics a show of performance skills more than a presentation of substantive ideas and policies. FDR's cozy weekly radio "Fireside Chats," intoned in a mellifluous and reassuring voice, set the standard in the 1930s. Later, the presidential debates of Kennedy and Nixon in 1960 brought the show to television, making "performance" on the small screen the gauge of political merit. Television gave the telegenic and adroit performer JFK an edge in the debate and in the election. That he should have frequently fraternized with Hollywood entertainers was only to be expected—if nearly unthinkable a generation earlier. When, two decades after Kennedy's election, the former movie actor and television "personality" Ronald Reagan took up residence in the White House—fielding a journalist's pointed question, "How can an actor be president?" with the deft and revealing reply, "How can a president not be an actor?"—the writing was on the wall: entertainment and politics had become pals.

The cult of celebrity also arose from the ascendancy of images and pseudo-events. Boorstin coined the definition of a "celebrity" as someone known simply for being well-known. And television supplied an ever-present mode of becoming that, if not for long—provoking Andy Warhol's quip, "In the future everybody will be famous for fifteen minutes." Nowadays, celebrity has become the measure of human worth for many Americans, and achieving celebrity is almost a sure ticket to a career in American politics for anyone—as well as the best revenge envisioned by discontented young males who try to gain fame by carrying out public shootings. The America of Boorstin's "images," "pseudo-events," and celebrity played into the Culture of Entertainment very well.

The second book I'll mention is *Amusing Ourselves to Death: Public Discourse in the Age of Show Business* (1985) by Neil Postman. A professor of Communications and social critic who published extensively on contemporary American culture, Postman described here (with a nod to Marshall McLuhan's fecund idea that "the medium is the message") how visual technologies, particularly television, have created a culture that hooks people on what television does. And what it does, almost exclusively, is entertain. That is, it seizes visual attention and plays with the mind while asking no effort from viewers. Yielding to that fact, even presumably non-entertainment offerings, like reporting the news and presenting "educational" programs, have learned to entertain in order to keep

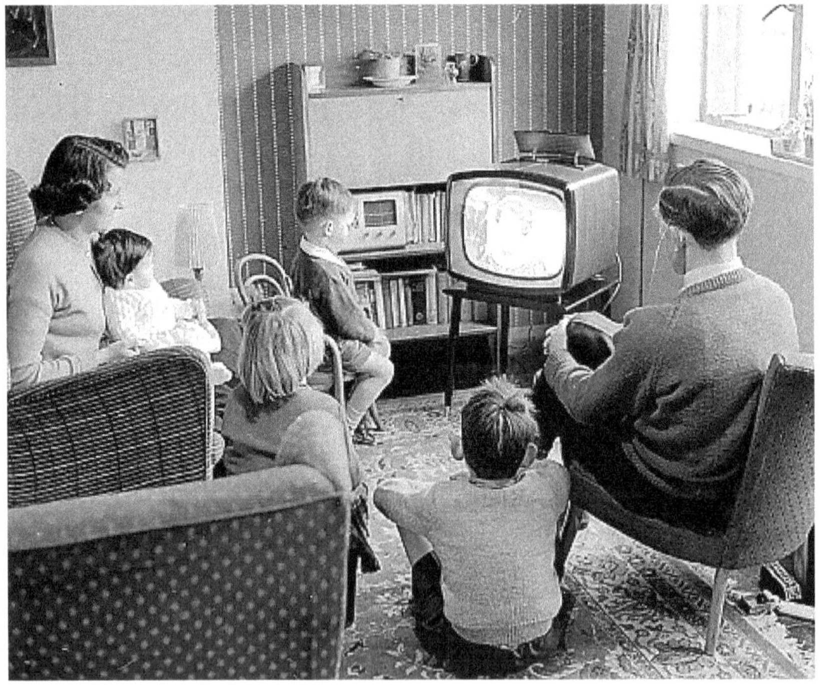

Fig. 48 — An ideal American family—white parents and their four well-behaved small children—of the 1950s gather in their suburban living room to watch television. The boxy television set is part of the family, bringing them happily together every evening. But not to socialize. Rather to be mesmerized.

viewers (see Fig. 48). Not only that, because television entertainment has become so pervasive in American life, it can lead viewers to expect the rest of life to be entertaining, too, shaping minds to respond to little else.

The expectation that life should be entertaining also brings an assumption that no experience should be more mentally taxing or coherent than television fare, with its abrupt shifts of scene or subject and its illogical interruptions of scheduled shows by strings of even more disjointed, yet entertainingly eye- and ear-catching, commercials. Television commercials could themselves be so entertaining that when an educational entrepreneur persuaded some school districts to install television sets in classrooms free of charge to broadcast ten-minute news programs along with two minutes of commercial advertising, the students gave their attention primarily to the flashy commercials, largely ignoring the news, no matter how disjointed the commercials were or "entertaining" the always-episodic news tried to be.

Although Postman does not dwell at length on it, I might point out that so-called "educational television" for children embraced entertainment with alacrity and ingenuity. The innovative *Sesame Street* cleverly staffed its entertaining instructional episodes with loveable, large-scale puppet animals called "Muppets" (see Fig. 49). Amid their cartoon-like capers, the Muppets, along with visiting persons (usually a "celebrity"), taught children about letters and words and numbers and so on. To juice the appeal and impact of its televised instruction, the show originally preceded some of its segments with (what else but?) commercials. "Educational" commercials, of course. "I suggested using commercials to teach letters and numbers," said Joan Ganz Cooney, a creator of the show, because commercials can teach children anything, and "television was teaching willy-nilly," missing an educational opportunity she was determined not to miss.[27] Young viewers would be told that, for instance, the next segment of fun stuff is "Brought to you by the letter G," then they would get some clever instruction about that letter. The show adopted other techniques of advertising, too, like rhyming jingles and catchy slogans. The Muppets themselves (with their creator Jim Henson) had actually come to *Sesame Street* from television advertising—of such products as coffee and dog food. And just as advertising

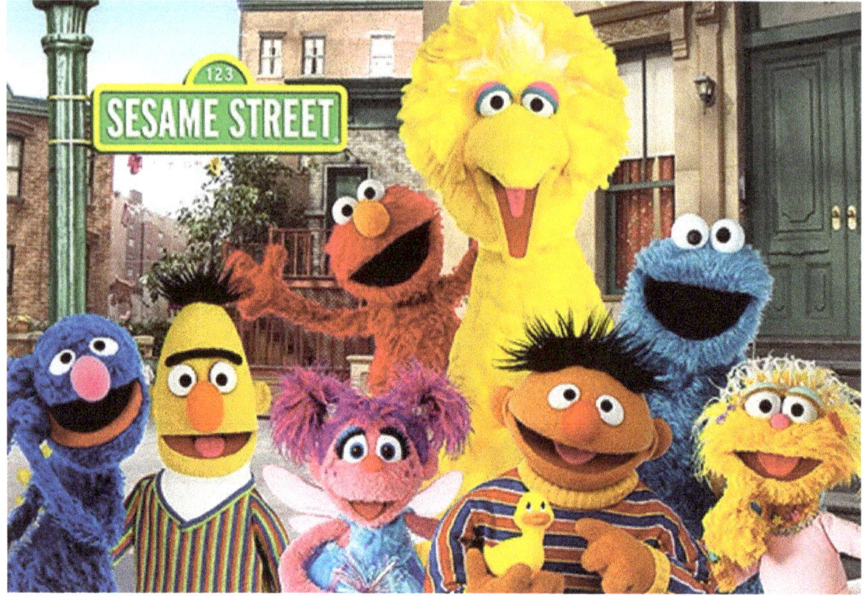

Fig. 49 — Some Muppets of Sesame Street. *Nearly two thousand Muppet characters have appeared on* Sesame Street *during the five-plus decades the show has been running since its launch in 1969. Among the most beloved "stars" of the show: (back to front, left to right) Elmo, Big Bird, the Cookie Monster, Grover, Bert, Abby Cadabby, Ernie, and Zoe. Each Muppet has a personality of its own, but I leave that for fans to explore.*

exploited low-art's powers to seize attention and sell products, the educational ingenuity of *Sesame Street* used entertaining advertising practices to capture children's gleeful interest for a few minutes in order to teach them elementary things. And it did this well.

But this was not all that *Sesame Street* taught them. Children also learned that education is—or *should* be—*entertaining*, namely, effortless, and fun, and that commercials are both beneficial and necessary in the world. For that matter, they learned that watching practically anything on television asks the mind not to work but simply to follow and respond to the shifting images and jolly patter on the screen wherever these might go. Which is to say, as more than one critic has remarked, *Sesame Street* taught children how to watch television, with all the ramifications that entails.

Although *Sesame Street* is hardly alone to blame, it is no surprise that in recent times students' attention spans and powers of concentration have diminished while their mental acceptance of inconsistencies and incoherence, along with their expectation to be entertained, have increased. Postman found evidence of this among his own students, who often threw ideas together in their comments and papers with little attempt at coherence, a defect the students either could not see or defended with a shrug as a natural way to think. If he overstates the responsibility of television itself for such aberrant intellectual practices, he nonetheless tells a chilling tale of what television in the "age of show business" is doing to us.

In the late 1990s, the critic Neal Gabler flogged entertainment even harder than Postman. In *Life: The Movie: How Entertainment Conquered Reality* (1998), he contended and abundantly illustrated how "entertainment has become the primary value of American life," and that, in his judgment, this has converted life itself into entertainment. By which he meant that the seductive pleasures of entertainment have infected practically everything we do, from religion to social life and politics. That infection has led people to identify themselves with entertainers and to think of themselves as performers in life modeled on celebrities and movie fantasies. This state of mind has created, in Gabler's words, a "world of post-reality," where, for many people, nothing is real except as a movie. But that is not "reality" at all. Like Postman with television, Gabler goes too far with the idea of life as a movie, but also like Postman, Gabler is not wrong to say that entertainment has become the air we breathe.

In 2017, the critic Kurt Andersen looked at the same landscape as Boorstin, Postman, and Gabler, but he did it through the long lens of American history from its origins. He found that a penchant for fantasy, or the inclination to prefer dreamworlds and imaginings to the world as it is and to try to live out those fantasies, has typified American culture from its earliest days. And he contends in *Fantasyland: How America Went Haywire: A 500-Year History* that this penchant has fully bloomed only in recent times with the open acceptance of untruth as truth and unreality as reality among a large segment of American society. Now, he concludes, we live in a "post-factual," "post-truth" society, where "being American means we can believe any damn thing we want." Andersen sees the mounting influence of entertainment as more of a symptom than a source of this current condition, whose igniting cause he finds chiefly in the radical relativism of the 1960s, later fueled by computer technologies that have handed everyone a torch to incinerate truth. Still, his "Fantasyland" of today and the Culture of Entertainment are one.

Confirming the reign of entertainment, a pair of academics published a five-hundred-plus-page textbook entitled *Entertainment and Society* that went through two editions in the first decade of the twenty-first century (2003, 2010). From their academic perch they viewed modern entertainment as a form of "constructed . . . leisure . . . produced with design and awareness of what it is and what it does." [28] In other words, unlike traditional leisure-time diversions, entertainment comes to us readymade and fashioned to exploit our desire to have a good time. That means consumer commerce and technology call the shots in entertainment today. The authors covered the waterfront of entertainment as they understood it, specifying its many types, identifying its links to other ingredients of culture, including religion, ethics, and law, and surveying academic theories of entertainment's effects. Calculating that there are no fewer than 48 distinct theories of "how people relate to and are affected by the media" that deliver entertainment, they sided with none of those theories, nor did they draw any conclusions of their own about the effects of entertainment on individuals and society. But then, the authors were writing an academic textbook, not a work of cultural criticism. Even so, they pulled out the stops in trying to make the nearly six-hundred-page book itself "entertaining" with offbeat pictures, quirky text arrangements, numerous boxes containing semi-related information and others marked by a cartoonish camera taking a flash photo next to the words "FLASH FACT" to present anecdotal details, and movie parlance scattered throughout, like "Fade to Black" instead of the prosaic Conclusion at the end of each chapter. Textbook though it may be, everything in the book's form and contents shows that entertainment in one form or another is everywhere, and that, whereas scholars might differ in how to interpret its effects, none concludes that entertainment simply washes over us leaving no traces.

Critics have continued to bemoan how entertainment is not only everywhere but that, as the author of a recent cover story in the *Atlantic* magazine put it, "Everything is Entertainment." This lengthy article charted the terrain of entertainment but added nothing new to the litany of telltale facts and resigned complaints that we have grown used to about the parlous condition of American culture. She did characterize what I call the Culture of Entertainment as the "Metaverse" of quasi-reality we live in, and if that gives anyone a new slant on the subject, so much the better.[29]

The last critics I will mention here are those who have bewailed the enveloping influence of entertainment as the Disneyfication of America. They (among them Kurt Andersen, who surely drew his title from Disney) mean that the "Fantasyland" of Disney entertainments has become a way of life for many Americans. And they have good reasons to think that. Just look at the Disney theme parks. These differed from traditional amusement parks, which offered a hodge-podge of rides and other diversions, by welcoming visitors into a fantasy world where everything you do or see, including the Disney staff, is related to a "theme"—or variety of themes—usually taken from Disney movies. The original Disney theme park in California now boasts nine themed "lands," such as Adventureland, Frontierland, Tomorrowland, and, of course, Fantasyland. In this pseudo-reality of entertainment, tens of thousands of people can spend the whole day, or several days at a time, living out the mind games of Disney fantasies. The Disney success inspired many imitators, and now theme parks are all over the place—Disney theme parks themselves nearly encircle the globe—and a widespread mentality wants, and even expects, more and more experiences to be like those of a theme park.

Naturally attuned to this contrived desire, the Disney Corporation hatched a new idea. Since Walt Disney himself had installed an idealized version of "Main Street, U.S.A." (c. 1910) in the original Disneyland, and variations on it would be the first of the "lands" encountered in all succeeding Disney theme parks, the Disney Corporation decided to take the next step. They constructed an entire actual town embodying the Disney fantasy of the perfect place to live. Planned and built in the 1990s and located, wouldn't you know, with a Main Street running to Disney World in Orlando, it was named Celebration, Florida (see Fig. 50). Celebration was to be the ideal Disney town, designed top to

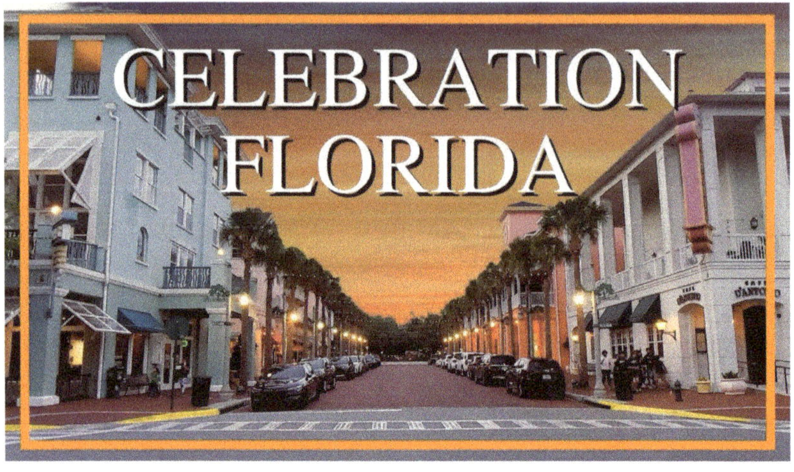

Fig. 50 — Title of YouTube video tour of Celebration, Florida, 2021.

This street in the city center displays the cinematic charms of the Disney town in colorful buildings and perfectly matched, symmetrical palm trees lining both sides of the street. And not a scrap of litter, or anything out of place, to be seen.

bottom like a Disney movie set with charming, immaculately tidy streets and historic houses, and managed to reflect the Disney brand, along with Disney rules for the inhabitants. It was a made-to-order instance of "life: the movie" for anyone who really wanted to live in a movie set (curiously, Gabler gives it only a passing footnote). Although Disney control of Celebration has diminished over time, as home to about eleven thousand people, it evidently still has the ideal small-town Disney atmosphere with residents who seem to have inculcated the Disney ethos and don't need Disney edicts to keep the movie running—although they have found that actuality can sometimes conflict with fantasy when the plumbing leaks, or when neighbors do not always behave according to the Disney script or, rather, to the covenants of the town. But whatever else can be said about Celebration, Florida, it certainly belongs to the Culture of Entertainment.

With the profuse evidence all around us and the many thoughtful writings illuminating how entertainment has come to pervade American culture, one might wonder if there is anything new to be said on the subject, or any new perspective that might yield fresh understanding.

Well, I want to give it a try. I will do this by playing out what the low-art experience and its mind games can tell us about the Culture of Entertainment and how this culture affects as it does. I will begin by briefly recalling what happens to us in the low-art experience in general. Then I will go to some of the principal effects of that experience in the Culture of Entertainment on minds, culture, and politics.

Mind Games of the Low-Art Experience

Of first importance, to reiterate an idea familiar here by now, the mind games of the art experience take us out of the real world, granting us freedom from that world's mental and emotional demands. But, while those mind games are generally the same in high art and low, we play them more freely in the low art experience. For that experience can take us farther outside the requirements of mental effort, emotional restraint, and seriousness than the high-art experience does. And with this trip goes a kind of mental passivity that judges nothing, barely rouses thought at all, and opens a door to the boundless liberty of fantasy where almost anything is possible. Consequently, when the mind games of the low-art experience become ubiquitous in life at large, the effects on minds and culture in the real world can be significant, and disturbing. We will look a little more closely into some of those effects by way of mental passivity and fantasy themselves.

Let's begin with mental passivity. Although, as Aristotle said, the passive pleasures of amusement can provide salutary rest from exertion, those pleasures can also nurture an appetite for the sweet passivity of inexertion itself—what the Italians agreeably call *il dolce far niente*, the sweetness of doing nothing. *Il dolce far niente* is not a bad thing in itself, but the appetite for passive pleasures turns bad when it dulls the appeal of more mentally stimulating and challenging pursuits. For this deprives us of the mental exercise we need to remain intellectually and emotionally vital human beings. Not only that, besides offering passive pleasures, the mind games of the low-art experience relax many of the rules that govern mental life overall in the real world. These rules include the logical laws of coherence and contradiction (i.e., ideas must cogently fit together, and two contradictory ideas cannot both be true at the same time and in the same way),* as well as respect for objective facts. Therefore, black can be white, up can be down, insanity can be sanity, magic can work, and all wishes can come true. That is to say, the mind games of the low-art experience and the mental passivity they bring—along with fantasy—make virtually anything possible. At the same time, those mind games tell us that nothing will have consequences, or, at any rate, not real-world consequences. And when anything is possible, but nothing has real-world consequences, we need not judge anything that happens and can just passively let it be and enjoy it. That's entertainment. Which gives it such appeal, and menacing appeal at that.

But the mind games of mental passivity can have even more pernicious results than this. These results occur through the fantasies that those mind games unleash. We have seen instances, like Emma Bovary and Mark David Chapman, where the fantasies inspired by the art experience can be so consuming that they impair one's life and harm others. But these cases display only the obvious damage unharnessed fantasy can do. The mind games of unrestrained fantasy can have subtler effects: they can alter our very sense of truth and reality.

The mind games of fantasy do this perhaps most adversely by rendering truth and reality completely subjective. If you want to think something is true, it is true for you, in your subjective fantasy. In Kurt Andersen's pithy words, nowadays "we can believe any damn thing we want." No justification is necessary—or is really possible. That might be innocent enough in the low-art experience of entertainment itself, but it can be threatening when taken outside that experience. For when we passively allow our fantasies to deny or ignore the objectivity of truth and reality, we can become disinclined, and possibly unable, to judge anything, however illogical, nutty, or pernicious it might be outside our fantasies. And this robs us of all defenses against anyone else's claims about truth and re-

---

* These logical laws (the second is a pillar of Aristotle's logic) are not universally accepted. Buddhism, for example, has developed theories of reality and ways of thinking more hospitable to logical incoherence and contradiction and therefore beyond the vaunted rationality of Western thought, which Buddhist thinkers have judged too confining to comprehend the complex nature of existence.

ality. We have no objective logical truths, no objective facts, no objective world to hold onto that could stir us to take a stand and say: "No. That is *not* true, *not* real." And we sink, with contented passivity and self-indulgent fantasy, into a maw of helpless subjectivity.* That might not cause us immediate grief, since we will have no way of judging our condition. But there is a price to be paid for the death of objectivity.

George Orwell grimly depicted that price in the novel *1984*. He showed it to be nothing less than the demise of human freedom and the extinction of genuine humanity. In that depressing, and depressingly prescient, novel, the State wields total control over citizens not only by having Big Brother keep track of everyone, but, more deeply, by banishing objective reality from their lives. For instance, the State denies the objectivity of historical facts, making them malleable to the State's wishes. And it is the official task of the pathetic anti-hero Winston Smith to rewrite history again and again, in his office at the Ministry of Truth, to meet the State's fluctuating demands. Winston does retain an ember of freedom in his own mind by telling himself that as long as he can say 2 + 2 = 4 he will have a glow of objective truth to reassure him. But in the end, even that small glimmer of objectivity is snuffed out. The state targets him as a subversive and eventually crushes his spirit. Finally, he concedes that if the State says 2 +2 = 5, then so it is.

Although in America we do not live under an all-powerful state like that in Orwell's novel, we can see objectivity yielding to subjectivity on all sides through passivity of mind and self-indulgent fantasies. Think about it: When the young insatiably hunger for the fleeting images and abbreviated messages of smart phones, glue their eyes to the incessantly

---

* Some readers might wonder how the dangers of subjectivity described here relate to the quite subjective art experience at the heart of this book. I would say that whereas the art experience and the idea of art that goes with it are rooted in the subjective experience of individuals, and therefore "art" has no meaning outside that experience, this is simply a pragmatic, empirical judgment about matters of value, not matters of fact. Although this book contends that the idea of "art" has no meaning outside the subjective art experience of individuals, this should not be construed to imply that the objects we label "art" do not exist objectively in the real world. The subjectivity of the art experience is the subjectivity of ideas, values, and judgments, and in no substantive way conflicts with the objectivity of logical and factual truth.

kinetic sensations of video games, let their thoughts flit from one idea to another with no sense of coherence or contradiction, have no patience or capacity to read long books or to think through much of anything, and embrace as a pseudo-righteous principle of tolerance that "you can think any damn thing you want"; when conspiracy theories making bizarre assertions about reality in defiance of all facts win support from nearly a third of the American people; when the most-watched network on American television is a so-called "news" network that attracts viewers to lap up almost nothing but fact-free conspiracy theories and factitious political propaganda; when viewers of that same network recoil in rage at its early—and accurate—announcement that Democrat Joe Biden had won Arizona in 2020, prompting the network "to protect the brand" by recommitting itself to broadcasting untruths to satisfy its ideologically besotted viewers; when an American president can tell blatant lies even about things that are obviously false (false, that is, to anyone who accepts facts), including his absurd claim that voter fraud had deprived him of reelection, and urge the rewriting of history to suit himself; when much of the country and almost an entire political party sides with this now-former president, even as he seeks another term in office amid multiple legal indictments for his misbehavior; well, then you know that the mind games of mental passivity have undone the ties to objectivity for many Americans and that the mind games of fantasy are fastening those ties to subjectivity. No wonder many critics have complained that we live in a subjective "post-truth" or "post-reality" world. As Daniel Boorstin remarked over sixty years ago, in the age of "pseudo-events," "the menace of unreality" haunts us all around.

But wait once more. We must ask: Have the mind games of entertainment, with the passivity of mind and penchant for fantasy they induce, actually weakened cognitive abilities to the point that people can no longer recognize logical incoherence, contradictions, and factual lies, or distinguish between objective truth and subjective fantasy? The first answer that comes to us will likely be: No, at least not for everybody, like the critics who try to alert people to the threats. But when we ponder this question a little more, we might well answer something like this:

Although the cognitive abilities might not have diminished in themselves, the habits of mind those abilities depend on to keep sharp probably have, at least for young people who have grown up—and those to follow—in the Culture of Entertainment. For instance, under the sway of omnipresent entertainment, the habit of mental discipline yields to a habit of passive response, the habit of effort yields to a habit of self-indulgence, the habit of sustained attention yields to a habit of impatient distraction.* And these kinds of substitute habits point to another, which is perhaps the most corrosive of all. It is the habit of mind that supplants *seriousness* with what, for want of a more precise and felicitous term, I will call *unseriousness*. And it touches everything in the Culture of Entertainment. I will go so far as to say that the habit of *unseriousness* could be the most insinuating and pernicious effect of the mind games we play in the low-art experience of entertainment.

By *unseriousness* I mean primarily an attitude of mind that disregards the consequences of actions and ideas, or that treats actions and ideas as

---

* In the provocative book, *The Shallows: What the Internet is Doing to Our Brains* (2010, 2020), Nicholas Carr makes the case that persistent use of computer technology, especially the Internet and smart phones, is actually altering the cognitive structure of the brain. For the experience of flitting about on the Internet or smart phones, garnering bits of information almost instantaneously and other such practices, neurologically strengthens some cognitive skills, like quick (if superficial) problem-solving, while letting others go fallow, like deep thought. Understandably, Carr is most concerned with the skills that go fallow. He sees this in unfortunate habits of mind like inattention, fragmented thought, shortened concentration, and a passive submission to sensations and "information." It is clear that Carr attributes to the neurological effects of computer technology much the same habits of mind I attribute to the mind games of entertainment. And for many of the same reasons. I do not go into neurology, but I would say that the Internet experience is analogous to the art experience in taking us out of the real world. Where is cyberspace if not outside the real world? The Internet experience also lets us do things we could not do in the real world. Actually, what we do in that experience, including with smart phones, is a kind of play—like the electronic games that served as the model for how we interact with the Internet. "The Internet is like a treasure hunt," observed the renowned French author Annie Ernaux in her memoir/novel *The Years*. It's an entertaining game of searching here and there for clues to the treasure, or of "browsing" just to see what you can find. Consequently, as I have implied a few times in these pages, it should not be difficult to see that what computer technology does to us belongs to the Culture of Entertainment, complementing the mind games of entertainment that emerged before this technology invaded our lives.

though they have no significant consequences. By contrast, *seriousness* is an attitude that, perhaps above all, views actions and ideas in the light of their potential consequences in the real world. *Unseriousness*, therefore, belongs to entertainment where nothing seems to have real-world consequences, whereas *seriousness* belongs to the real world where consequences do matter. And more, I would say that when actions and ideas have real-world consequences, those actions and ideas, as well as their consequences, are themselves *serious*. By the same measure, when actions and ideas have no real-world consequences but only consequences outside the real world, those ideas, actions, and consequences are all in themselves *unserious*. That is a rather inelegant way of understanding these terms, but it captures the nub of the issue. Now I must add a bit of a tangle: We can be *serious* about actions and ideas that have *unserious* consequences, just as we can be *unserious* about actions and ideas that have *serious* consequences. This is not mere wordplay either. It is, I could say, a *serious* truth. A glance at play itself will help untangle the tangle.

Unseriousness *and Play*

"Play," in the sense of child's play, as well as of diverting adult games, is inherently *unserious* because it takes place outside the real world and has no real-world consequences. But we can nonetheless engage in play with an attitude of *seriousness*. Think of Huizinga's son's game of trains. The boy played that game very *seriously*, with strict rules that could not be violated without wrecking the game. Those rules required that the chairs believe they were part of a "real" train the boy was pulling as the engine. And, as he warned, if his father kissed him, the rules of the game would be broken and then "the carriages won't think it's real." The lad knew it was all only child's play and not part of the real world, but within the frame of the game he treated everything as *seriously* as if it were real. And he was determined to ensure that the other "players" shared that *seriousness*. We could say he played his game with *serious unseriousness* and *unserious seriousness,* that is to say, he played an *unserious* game *seriously*, and so his *seriousness* was ultimately *unserious*.

Now go from child's play to competitive games. Here play starts getting more complicated. These are games with very specific rules for how to play, and the players should take the rules and the game very *seriously*. If they don't take them *seriously*, the game falls apart; and no one wants to play any game with someone who is *unserious* about it—any more than Huizinga's son wanted his "players" to lose the *seriousness* of his game. Competitive games also have *unserious* consequences that the players can treat *seriously*: they play to win, not to lose. But the players know that the consequences of winning and losing occur only within the frame of the game outside the real world. So, however *seriously* the players play the game, they recognize that it is all, even winning and losing, essentially *unserious*, and when the game ends they can return to the real world having simply had a good time playing the game with *unserious seriousness*.

But that *unserious seriousness* changes when the same kind of competitive game becomes a professional activity. For then the game belongs to the real world for the players and many others. Compare amateur and professional baseball. They have essentially the same rules and produce the same consequences: winning or losing. But, while the consequences of who wins or loses an amateur game remain within the frame of the game, the consequences of who wins or loses a professional game do not end there. A great deal can be at stake in the real world for winners and losers, including the careers of the players, ticket sales, television rights, and so on. Professional baseball—like other professional sports, which now number all kinds of formerly amateur activities, such as skateboarding and beach volleyball—is *serious* business with *serious* real-world consequences for many people, not an *unserious* game with *unserious* consequences outside the world. However *seriously* an amateur might play a game, it remains just a game, whereas the professional is not merely playing an *unserious* game; he or she is not really even *playing* a game, no matter how enjoyable the activity might be, but is *working* at *serious* business.*

---

* The actor Brian Cox, best known recently for his central role in the *serious*, highly successful television series *Succession*, said that professional actors often take their "work" too *seriously*. "It's a game," he told the *New York Times*. "It's playing. It's what kids do . . . They have the natural instinct of play, and we [actors] forget about what playing is about." (Quoted in article on *Succession*, *New York Times*, April 10, 2023, online.)

One more twist. And this will return us to how the mind games of entertainment can foster an attitude of *unseriousness*. The twist is that we can treat *serious* things with an attitude of *unseriousness*. I indicated something like this can happen if a player does not play a game with the *seriousness* it requires, a *seriousness* that intensifies in professional games owing to their real-world consequences—if a professional player plays with nonchalant *unseriousness* despite the game's *serious* real-world consequences, bad things will happen for that player and others. It is this kind of *unseriousness* about *serious* consequences that will occupy us, because here we see how the attitude of *unseriousness* can have *serious* and damaging real-world consequences.

And with that, we leave play and the rhetorical tangle of *seriousness* and *unseriousness* for the Culture of Entertainment and how it brings an *unseriousness* of mind that can have *serious* consequences in the real world. As a prelude, I will touch on some anticipations of this attitude of *unseriousness* within the artworld.

Unseriousness *in the Artworld*

We begin by returning to the aesthete Oscar Wilde. He exalted art as the meaning of life, stripping ordinary existence of any substantive meaning of its own and giving him license to make fun of nearly everything—except maybe beauty, although he had some fun with that too. He demonstrated his aesthete's creed from his first reported witticism, "I find it harder and harder to live up to my blue China," on through a lifelong string of clever phrases and catchy quips, down to the last, "My wallpaper and I are fighting a duel to the death; one of us has to go." And in that frivolous spirit he derided *seriousness* as a folly of stuffy Victorians, while endorsing frivolity as an amusing way of life with no consequences to care about. As he described the theme of his most popular play, *The Importance of Being Earnest*: "we should treat all trivial things very seriously, and all the serious things of life with sincere and studied triviality." But in time he paid a heavy price for this *unserious* attitude when his cavalier behavior brought *serious* consequences in the real world: he was convicted of homosexual "Gross Indecency" and cast into Reading Jail, ringing down the curtain on his scintillating career.

Following Wilde, even the *seriousness* of art would become the butt of jest among artists. We could start with Alfred Jarry's nonsensical comedy *Ubu Roi*, an anti-theater jape that premiered in Paris a year after Wilde's *Earnest* in London, shocking audiences with its first word, *merdre* (never heard before on stage), and proceeding with obscene and madcap antics to pillory every social norm from morals to art. A couple of decades after *Ubu* came Marcel Duchamp's poke-in-the-eye-of-art urinal that he displayed in 1917 as *Fountain*, the first of his many "readymade" "artworks" flouting conventional ideas of what "art" can be (see Fig. 14). At the same time, the zany creations of Dadaism melded a mystical aesthetics with ridicule of sober-minded art and of a society that had brought the madness of World War I. On the heels of Dada's artistic improprieties came Surrealism, which dealt in dreamlike images (inspired by the "metaphysical" paintings of Giorgio de Chirico, many of which he would cavalierly replicate; see Appendix) stressing incongruity and irrationality, which produced such curiosities as the artist/showman Salvador Dali's tongue-in-cheek *Rainy Taxi*, an actual taxi with rain streaming down inside over two female mannequins.

Whatever the *serious* intentions of such artists, the pranks they produced with a wink helped to undermine the *seriousness* of high art and the very idea of *seriousness* itself. American Pop Art capped this tradition in the 1950s and 1960s with the likes of Roy Lichtenstein's paintings of cartoons, Robert Rauschenberg's soft sculptures of hamburgers, and Andy Warhol's *Campbell's Soup Cans* and *Brillo Boxes*. The jester of that movement, Warhol, brashly turned the very idea of artistic creation into something of a joke. After gaining notoriety with his takeoffs on consumer products, he pursued a life of *unseriousness* in a culture he saw suited to it. At his so-called Factory, he ground out silkscreen images of prominent figures, mainly popular performers, and pointless films of people sleeping, and invented the "Superstar" as a mockingly made-up "celebrity." Along the way, he playfully reported in a book of his "philosophy" that "After I did the thing called 'art', or whatever it's called, I went into business art" because "business is the best art." A born entertainer and spiritual heir of P. T. Barnum, Warhol personified entertainment's *unseriousness* while cashing in on it. And he was completely at home in the Culture of Entertainment that he brazenly promoted, jocularly exemplified, and profited from handsomely.

Warhol and his fellow Pop Artists also helped usher in the artistic movement of Postmodernism, which spurned the more *serious* pretentions of Modernism for a jaunty eclecticism that gleefully joined commerce, pop culture, and art with a glib irony and cheeky self-consciousness. Many modernists had drawn on commerce and pop culture, but they had usually done that with *serious* high artistic aspirations

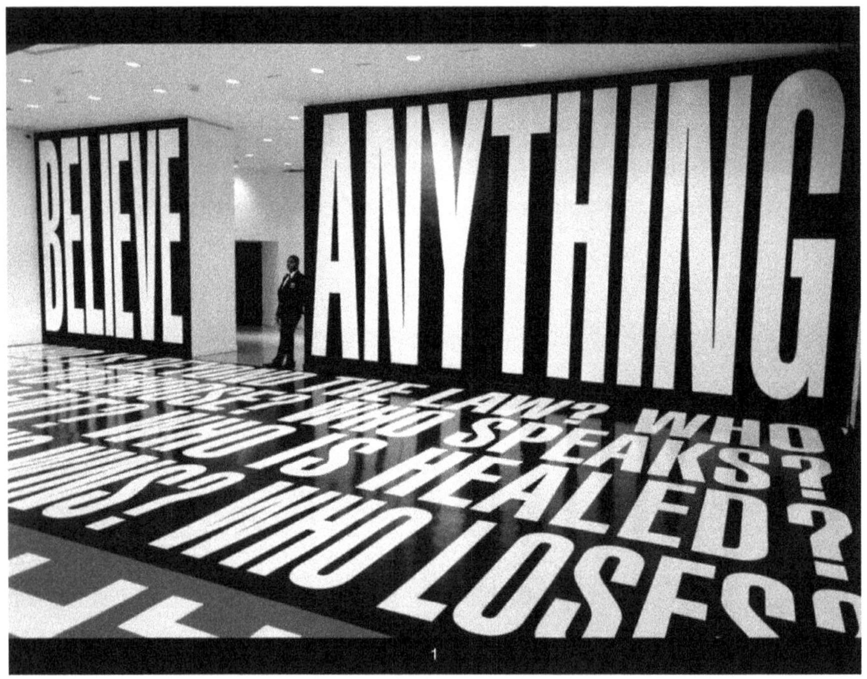

Fig. 51 — "KNOW NOTHING. BELIEVE ANYTHING. FORGET EVERYTHING." (untitled), Barbara Kruger.

Perhaps the quintessentially postmodern artwork, Kruger's first artistic version appeared in a quite surrealist work of 1987 consisting of a black-and-white photograph of a woman lying in a physician's chair having some kind of eye exam as three red stripes stamped with the six words run across the top, the bottom, and the center of the photograph. Kruger recycled those words again and again, and in 2013 organized an exhibition (seen here in part) largely around them. They are probably as much identified with her as her ironic, jokey, postmodern jab at consumerism in another artwork of 1987 that superimposed on a black-and-white photograph of a grasping hand the words in bold red letters: "I Shop Therefore I Am."

(evident in the Museum of Modern Art's exhibit "High and Low: Modern Art and Popular Culture"). The self-consciously radical ideology of Postmodernism rejected such *seriousness* and promoted *unseriousness* as the apt postmodern cast of mind. This ideology also produced fads in philosophy and literary theory, spawned by *à la mode* French intellectuals like Jacques Derrida and Jean Baudrillard, that all but banished objective truth altogether. All of these postmodernist ideas sanctioned every subjective and relativistic idea of truth, just as they allowed anything to be art (see Fig. 51). As the critic Denis Donoghue astutely concluded (in a survey of the subject for the *New York Times Book Review* in 1986), "there is a certain weightlessness in postmodernism that makes it possible for an artist to do anything that he chooses . . . like a game without rules." And *a game without rules* is inherently *unserious*. The title of the encyclopedic and emblematic postmodern novel by David Foster Wallace captured the ironic, amused, and *unserious* postmodern spirit of the times: *Infinite Jest* (1996).

The *unseriousness* of Postmodernism could be said to crown the tradition that had undermined, where it had not overtly assailed, the *seriousness* of art in the West. This *unseriousness* fit the *unseriousness* of the Culture of Entertainment as though they had been made for each other. And to a degree they were. But Postmodernism by that name was a phase of culture, whereas the Culture of Entertainment, by any name, has been rising for a long time and has long outlasted the heyday of Postmodernism. At all events, we now take up the attitude of *unseriousness* that the Culture of Entertainment fosters, and a few troubling instances of its *serious* consequences in the real world.

The Unseriousness *of Entertainment and Its Consequences*

Begin here: Entertainment promotes an attitude of *unseriousness* simply by being entertainment. For when the mind games of the art experience take us into the frame of entertainment we arrive in a realm of fantasy outside the world, where the intellect goes passive and fantasy goes to town, where anything is possible and yet nothing really matters because nothing has real-world consequences. This means nothing within the frame requires any more *seriousness* than a child's game. The reigning rule in the mind games of entertainment, like child's play, is that the real-world not intrude to dissolve the frame. That rule shields the entertainment experience from real-world threats that could break the frame, such as contradictions, incoherence, truth, facts, or unsettling realities in any form. And the more of that experience and its mind games we indulge in, the more likely we will be to carry their effects into the real world with us, whether we know it or not. When that happens, we can treat life itself as though it is mere entertainment with no *serious* consequences. This shows up in a "So what?" response to nearly anything, regardless of how unintelligible or ridiculous or grave—just as we accept the "movie logic" of many movies, with their sudden shifts of scenes, illogical plot lines, rambling action sequences, and tacked-on endings, all epitomized in the very title of the self-consciously incoherent film awarded the Oscar for Best Picture of 2022: *Everything, Everywhere, All at Once*. To outrageous ideas and denials of facts, to contradictions and lies, to the infection of our cultural life by entertainment, we tend more and more to shrug, chuckle, and, in effect, say, "So what?"

The author Hermann Hesse had anticipated this attitude back in the 1920s in a memorable scene of his novel *Steppenwolf*. The book tells the strange story of a man named Harry Haller who is "caught between two ages": the fading age of high culture that he reveres, exemplified by monumental figures like Goethe and Mozart, and the new age of vulgar popular culture surrounding him with jazz clubs, dance halls, and other allurements to shallow sensuous and sensual pleasures, which at once disgust and entice him. That ambivalence toward popular culture reflects a conflict he recognizes within himself between an ascetic intellectuality and the instinctual appetites he identifies with a wolf of the Steppes. Through one dreamlike episode after another in the "Magic Theater for Madmen Only," he struggles with himself and with his times. Toward the end, his hero Mozart appears and reappears, always laughing. In his last entrance, Mozart carries a portable radio that distortedly, scratchily, hideously blares out a performance of music by Handel. Harry Haller is appalled that Mozart, of all people, would "inflict this mess" on anyone, this desecration of great music, this "victorious weapon in the war of extermination against art." But Mozart only laughs and chides Harry for taking things too *seriously*. Instead of being so *serious*, Mozart scoffs, Harry "must apprehend the humor of life, its gallows-humor." Then he will "learn to listen to more of the cursed radio music of life and to reverence the spirit behind it and to laugh at its distortions" (see Fig. 47). After all, it doesn't really matter.*

Learn to laugh at the radio music of life. That could be a credo of the Culture of Entertainment. Don't take anything too *seriously* because nothing within the frame of entertainment has real-world consequences. And in the Culture of Entertainment, that frame is coming to enclose almost everything.

We might object that, if people were to treat everything that happens in the real world as *unseriously* as entertainment, they would eventually pay a price, because what happens in the real world can have *serious* consequences. And we would be right. For, as suggested earlier, the attitude of *unseriousness* can in itself have very *serious* real-world consequences. This could well be the most insidious effect that the mind games of entertainment can have.

As a troubling example, think of the young males who act out their resentments and fantasies with dramatic acts of violence. We have seen this in Mark David Chapman and John Hinckley, as well as in the perpetrators of mass shootings that have become achingly familiar in recent years. These young men might have been deadly *serious* about their intent to kill, but I dare say this *seriousness* was for them as much or more

---

* Were a reader to ask how Laurence Sterne's celebration of laughter in *Tristram Shandy* compares to the laughter of Hesse's Mozart at the radio music of life, here is what I would say: Laughing at the radio music of life amounts to a thin and resigned cynical laughter expressing a sense that nothing matters in this world, so we might as well shrug, chuckle, and go on our way; by contrast, Sterne celebrated good-hearted laughter that affirms human life because that life *does* matter, and good-hearted laughter helps us live it well. If readers also want to know how Sterne's laughter goes with the attitude of *seriousness* that could seem at odds with it, I might say this: The good-hearted laughter Sterne extolls is *serious* laughter, for he sees that this laughter has *serious* consequences in the world, namely, good-hearted laughter makes the world better, whereas cruel laughter, sardonic laughter, resigned and cynical laughter do not. If this means that Sterne's *Tristram Shandy* belongs more to high art than to low, so be it.

that of a playing a game than it was the *seriousness* of weighing consequences in the real world. That is to say, a certain *unseriousness* colored their attitude toward the real-world consequences of their actions. To punch a previous point, they saw killing people as a performance guaranteed to make them famous in a society they believed values celebrity above all other human qualities—a performance that would make them "stars" in the pseudo-reality of their own reality show outside the real world. So, as *seriously* as these killers might take their performances and their hopes of becoming celebrities, they are quite *unserious* about the *serious* real-world consequences of their acts for other people.

We can see a sickeningly perverse, and painfully apposite, variation on treating *serious* real-world consequences with the *unseriousness* of entertainment in the case of the rabid conspiracy theorist Alex Jones. He had made a fortune purveying shameless falsehoods and groundless accusations on the radio to gullible Americans for years. Then, in late 2012 he added an unimaginably wicked one. He started broadcasting crazy assertions that the horrendous Sandy Hook school mass shooting, which had just taken the lives of twenty children and six adults, was itself nothing but theater and that the grieving families were only playing roles. "It's as phony as a three-dollar bill," he declared, a setup by the government "to get our guns."[30] In making these heated charges, he was, of course, performing for a radio audience that put money in his pocket—lots of it. And he was doing this with a "So what?" indifference toward not only the falseness of his words but to the real-world consequences those words could have. Jones thought of this as entertainment only pretending to be *serious*—it was the *unserious seriousness* of a game, the game of entertainment. But his avid listeners took him very *seriously*, or, rather, they let the mind games of entertainment become their reality—just as they had accepted his other fantastic conspiracy theories—and some of them started harassing the Sandy Hook parents with death threats and other nastiness. Eventually, resolute parents took Jones to court, and ten years after the tragedy they won substantial damages for the real-world consequences of his words. Although he finally grudgingly—and *unseriously*—apologized, he seemed baffled and affronted that his multi-million-dollar media empire could be threatened in the *real world* over what he regarded as an entertainment that could not do anyone, least of all him, any harm. Or he didn't care—except for harm to himself.

And Jones's haughty *unseriousness* would not die. He defiantly resisted paying the damages by placing his financial resources in the hands of allies and shielding himself behind bankruptcy laws, assuring his addled fans that he would fearlessly carry on his radio show and that the "jerks" who had taken him to court would get nothing. He might prove right in the end. But could this whole affair have happened before the Culture of Entertainment made *unseriousness* about the real-world consequences of practically anything—except making money—a familiar way of thinking? Not likely.

The case of Alex Jones made news because courageous parents managed to hold him accountable for the *serious* consequences of his *unseriousness* in treating everything as entertainment. Countless other performers of harmful *unseriousness* for personal gain have escaped that fate as they have purveyed politically charged lies for profit in the guise of entertainment. No one proved this more conspicuously or arrogantly than Rush Limbaugh. This witty, hate-mongering, right-wing ideologue, whose blather reigned on talk radio for two decades, persistently brushed away criticism of his false and violent rhetoric with the glib defense that he was just an "entertainer." Limbaugh's popularity, like that of Alex Jones and other political "entertainers," demonstrates how effective, deceptive, and dangerous the attitude of *unseriousness* can be when masked as entertainment and feigning *seriousness*. But nowhere are the real-world consequences of this attitude more prominent—in no small part owing to those political "entertainers"—than in our recent political life. Consequences that for many people are ominously *serious*, but for other people are almost laughably *unserious*.

The political career of Donald Trump supplies more evidence of this than anyone could need or want. But because that career exemplifies, with historic reverberations, the damage the mind games of entertainment and their attitude of *unseriousness* can do, I will let a sampling from Trump's presidency, culminating in the events of January 6, 2021, take us to the end of these reflections on politics in the Culture of Entertainment. The chapter will then close with a short coda on the place in this culture of Artificial Intelligence and Virtual Reality devices, followed by an Epilogue on some prospects for the future.

The Politics of Entertainment and Unseriousness

It is no surprise that Trump launched his political career from his role as host of a so-called reality television show that feigned reality with the *serious unseriousness* of a game. In fact, this was a game, where purportedly uncoached contestants vied for positions in Trump's business empire. The host's performance climaxed each week with a histrionic hand gesture and the exclamation "You're fired!" as he winnowed the contestants down to the winner. If the payoff for the winner had a shadow of reality, it was a shadow in an empire of lies, fraud, and Trump's craven pursuit of wealth and celebrity, as Trump's competitors well knew and as subsequent events and legal cases have proven. Going from a television "reality" game show to politics was a short step for this tireless performer, of course, since so much of political life had itself become something of a reality show. And he performed politically with his own audacious style and the entertainer's *unseriousness* as someone born to play the part. He demonstrated this right off the bat. For instance, after launching his campaign for president, he boasted at a rally in January 2016 that he was already so popular he "could stand in the middle of Fifth Avenue and shoot somebody, and I wouldn't lose any voters, OK?" He could be *unserious* even about shooting people! But he must have been right, for he went on to win the election and become president, or, as pundits wryly observed, Entertainer-in-Chief.

Outrageous assertions and bald-faced lies—which he learned from the writer who wrote his book *The Art of the Deal* for him to euphemize, or misrepresent, as "truthful hyperbole"—typified his style, for sure, as it had his business career and personal life. But his political devotees persistently defended him by saying, "We take what he says *seriously* but not literally." In other words: "He doesn't mean what he says and is only putting on a show, so his words don't really matter and we can attach *seriousness* to any of them we choose." Such *unserious seriousness* must have come as easily to them as it did to him. One might well wonder if either he or they truly believed anything he said. But then, the point is not if he believed what he said, but that *he didn't care* about the consequences of his words—other than winning fans and "ratings" (in politics no less than on television). A journalist who had closely observed Trump as president and his allies concluded that none of them seemed to care. "The truth of this scam, or 'joke,'" he wrote of Trump's performance, "was fully evident inside the club" where everyone "got the joke."[31] And "'Getting the joke,'" added a *New York Times* columnist, meant "understanding that nothing you say need be true, that nobody expects it to be true."[32] A former Republican strategist saw the same cavalier attitude and named the supporters around the president "Nothing Matters Republicans." For they thought of themselves playing "some big game devoid of real-world consequences," where everything that happens is "all part of the Game."[33]

Some big game devoid of real-world consequences. Exactly. But that game turned out to have very *serious* real-world consequences, indeed. Historic consequences at that. For on January 6, 2021, Trump's *unserious* "game" of politics as entertainment turned into an attack on the nation's Capitol and on the tradition of American democracy unlike anything seen before. The president and his supporters might laugh away those events or otherwise dismiss them as not really *serious.* But history will not—short of successful Orwellian efforts to rewrite it, which Trump and his allies would eagerly do if given the chance. I will conclude with a brief look at the events of that remarkable day and their aftermath as salient symptoms of the insidious *unseriousness* that marks the mind games of the Culture of Entertainment.

On the morning of January 6, 2021, a crowd of some thirty thousand people gathered on the ellipse south of the White House in Washington, D.C., and at least that many more stood beyond the ellipse toward the Washington monument, for a rally by the outgoing president to protest the election results that had brought his defeat. And, just as four years earlier he had boasted that the crowd at his inauguration had been of record size, vastly larger than in fact it was, as anyone could see, now he

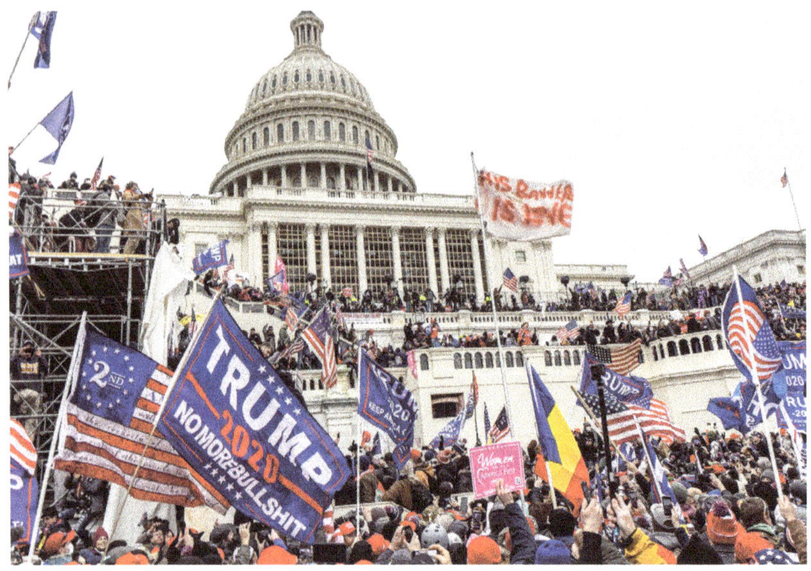

Fig. 52 A — The assault on the Capitol by crazed and celebratory Trump supporters, January 6, 2021. (Photo: Alex Kent, Louisiana Illuminator, *January 8, 2021.)*

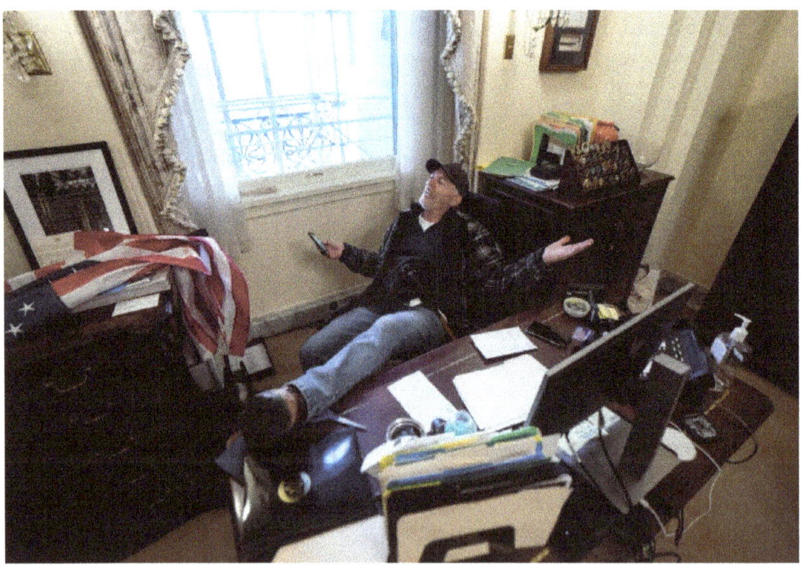

Fig. 52 B — A rioter who invaded the Capitol lounging theatrically and grinning proudly in the desk chair of Speaker of the House, Nancy Pelosi, January 6, 2021—obligatory American flag draped nearby, and cell phone at the ready to "share" the triumph. He (Richard "Bigo" Barnett) later claimed that he had been pushed inside the Capitol against his will by the crowd, and his lawyers contended he had then simply wandered into Pelosi's office while looking for a bathroom. A jury quickly found his defense laughable. He was convicted and sentenced to four-and-a-half years in prison for his actions that day.

perversely insisted—as he had been doing since the election, but now more angrily and ostentatiously—that he had actually won the election by a landslide, which was stolen from him by fraud. And he urged the crowd to "Stop the Steal" (a marketing slogan like the one he had copyrighted during his first campaign, "Make America Great Again," popularized as MAGA) of his victory by marching to the Capitol building to prevent the vice president and Congress from certifying the election results, a symbolic procedure required by the Constitution. He vowed to lead them there, but Secret Service agents prevented him for security reasons, provoking his petulant rage and indignant shouts that he was the president and should get his way, and that he would not be in danger anyway because "These are my people." Were they ever. Thousands of them charged up to the Capitol and some two thousand stormed the building, overwhelming the police, breaking in through doors and windows then racing down hallways, ransacking offices, and furiously searching for the vice president, whom the president had accused of betrayal for refusing to abandon the ceremonial duty of completing the certification (see Fig. 52 A).

Did Trump really believe he had won the election but that it had been stolen from him by fraudulent voting? Did he really believe he could change the results by getting his followers to storm the Capitol, seize the vice president, and stop the congressional certification? Did he actually grasp what he was urging them to do and what would happen if they did it? On the evidence of people around him, he actually knew he had lost the election and had vented his rage and dismay at that reality. But, again, *he didn't care* about the facts or the potentially bad consequences of his words or actions. For him, it was all part of the "game," the entertainment, the narcissistic performance of his presidency, and he wanted the performance to go on, viewing the consequences of his words and actions with the airy *unseriousness* of Entertainer-in-Chief.

Even the rioters who had taken those words *seriously* enough to act on them seem to have done so with only the *unserious seriousness* and *serious unseriousness* of a game or an entertainment. Most sported the bright red MAGA hats signaling membership on the Trump team; some who invaded the Capitol building also wore colorful regalia of their rebellion; and many happily posed for pictures in conquered congressional offices (see Fig. 52 B), several of them ostentatiously waving or wrapped in American flags. A number of their leaders were, to be sure, long-standing white-nationalist "patriots" animated by racial grievances and an anti-democratic ideology. And for three decades right-wing authors, pundits, radio talk show hosts, and the most popular cable news network had been purveying screeds of hatred and fabricated accusations of treason, hostility to the true America, and other nefarious offenses committed by the political Left. Perhaps the white nationalists did believe the vicious ideology they acted on. But did the right-wing-media demagogues believe the incendiary messages they had been broadcasting? Once again, more to the point: Did they care? It seems that they neither wholly believed it nor did they care. They had learned they could, like Rush Limbaugh and Alex Jones, make a lot of money from their "entertaining" performances, which was apparently the only real-world consequence that mattered to them, and that if they muddied the waters with too much truth, the audiences they had won with provocative lies and phony outrage might leave them.

Fox News discovered this on election night 2020 after reporting, prior to other networks, that Democrat Joe Biden had won Arizona. This instance of political integrity by the news division of Fox (by contrast to the factitious, money-making ideological shows) prompted defections from the network by viewers deaf to undesirable realities, driving down ratings and alarming executives, who hastily decided that, above all, they had to "protect the brand." Pandering to those viewers, Fox then fell in line with the Big Lie that Trump had won reelection but that his victory had been stolen by fraud. Fox commentators even falsely blamed a voting machine company for helping to perpetrate that fraud.

But that last accusation proved to be an untruth too far. The voting machine company sued Fox for defamation, and the discovery process prior to the trial revealed (through emails and text messages) that, as Fox executives had scrambled to restore their top ratings after the election, no one at Fox really believed the Great Lie or the charges against the voting machine company. Even so, that didn't matter to Fox executives who saw that to "protect the brand" they would have to give their viewers what they wanted. And those viewers wanted politically appealing untruth posing as truth. If that included false charges against a voting machine company and the American election system, "So what?" But these revelations became such a public relations embarrassment for Fox that executives suddenly settled the law suit to curtail the damage only hours before the trial was about to begin. To further curb the self-inflicted cost, Fox also fired the popular commentator Tucker Carlson, who had most blatantly repeated lies on the air about the alleged election fraud, lies contradicted by his own private communications (disclosing, in addition, his intense racism, which the network feared would further weaken its legal defense). Still, Fox admitted no wrongdoing in disseminating the reckless falsehoods that would lead to the events of January 6th.[34]

At all events, the rioters who assaulted the Capitol that day did not come from out of the blue. They had plenty of exploitative, self-serving, and disingenuous media "entertainers" to egg them on. They also had orders from a president whose lies they had chosen to believe, and who had urged them to become performers in the reality show of his Big Lie. And while the assault went on, this president did exactly what we might expect him to do: he sat watching that reality show unfold on television in events he had set in motion. That he would rebuff advice to call off the rioters was entirely in character. He wanted to wait for the end of the show to see if it would turn out according to his script. Finally, hours later, conceding that the show was not going to wind up that way, he reluctantly yielded. But he did not change his tune, or his performance. Even as he told his rioting followers in a televised address to go home, he praised them for their actions and repeated the Big Lie that the election had been stolen from him.

For Trump, the events of January 6th amounted to little more than another episode in the reality show of his presidency—if an episode that his irresponsible words could not, in the end, quite bring to the denouement he had desired. He viewed those events (on television, no less) as an entertainment with no *serious* consequences in the real world. The rioters seem to have thought that way too. For, besides cavorting inside the Capitol with the *unseriousness* of entertainment, they evidently thought their actions would have no *serious* adverse consequences *for them* in the real world. When arrested on the evidence of their filmed "performances" they lied about what they had done as readily as Trump could lie about anything, claiming they had merely engaged in a peaceful protest. One rioter cagily asserted that he didn't even know the U.S. Congress met in the Capitol. For them, the show was not really over, just moving on to another episode. And any consequences of their actions were part of the entertainment, outside the real world. Or we could say that, in the mind games they were playing, the show had *become* the real world. The *unseriousness* of entertainment reigned in their minds, leading them, like Trump himself, to treat even the *serious* real-world consequences of their actions that day with that same invincible *unseriousness*.

This attitude would also infect—and for many of the same reasons—most of the president's political party and congressional Republicans in the aftermath of the Capitol invasion. The Minority Leader (soon to become Speaker, but at the cost of draconian concessions to right-wing extremists, who ousted him nine months later for not sufficiently submitting to their their desires) in the House of Representatives, Kevin McCarthy, at first deplored the events and exhorted the president to put an end to them. But before long, he, like so many of his colleagues, would change his mind and dismiss what happened at the Capitol that day as nothing but a political protest of no special import and to be forgotten. For these politicians, like the rest of the now-former-president's supporters, the events of January 6th had no *serious* real-world consequences to be concerned about after all.

When we ask how McCarthy and many of his Republican colleagues could have so readily changed their minds, the answer is not far to seek. Their voters (and some of those colleagues) demanded it. In thrall to the drumbeat of right-wing propaganda and to the conspiracy theories that thrive in a fact-free environment, and to the mind games of entertainment that had let them accept the Entertainer-in-Chief's mendacious performances and haughty *unseriousness*, those voters did not care about consequences of the president's performance that day or any other. They just wanted the performance to go on. And they would punish any politician who didn't serve their wishes, just as viewers (who were, of course, many of the same people) would punish Fox News for reporting anything contrary to the ideological propaganda the "brand" was known for. So, whatever rationalizations Republican leaders told themselves, they decided to support Trump and play the "big game devoid of real-world consequences"—devoid of such consequences, that is, except for placating voters and selfishly clinging to political power. They made the same concession to those voters that Fox did to its viewers: what ratings and profits were to Fox and other right-wing media outlets, votes and power were to Republican politicians, truth be damned.

The aftermath of January 6th for these Republicans, like Trump, therefore became very much a netherworld of impervious unreality, where the president was still victorious, where election fraud by the Left had stolen the victory, where such (imaginary) fraud must be prevented everywhere in the future by curtailing voting access, and where the events of January 6th didn't really matter. Kevin McCarthy redoubled his defense of the indefensible, as did the right-wing media led by Fox News, which aired ever more strident versions of that defense—despite private rejection of the Big Lie by even its most extreme commentators, as we have seen. McCarthy would even give one of those commentators, Tucker Carlson, reams of unpublished testimony from the subsequent congressional investigation of the Capitol assault, which Carlson edited and broadcast to support the absurd claim (popular among Fox viewers and Republican politicians) that no assault had occurred but that the events amounted to nothing more than the curious prowling of "orderly and meek" sightseers.[35] These persistent public denials of reality attest again that in the entertainment world of Fox News—which included most Republicans and much of the country—there were (and are) no *serious* real-world consequences of anything to care about except television ratings. And that so many Americans live in that world can only mean the mind games of entertainment that foster the attitude of *unseriousness* have become widely habitual.

But the consequences of January 6th were *serious* indeed—even, as it turned out, for Fox News when the network had to pay nearly a billion dollars to settle the defamation suit brought by the falsely accused voting machine company, although these legal consequences were slight compared to the threat to American democracy. As many critics have painfully observed, for the first time in American history, a president defeated at the polls had refused to concede and peacefully pass the baton to the victor. Instead of following tradition, he used every shenanigan he and his allies could come up with to hang onto power, marshalling ever more lies, assailing the democratic election system, and pressuring public officials to change ballot counts, all culminating in the rebellious riot of his fanatical fans who assaulted the Capitol. The congressional investigation into the events of January 6th gathered copious evidence of every step the president took toward his desired goal. And the dramatic public hearings that presented the evidence made the disturbing facts undeniable—at least to anyone living in the real world.

And yet, those hearings possessed a certain irony. An irony that must be acknowledged. It is this: Determined to drive home to the American people the truth of the president's errant actions, the committee holding the hearings knew that this truth would have to be presented on television, and as nothing less than entertainment. Otherwise, the public's attention would flag. The hearings would therefore use entertainment to demonstrate that the president who had risen to national prominence on the *unseriousness* of entertainment, and had governed as a kind of entertainer, had actually done the country *serious* harm in the real world. A nice irony, to be sure. And one possible only in a Culture of Entertainment. To achieve its purpose, the committee hired a television producer to create a compelling TV drama. Under his adroit guidance, staff members distilled countless hours of testimony and bushels of documents, punctuated with memorable appearances by firsthand observers of the president's behavior, into several professionally produced episodes arranged by theme and presented like a television series, complete with nifty titles and teasers for the next episode. It was, indubitably, arresting entertainment, and *serious* entertainment, or as *serious* as television entertainment can get. But, presented as entertainment, notwithstanding its *serious* drama, the hearings made one wonder if they would produce the *serious* consequences in the real world that the committee had intended or if, instead, the hearings would become just last year's ephemeral entertainment.

Predictably, and with no sense of irony, Trump and his followers denounced the hearings as nothing but a partisan show, a mere TV entertainment. And, although hit with a host of legal prosecutions for his election-related misdeeds, he went on theatrically to campaign for a return of his reality show to the White House, intoning the same Big Lie and rallying his troops to redress his fraudulent loss and send him there for a second act in 2024.

(As of the time this book went to press in early 2024, Trump had been charged with ninety-one felony counts in criminal trials from New York, Washington, D.C., Georgia, and Florida for his actions to overturn the election and other violations of the law—in addition to civil charges in New York for business fraud. And yet, he was not only overwhelmingly favored to win the Republican nomination for President but he led in polls to defeat President Biden in a rematch, promising to get revenge on the "vermin" who had opposed him and even to "terminate" the Constitution. His second act would surely spell the end of American democracy as we have known it since the Founding. But his addled followers didn't care. So, whatever Trump's future in American political life, the attitude of *unseriousness* that he thrived on and encouraged is likely to persist.)

The behavior of Trump as president and especially from the election to January 6th and its aftermath—to which we could add the years from then to 2024—has elicited many sober judgments condemning him as narcissistic, autocratic, contemptuous of the Constitution, dangerously ignorant of the international world, indifferent to facts and reality, and a threat to America's democratic institutions and traditions such as the country has never seen, and more. Such judgments are all accurate. But threaded through all of Trump's behavior, I would say, is also—and nothing is more pronounced or consequential than this—the attitude of *unseriousness* that goes with the Culture of Entertainment.

I would add the charge that Trump's career and the events of January 6th, as well as the aftermath of those events and the televised congressional hearings examining those events and their causes, demonstrate one thing for certain. It is that American political life increasingly inhabits the Culture of Entertainment. And this fact (as I think of it) presents us with two political alternatives: Will the *serious* reality of Trump's wayward political career and the events of January 6th prove to be salutary warnings of the fragility of American democracy, despite the Culture of Entertainment with its insidious attitude of *unseriousness*? Or will that culture and its *unseriousness* strengthen their hold and strangle American democracy as though it doesn't matter anymore, because in the Culture of Entertainment nothing has real-world consequences? We should think very *seriously* about those alternatives.

Conclusion

By now any reader is bound to ask: Are the mind games of entertainment alone to blame for the events of January 6th and everything else identified here as sorry conditions of our times, from the decline of effort and objectivity to the ascent of *unseriousness*? And, as with the previous question about entertainment impairing cognitive abilities, we must answer: No. All historical events and situations arise from multiple causes. But we should also ask: Would the events and those conditions have come to pass without the pervasive effects of entertainment? Again, the answer must be: No. As historians would say, entertainment might not be the *sufficient* cause (enough by itself) of our situation, but it is a *necessary* cause (without it the events and conditions would not have occurred). For who can honestly doubt that a society as awash in entertainment as ours would show widespread signs of what we could call the entertainment mentality, with its mind games that take us out of the world, encourage mental passivity and stimulate fantasy, freely deny or disregard facts, logic, and objectivity, and foster an attitude of *unseriousness*? And who can doubt that these signs would show up across the culture and deeply affect politics? Add to these probable results, the likelihood that, with new technologies of communications and entertainment arriving almost daily in a rising tide, we will sink ever deeper beneath the waves of the Culture of Entertainment.

That tide of novel technologies has even brought two perfect symbols of that culture and the mind games of entertainment. Both are very recent inventions. One is Artificial Intelligence (AI). AI can do astonishing things with unimaginable quantities of information extending from mere facts to sounds, pictures, and words. And with a few cues it can create alternative realities, or unreal realities, indistinguishable from the real thing—like writing documents, composing music and poetry, and fashioning entire artificial worlds. These powers render AI capable of doing much good, such as aiding doctors in diagnosing and treating disease. But it can also be a frightening tool of misinformation and misrepresentation, like creating videos of actual people doing things they would never do in reality. AI therefore almost entirely blurs the line, made fuzzy already by older technologies, commerce, and art, between truth and illusion, reality and fantasy, life and art. Appropriately named, *Artificial* Intelligence all but completes the passage from a world of nature and actual things to a world of images and technological artifice. In the future, AI will make it harder and harder even to think about such distinctions. And could discourage even trying—adding yet another "So what?" to the Culture of Entertainment.

The second new technological symbol of the Culture of Entertainment—and its enticements through mind games to escape the real world's demands and *serious* consequences—is a relative of AI. It is known as "Virtual Reality." Going far beyond the pseudo-reality of so-called "reality television," we can now steep ourselves in Virtual Reality provided by devices that we can strap on like futuristic goggles. These ingenious Virtual Reality machines enable entertainment and its mind games to take us farther outside the restraints of the real world than ever. They make it possible for people to live mentally in a "Virtual Reality" of anything they desire. Do you want to be in a movie or in a perfect world or be a princess or a heroic warrior or a great lover? Just strap on the machine—or strap yourself into a special equipped chair or into a full-body device, as some machines allow—and you can be, at least in your mind and senses. All you have to do is let your fantasies fly and the machine will take you away, playing the mind games of entertainment with you. Or, to save yourself even the trouble of generating your own fantasies, you can get them supplied by the machine on all kinds of themes (see Fig. 53).

Like AI, Virtual Reality machines bridge the distance between reality

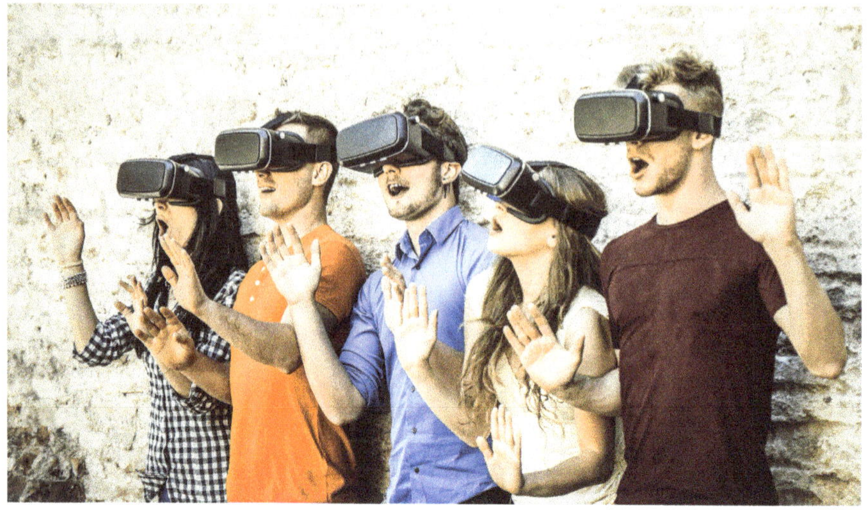

Fig. 53 — Virtual Reality headsets take people out of the real world into a world of fantasy more "realistic" than any before. Such devices almost play the mind games of entertainment for us. (Advertisement for Toucan Systems, Virtual Reality equipment, 2019.)

and unreality. And if AI will make it ever more difficult to distinguish reality from unreality, Virtual Reality machines will make it ever easier not to care. The Culture of Entertainment has only to implant AI mechanisms and Virtual Reality devices inside peoples' heads to make its triumph over traditional reality and humanity complete. And, of course, no one will notice, or care. How could they?*

To be sure, as history moves on it will bring new permutations of the Culture of Entertainment. And, who knows, that culture might even one day run its course and expire. Think about that. Could it happen? How? A few thoughts on possibilities in the Epilogue will bring this little book to a close.

* This might not be too far from Aldous Huxley's dystopian vision in *Brave New World*, but Huxley did not foresee the Culture of Entertainment with its mind games and its inventive technologies as the road to dystopia.

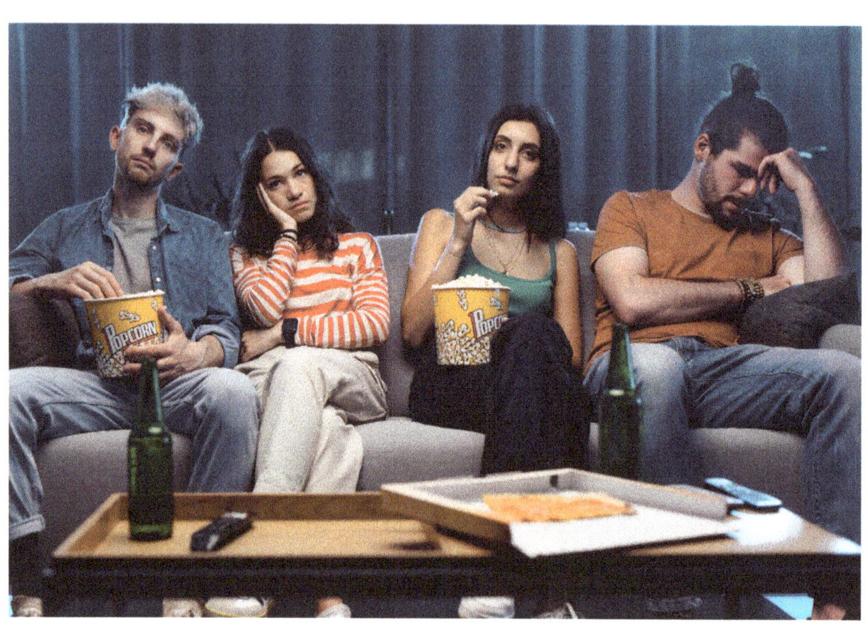

Fig. 54 — Young people bored by the television they watch, but they cannot seem to bring themselves to turn it off, as though numbed into submission to whatever flickers across the screen. A scene foreshadowed by that of the contentedly mesmerized family gathered around a TV in its early days (see Fig. 48).

Epilogue: What Now?

"So what?"

Although we could live without art and the art experience, both high and low, we could not live well. For, as shown above, in freeing us from demands of the real world, the art experience and its mind games allow us to do things we could not otherwise do, or not do as beneficially, from enjoying the ready pleasures of low art to engaging in the more demanding stimulations of high art. But, as we have also seen, even some benefits of the art experience can become too much of a good thing. The high-art experience can, for instance, become an end in itself, making the love of art and aesthetics the very meaning of life, diminishing the value of everything else. But the low-art experience can do more harm than that. This harm derives from the very nature of low art, which thrives on the human hunger for pleasurable escape from the burdens of the real world. That escape in itself is not a bad thing, and might even be salutary—remember Aristotle's idea of "amusement" as necessary rest from toil. But when we make it an end in itself. bad things can happen. For in enticing us to escape as far outside the real world as the mind games of low art can take us, those mind games can induce habits of mental laxness, an insatiable appetite for passive pleasures and unbridled fantasy, and a corrosive attitude of *unseriousness* toward the consequences of anything. Is this not, in fact, what the low-art experience—promoted by the far-reaching commercial entertainment industry—has increasingly shaped people to want: escape from the real world's challenges and consequences through entertainment? And is this not increasingly the very purpose of life in the Culture of Entertainment?

These questions bring us back to those posed at the end of the previous chapter: Is there any reason to think this condition will not continue? Could something happen, or be done, to change our course? Perhaps there is. I have no intention of trying to spell out remedies. Instead, I'll just identify a couple of possibilities. Here is one: Boredom.

For all of its appealing enticements, easy gratifications, and the necessary reprieve it provides from the effort of living in the real world, the low-art experience of entertainment cannot truly fulfill our lives any more than can resting from toil. Human beings need many kinds of stimulation, not just the largely passive pleasures supplied by commercial entertainments, whatever ephemeral excitements these might deliver. How long, for instance, can anyone watch television or listen to pop music without getting restless? Even with the physical lethargy and mental inertia that large doses of entertainment can induce, making it hard to do anything else, in time, a certain sense of surfeit likely sets in, along with at least a hint of self-disgust from sloth, followed by a yen for some kind of activity. That betrays boredom (see Fig. 54).

Paradoxically, since the Culture of Entertainment has tended to lessen concentration and shorten attention spans, we would expect boredom to set in faster than ever. And it does—like the students in a music appreciation class who complained that Chopin's "Minute Waltz" was "boring," prompting the teacher to exclaim: "How can you get bored in one minute?" (An apocryphal anecdote, no doubt, since Chopin wrote a *miniature* waltz, to be played in a couple of minutes, never in one minute). Well, one or two minutes with insufficient thrills, of the kind those students had become habituated to by entertainment in all its modern varieties, was too long for them to bear. That habituation is surely a principal reason the entertainment industry constantly ups the ante of superficial stimulation with ever more sensorily exciting movies, offbeat television fare on countless channels, spectacular and deafening pop music concerts, mesmerizing video games, exciting theme park activities, as well as technological novelties like Virtual Reality machines. But, as just observed, increased doses of superficial stimulation could turn out to be an intolerably boring way for people to spend their time, even if it gives them escape into entertainment from the exigencies of the real world.

Consequently, the day might come when enough people will get bored with the Culture of Entertainment and all it—largely through its corporate promoters—deploys to hold their attention. They will want more genuine and lasting gratifications, more satisfying mental, emotional, and imaginative stimulation, and more art experiences suited to the real world than are the fleeting escapist pleasures of entertainment. And they will cry: *Wake up* from the entertainment-induced sleep that amounts to a kind of cultural death! *No more* entertainment everywhere. *No more* pursuit of mere passive pleasures. *No more* omnipresent inducements to mental laxness and effortlessness. *No more* life-sapping lethargy and dulling of the senses from artificial overstimulation. *No more* exaltation of fantasy over reality. *No more* cult of appearances and celebrity. *No more* blurring of distinctions between truth and falsehood. *No more* dismissive unseriousness toward real-world consequences of actions and ideas. *No more* laughing at the radio music of life as though nothing matters.

A cultural revolution like that might be a lot to expect from boredom. But history has seen epidemics of boredom, or *ennui* as the French call it with a cutting edge, that have erupted to dramatic ends. World War I was perhaps the most historic of these, following upon decades of complaints about cultural decline and mutterings of *ennui* among the young rising to a crescendo of martial fervor. As the bold Futurist F. T. Marinetti declared in a book title of 1909, *War: The Only Hygiene of the World*. Young men all over Europe rallied to the call, feeling bored with peacetime and hungering for heroics and cultural renewal. "Come and die," exulted the poet Rupert Brooke to a friend as he embarked for embattled shores, "It'll be great fun"—he did die, but it wasn't much fun in the grotesque and mismanaged war, as his decimated generation of eager young warriors soon learned. Later, the cultural revolution of the 1960s was also fueled by a younger generation bored with things as they were, angered at an "Establishment" deaf to their voices, and yearning for an ideal world. Perhaps boredom like that could mount high enough to overthrow or undermine the Culture of Entertainment.

Besides boredom, there are other potential sources of change, too. These are pretty obvious and come down to awakening people to what is happening to them. That could start with opening their eyes to the mind games of the art experience, high and low, how we play them, and how they play us, for good and ill. And above all, how the mind games of the entertainment experience can give us such thorough freedom from the mental demands of the real world that they can instill habits of mind that work against us in the real world, impairing our ability to live full lives in that world, eroding the integrity of politics, and undoing sinews of a serious culture.

In fact, many colleges now offer courses along those lines. These can be found mainly in Communications departments that study the influence of the media and entertainment on American life. The critic Neil Postman was a pioneer of such courses. The authors of the encyclopedic textbook *Entertainment and Society: Influences, Impacts, and Innovations* wrote it for similar courses to lay out manifold issues involved in understanding the Culture of Entertainment. We have also seen some of the critical books that have ably targeted entertainment for damaging American society. We can only hope that, through such books and academic courses, or by whatever means, one day we will have a populace aware of the subtle powers and insidious perils—mental, emotional, cultural, political—of the Culture of Entertainment and the mind games it thrives on, and that people will act to curtail those powers and head off those perils. That would entail, among other things, working to preserve the objective reality of truth and falsehood, ensuring respect for the difference between reality and fantasy, and banishing the attitude of *unseriousness* that dismisses real-world consequences of actions, ideas, and of entertainment itself. That is a happy prospect.

And yet, to be *realistic*, I fear that neither boredom nor schooling nor critical books will be enough. For the Culture of Entertainment has showed remarkable resilience and capacities to offer new enticements to an all too malleable human nature. After all, as numerous critics have illustrated, that culture has invaded the schools and has made concentrated reading and deep thought ever harder to muster. We must also recognize that the Culture of Entertainment has gained sway not so much because people are unaware of entertainment's powers and perils as because consumer capitalism, which did so much to create that culture, has a very large financial stake in making it continue to flourish. This stake extends well beyond the economics of the entertainment industry itself, which churns out movies, television programs, video games, theme parks, and other "entertaining" diversions that people pay to enjoy. Practically everything that consumer capitalism touches, from marketing products to inventing new technologies, from rewarding celebrity to financing political campaigns, from lobbying Congress to running the mass media, has a share in that stake. In other words, everything in American society is economically tied to the Culture of Entertainment. For consumer capitalism, with its inherent, self-justifying need to expand, is the engine of the American economy, with all of the ramifications that has for American society and culture. Therefore, as alert as citizens might become to the wiles of entertainment, until those citizens manage to get consumer capitalism itself to change and to curtail the expansion of entertainment, the Culture of Entertainment and the mentality its mind games nurture will continue to prosper.

I must conclude, then, that anyone who believes the Culture of Entertainment will fade or crumble any time soon only confirms the grip of this culture in wish-fulfilling fantasies born of the mind games that take us out of the real world to where anything is possible. More likely than the possibility that the Culture of Entertainment will disappear is that one day we will simply shrug and say, "So what?" about everything in this culture, including what it does to us. And we will learn to laugh at it all as the inescapable radio music of life. But, to paraphrase Hesse's Mozart, this will be gallows laughter. (For a classic take on gallows humor, see Fig. 55.)

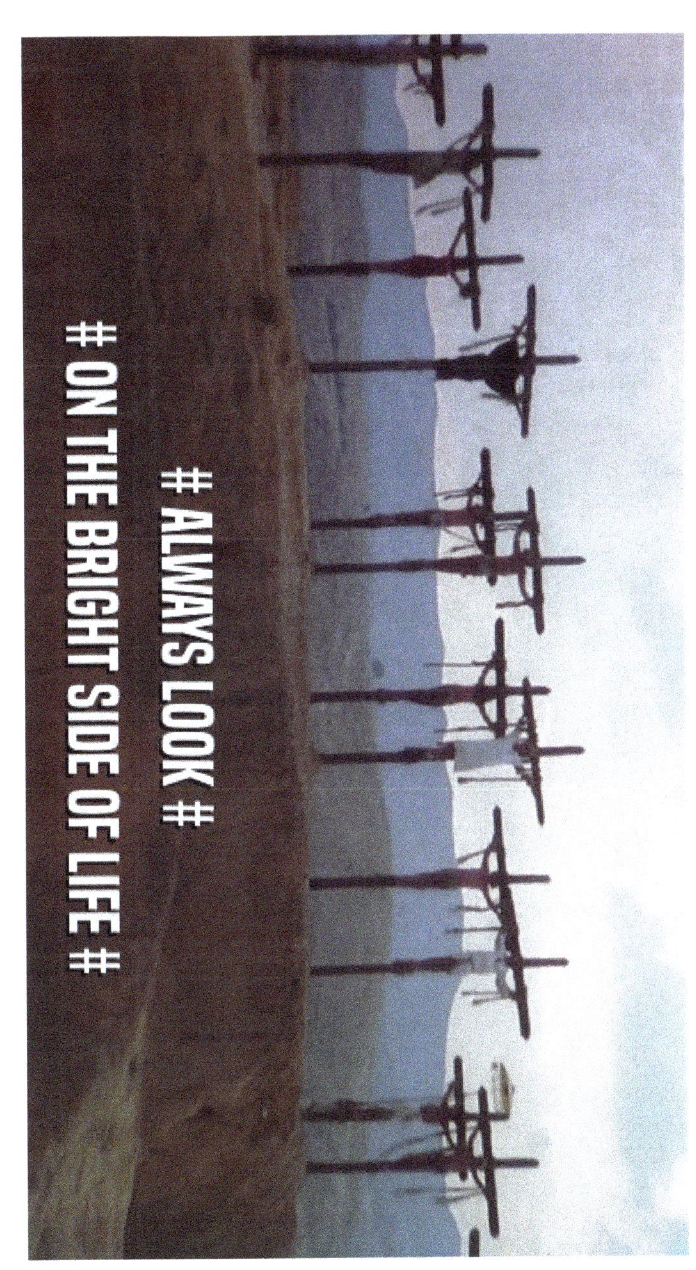

Fig. 55 — The final scene of Monty Python's The Life of Brian.

Here the hero, Brian, and genial fellow rebels against Roman rule are crucified for their subversive doings. But their condemnation to an inevitably slow and painful death on the cross does not daunt their spirits. And from their crosses they all break into the song, "Always Look on the Bright Side of Life." Who can resist gallows laughter at that? But this will be hearty, rather than hopeless, laughter.

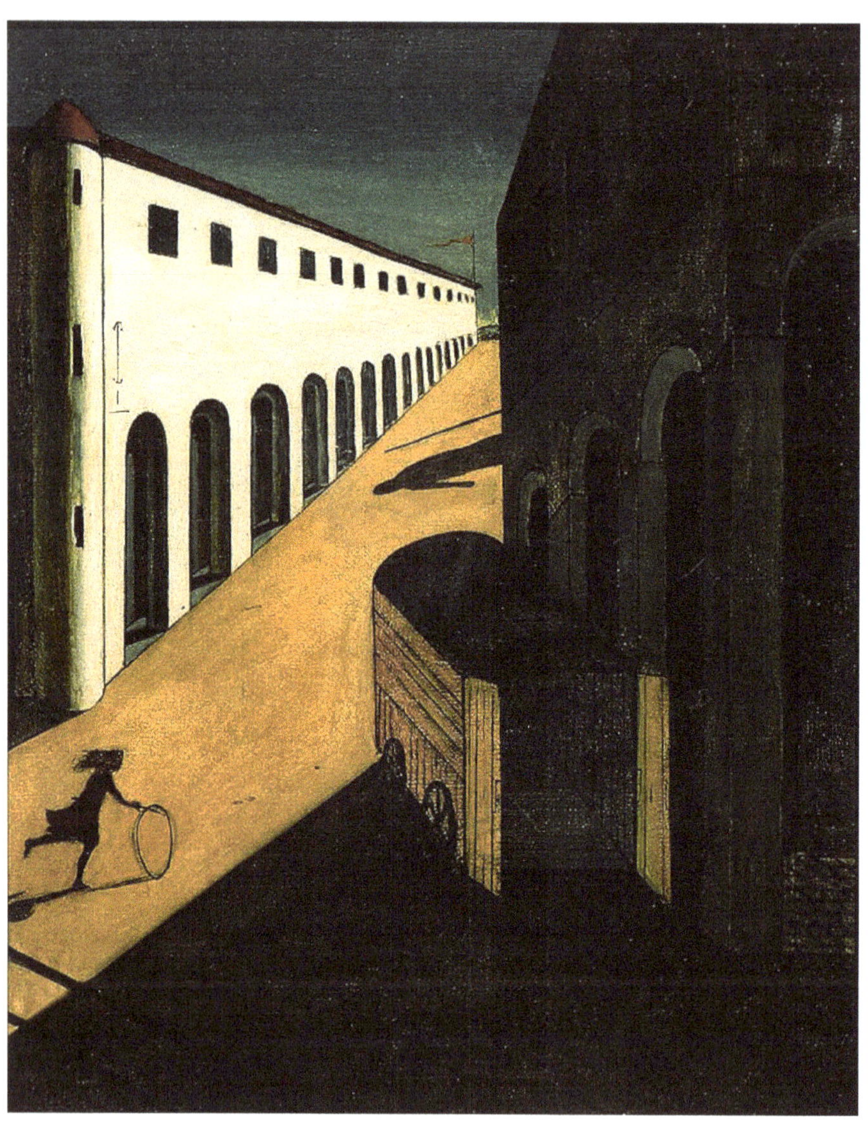

Fig. 56 — Giorgio de Chirico, The Mystery and Melancholy of a Street, *1914.*

Appendix

Giorgio de Chirico, The Mystery and Melancholy of a Street

Giorgio de Chirico (1888–1978), influential modernist, resolute individualist, thinker among artists, and arguably the greatest Italian painter of the twentieth century, was born in the northeastern section of Greece known as Thessaly. Although his parents were Italian, they were both born in Turkey, and they raised Giorgio and his two younger siblings in Greece, where their father worked as an engineer and socialized with people of many nationalities until his death in 1905, after which the family moved to Munich, Germany. De Chirico lived in Munich for about three years, studying art, becoming enamored of Arnold Böcklin's bizarre symbolist paintings, and discovering the eccentric philosophy of Friedrich Nietzsche. Munich would also be the first of several European cities—notably Paris, Florence, Ferrera, and Rome—that Giorgio would call home, for a time. This cosmopolitan heritage and existence gave Giorgio an individualistic perspective on life, along with a vague sense of alienation, of being an outsider not belonging quite anywhere. That sensibility would affect his character, his art, and his career.

During the course of his long life, de Chirico's works passed through a variety of artistic styles, from the traditional drawings of his years at art school and the paintings that followed, through his weird Böcklinesque experiments, his unique and influential early modernist works, and the classical/Baroque works of subsequent decades, to his late works, when he returned to some characteristics of his early art and also painted some fanciful cartoon-like canvases. And yet a certain taste for the classical Greek aesthetic of order and clarity and for Greek imagery stayed with him from the beginning. That, combined with an inclination—most evident in his youth—toward the enigmatic, the dreamlike, and an air of strangeness and alienation, as well inspiration from his quasi-mystical impressions of Nietzsche, whom he considered "the most profound poet," yielded the paintings of his early maturity by which he is still best known today.

Originating in Florence and painted between 1910 and 1919, mainly in Paris, the first few of these works struck de Chirico's soon-to-be friend, the poet and critic Guillaume Apollinaire as "strangely metaphysical paintings."[36] And they are. Although Apollinaire might not have been the first to view them as "metaphysical"—de Chirico's reading of Nietzsche seems to have already led him to think of them that way, as representing an inner reality—Apollinaire made "metaphysical" the public identity of de Chirico's works of this period. And, among them, the paintings of 1912–1914 set in piazzas are particularly "strange." By the artist's intention (e.g., see Fig. 56).

Possessing a distinctive "metaphysical" atmosphere, or *Stimmung*—a word de Chirico had learned from Nietzsche that the painter said "could be translated as atmosphere in a moral sense"—these early paintings were like none before them. For the "moral sense" of *Stimmung* meant to de Chirico a metaphysics of "strange and profound poetry, infinitely mysterious and solitary."[37] He could have added "enigmatic," for, as he wrote in a Latin inscription at the bottom of his first self-portrait (1911), "And what shall I love if not what is enigma," a sentiment he echoed near the same time in vowing "to represent everything in the world as an enigma."[38] He went on to do just that. "My paintings are small," he wrote to a friend after embarking on his journey into the metaphysical terrain, "but each one is an enigma."[39] And he named his first metaphysical painting, recalling an autumn afternoon in the Piazza Santa Croce in Florence, *Enigma of an Autumn Afternoon* (1910). He would similarly name other paintings in those years.

As mysterious enigmas, de Chirico's metaphysical paintings cannot be interpreted as one might do the works of other painters, for the images we see, even though recognizable, belong to the inner world of *Stimmung*, the atmosphere of strangeness and mystery. They have no other "meaning." Of course, one might interpret them aesthetically to explain how the artist organized forms and light and color to produce true works of art. But de Chirico did not concern himself primarily with such things. He occupied himself much more, at least in the beginning, with the "strange" and "infinitely mysterious" *Stimmung* that defies rational explanation or analysis. As he wrote during the heyday of his metaphysical period, "To be really immortal, a work of art must go completely beyond the limits of the human: good sense and logic will be missing from it. In this way it will come close to the dream state, and also the mentality of children."[40] No wonder the surrealists adopted de Chirico, viewing his metaphysical paintings as precursors of their own irrationally dreamlike artworks—until they turned against him for incorrigibly moving on in the 1920s to other styles, although they still praised the surrealistic idiosyncrasies of his stream-of-consciousness novel, *Hebdomeros* (1929), which he dubbed only "metaphysical."

And now the painting on the cover of this book, *The Mystery and Melancholy of a Street* (1914) (see Fig. 56). Perhaps de Chirico's most evocatively mysterious metaphysical painting, it is enigmatic, to be sure. Our eyes first fall on the stretch of a sunlit street extending into the distance, bordered on the left by a long, white, sunny, arcaded building that runs in dramatic perspective the length of the street to the horizon and holds a small banner on its roof at the end. On the other side, the street is bordered by shadows cast from another arcaded building that obstructs our view of where the street probably opens onto a piazza. In the street, we see only dark shadows cast by two figures in what must be a late, bright afternoon sun. The figure and shadow we probably first notice are those of a silhouetted young girl running, with hair flying, into the street from the lower left, rolling a large hoop with a stick. The second shadow our eyes pick out comes from a tall figure resembling a statue, along with a staff, standing in the piazza behind the arcaded building on the right. This same building is itself shrouded in shadows, which it throws across the bottom portion of the picture at an angle toward the running girl. In that shadow also stands a wooden van or wagon like those used to cart horses or to carry circus animals and paraphernalia. Its doors at one end lie open, revealing nothing at all inside. Curiously, although resting in the shadow, the van (or the side of it we see—with words on it added for the cover) is softly illuminated by no identifiable light source, unless it could be sunlight reflecting from the bright yellow street, and yet, that would brighten more than the van alone. One of the enigmas.

The contrast of sunlight and shadows certainly does strike the eye. And the more we think about what we see the more we wonder. The running girl is evidently having a good time playing with her hoop, yet she is very much alone, the only living thing to be seen in the vacant street and its adjacent arcades, and she seems to be moving toward the rather ominous figure in the piazza. A mystery in that. And the two arcaded buildings that frame the street almost dominate the scene. Why? Anyone who has seen many of de Chirico's paintings knows that arcades were an ever-present motif in his metaphysical works. Arcades seem to have entered his consciousness from seeing them often in Roman architecture and aqueducts. They might have suggested to him the passage of time and space with their gracefully repetitious forms, mirroring Nietzsche's notion of timelessness in the "Eternal Return," which had captivated the young painter. And, framing the young girl running alone with her hoop on the empty street as they do, the silent arcades might be said to enhance the enigmatic melancholy of the scene. In fact, de Chirico considered arcades particularly enigmatic. And when he said of them, "The *Roman* arcade . . . speaks in enigmas full of strangely Roman poetry, of shadows on old walls,"[41] he could have been speaking of what we see in *The Mystery and Melancholy of a Street*.

But the closer we look at this picture the more we will also see how de Chirico has put the contents ajar. The eye naturally follows the prominent white building as its dozen arcades roll predictably toward the horizon in diminishing perspective. There may be something aesthetically pleasing in that. But when we look at the dark arcaded building and the van in the shadows on the near right we might grow unsettled as we discern that the perspectives of their forms go haywire. Not only does the perspective of the dark building clash with that of the white one across the street in divergent vanishing points, it clashes with itself—the roofline perspective goes to one vanishing point and that of the foreshortened arcades go to another. And the perspectives of the van go still elsewhere. It is as though the sunlight side of the painting satisfies expectations and gives one a feeling of calm whereas the shadowy side disorients and stirs puzzlement, even disquiet. But I wouldn't count on that as de Chirico's explicit intent.

Light and dark, shadows and arcades, a vacant street and a concealed piazza, a girl playing alone and a hidden statue, they are all enigmas. To ask what they, or the enigmas in any of de Chirico's metaphysical paintings, "mean" is futile. Except to answer that they create the *Stimmung*. And the *Stimmung*, the atmosphere, of this painting is, as the name says, *The Mystery and Melancholy of a Street*. Let the mind games of the art experience take it from there.

A Note on de Chirico, Copies, and Fakes

As observed in Chapter I, de Chirico first copied or replicated one of his paintings—*The Disquieting Muses* (see Fig. 8)—in 1924 for his surrealist friend Paul Éluard when the owner of the original refused to sell it. Fabio Benzi demonstrates that Éluard's fellow surrealist, André Breton, a great admirer of de Chirico's metaphysical works, had arranged for the replica to be made. But de Chirico would regret this act of friendship. For the surrealists soon turned against him for refusing to work in their idiom and moving on from his quasi-surrealist metaphysical works. But there was more to the break between de Chirico and the surrealists than that. As Benzi details the story, Breton launched a crusade to diminish de Chirico's artistic stature and discredit him as an artist, labeling him a cheap copyist and something of a fraud. Adroit publicist that Breton was, he managed to stamp de Chirico in much of the artworld as just that. Naturally this embittered de Chirico against not only the surrealists but against the artworld—except for allies like Marcel Duchamp and Jean Cocteau—and especially against dealers and critics. This—together with the persistent indifference, if not disdain, of the artworld, with its worship of Modernism, toward his works after the metaphysical period, limiting his sales of anything new he created—induced de Chirico to make replicas of his saleable metaphysical paintings and date them to confuse venal dealers and crass collectors. There can be no doubt that de Chirico had cause to be aggrieved. Even so, although he professed in his *Memories of My Life* (Part I, 1945) to have had "total scorn for the opinions of other people," he probably cared too much about those opinions, never seeming to forget the people who had wronged him, often ascribing their motives to envy of his genius. Reading those *Memories*, one cannot help but see at least a hint of paranoia in de Chirico's grandiose self-perceptions and his accusations of enemies.

At all events, de Chirico's practice of replicating some of his metaphysical works, and doing so unabashedly in later years, also stimulated the creation of outright fakes by other hands. In fact, de Chirico and that master of reproduction, Auguste Rodin, became two of the modern artists most susceptible to forgeries or fakes. The de Chirico fakes confused the art market even more than his replicas did, since fakes could be particularly difficult to distinguish from his own replicas. Fakes even showed up in exhibitions and catalogues of de Chirico's actual works. All of this added more fuel to de Chirico's hostility toward the artworld.

The mind games of the art experience had been challenging enough for viewers amid the enigmas of de Chirico's metaphysical paintings themselves—de Chirico declared in his memoirs that "nobody has ever understood them." The copies and especially the fakes compounded the challenges. (I might note here that de Chirico made replicas of *The Mystery and Melancholy of a Street* into the 1960s—such as the one on display in the Carlo Bilotti Museum in Rome, post-dated to 1948, as acknowledged by the museum, but looking very much like a fake, with its hastily drawn running girl and shadow of the statue, truncated building on the left, and baggage strewn about and inside the wheelless van in the lower center [see Fig. 57]. The original, seen on this book's cover and in Fig. 56, appears to be held in an anonymous private collection.)

Vexed as he was by his enemies and by the proliferation of fakes, in

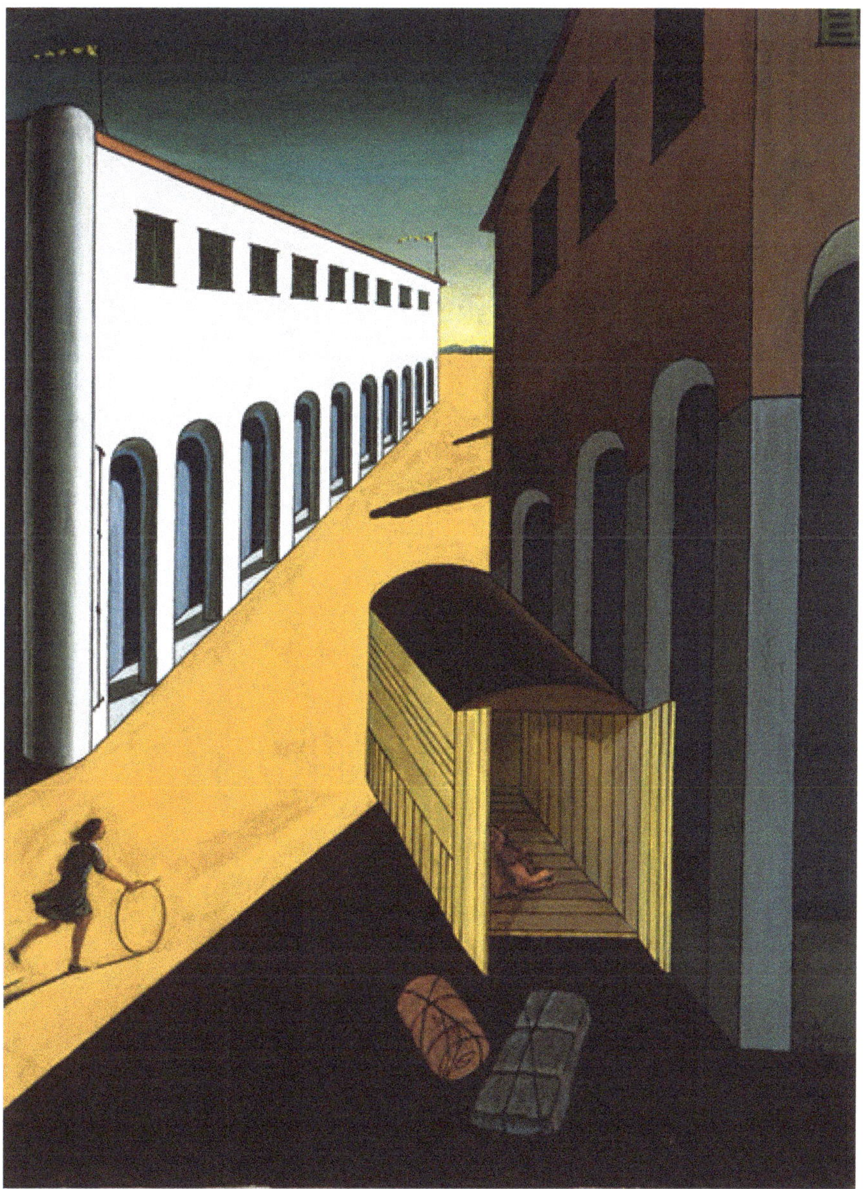

Fig. 57 — Giorgio de Chirico, The Mystery and Melancholy of a Street, *a replica dated 1948 but painted in the 1960s.*

his last decade de Chirico seems to have stopped making replicas of his older works and returned to some metaphysical themes of his youth, reimagining them anew. He also produced numerous playfully cartoonish fantasies that critics have identified with the spirit of Pop Art—just as they have his replicas. Those were mind games of art that he could happily play as his career drew to a close.

Endnotes

The Endnotes include references mainly for some important quotations whose source is not identified, however generally, in the text.

Chapter I

1. Joshua Reynolds, *Discourses on Art*, Discourse VII.
2. Joshua Reynolds, *Discourses on Art*, Discourse VI.
3. Samuel Johnson, *The Rambler*, No. 125.
4. *The Poetry and Prose of William Blake*, ed. David V. Erdman (Doubleday, 1965), pp. 645, 647.
5. Ibid., 650.
6. Samuel Taylor Coleridge, *Biographia Literaria*, ch. 13.
7. Imanuel Kant, *Critique of Judgment*, SS 46.
8. Artur C. Danto, *After the End of Art: Contemporary Art and the Pale of History* (Princeton University Press, 1997), p. 35.
9. David J. Getsy (Art History professor, University of Virginia), "The Materiality and Mythology of Rodin's Touch," DavidGesty.com.
10. Achille Bonito Oliva, "Industrial Metaphysics: An Interview with Andy Warhol" (Marisa del Re Gallery, Inc., New York, 1985), in *Andy Warhol (After de Chirico)* (Waddington Galleries, 1998), p. 8.
11. Both quotations from Richard Meyer, "The Supreme Court Is Wrong About Andy Warhol," *New York Times*, June 10, 2023, A18.
12. Danto, *After the End*, p. 47.
13. Danto, "The Artworld," *Journal of Philosophy*, Oct. 1964 ; the Duchamp quotation in the footnote comes from Tim Martin, *Essential Surrealists* (Paragon, 2000), p. 42.
14. Nelson Goodman, "When Is Art?," in *Ways of World Making* (Hackett, 1978).
15. Plato, *Republic*, X, 607a; IV, 424b-c; IV, 424 d-e.

16. Aristotle, *Politics*, VIII, vii; *Poetics*, ch. 6.

Chapter II

17. Quoted in Fabio Benzi, *Giorgio de Chirico: Life and Paintings*, trans., Christopher Adams and David Smith Rizzoli Electa, 2023, p. 417.

Chapter III

18. The accounts of Chapman's and Hinckley's actions and motives come mainly from numerous news reports at the time and later.
19. See e.g., *The Violence Project: How to Stop a Mass Shooting Epidemic* (2021) by Jillian Peterson and James Densley, interviewed in *Politico* May 27, 2022; *Mass Shootings: Media, Myths, and Realities*, by Jaclyn Schildkraut and H. Jayme Elsass (2016).

Chapter IV

20. Plato, *Republic*, II, III, IV, X, passim.
21. Aristotle, *Politics*, VIII.
22. Aristotle, *Politics*, VIII, vii.
23. Henry Raynor, *Music and Society Since 1815* (Taplinger, 1978), pp. 35, vii.
24. Both quotations, Edward E. Lowinsky, "Taste, Style , and Ideology in Eighteenth-Century Music," in *Aspects of the Eighteenth Century*, ed. Earl R. Wasserman (Johns Hopkins Press, 1965), p. 164.
25. Quoted in Ibid., p. 191.
26. *Baltimore Patriot*, May 25, 1844. The full newspaper story and its historical context were later reported by an eye-witness and companion of Morse, who had also been in attendance at Morse's first official demonstration of his machine, John W. Kirk, *Scribner's Magazine,* March 1892. Available online, "The First News Message by Telegraph," todayinsci.com.

Chapter V

27. "Muppet characters in advertising," fandom.muppet.com/wiki.
28. Shay Sayre and Cynthia King, *Entertainment and Society: Influences,*

Impacts, and Innovations, Second Edition (Routledge, 2010), p.5. On theories of the effects of media and entertainment, ch. 5, passim.

29. Megan Garber, "We're Already in the Metaverse. Reality Is Blurring. Boredom Is Intolerable. And Everything Is Entertainment," *Atlantic*, March 2023.
30. "Here's what Jones has said about Sandy Hook," *New York Times*, September 22, 2022, online.
31. Mark Leibovich, *Thank You for Your Servitude: Donald Trump's Washington and the Price of Submission* (Penguin Press, 2022).
32. Carlos Lozada, "The Inside Joke that Became Trump's Big Lie," *New York Times*, September 22, 2022.
33. Tim Miller, *Why We Did It: A Travelogue from the Republican Road to Hell* (Harper Collins, 2022).
34. See, e.g., Jeremy W. Peters, "Inside the 3 Months that Could Cost Fox $1.6 Billion," *New York Times*, March 20, 2023, online; Mark Mwachiro, "Latest Court Filings From Dominion Show Fox News Works Hard to Protect Its Brand," tvnewser, February 17, 2023.
35. Tucker Carlson, quoted in "'The Whole Thing Seems Insane': New Documents on Fox and the Election," *New York Times*, March 7, 2023, online.

Appendix

36. Apollinaire, "La vie artistique," *L'Intransigeant*, September 10, 1913, quoted in Benzi, *Giorgio de Chirico: Life and Paintings*, op. cit., p. 124.
37. Quoted in Benzi, Ibid., p. 70.
38. Ibid., p. 69.
39. Ibid., p. 83.
40. Ibid., p. 177.
41. Ibid., p. 109.

Index

Because the table of contents is quite detailed, the Index need not be. And because certain subjects run through the book, the Index refers to those subjects—such as mind games, art, entertainment, high art, low art—only to point out a few particularly useful references.

R

S

T

U, V

W

www.ingramcontent.com/pod-product-compliance
Ingram Content Group UK Ltd.
Pitfield, Milton Keynes, MK11 3LW, UK
UKHW062312290726
14090UKWH00018B/1029